STRUCTURED *BASIC* AND BEYOND

D0873493

COMPUTER SOFTWARE ENGINEERING SERIES

Ellis Horowitz, Editor
University of Southern California

Wayne Amsbury
Structured BASIC and Beyond

Peter Calingaert
Assemblers, Compilers, and Program Translation

M.S. Carberry, H.M. Khalil, J.F. Leathrum, J.S. Levy
Foundations of Computer Science

Shimon Even
Graph Algorithms

W. Findlay and D.A. Watt
Pascal: An Introduction to Methodical Programming

Ellis Horowitz and Sartaj Sahni
Fundamentals of Computer Algorithms

Ellis Horowitz and Sartaj Sahni
Fundamentals of Data Structures

Tom Logsdon
Computers and Social Controversy

Jeffrey D. Ullman
Principles of Database Systems

STRUCTURED *BASIC* AND BEYOND

WAYNE AMSBURY

Northwest Missouri State University

Computer Science Press

Computer Science Press, Inc.
9125 Fall River Lane
Potomac, Maryland 20854

1   2   3   4   5   6 Printing   Year 85   84   83   82   81   80

Library of Congress Cataloging in Publication Data

Amsbury, Wayne, 1935–
    Structured BASIC and beyond.

    (Computer software engineering series)
    Bibliography: p.
    Includes index.
    1.   Basic (Computer program language)   I.   Title.
II. Series.
QA76.73.B3A57   001.64 ′24   80-18382
ISBN 0-914894-16-1

ACKNOWLEDGEMENTS

Among the family, friends, and colleagues who helped to make this book possible, there are four who deserve special notice: Burl Amsbury, Carlene Amsbury, Gary McDonald, and Rose Wallace.

Thank You

PREFACE

This book is founded on two philosophies: a philosophy of programming, and a philosophy of teaching that programming philosophy.

A PHILOSOPHY OF PROGRAMMING

Programming is a largely language-independent activity, the heart of which is to develop a logical structure which solves a given problem. The logical structure must be one which can be readily translated into a program, but for most problems, the same structure will serve for a program in BASIC, FORTRAN, PL/I, Pascal, or ALGOL. That structure can be portable, not only from machine to machine, but language to language. In contrast, the listing of a finished program seldom is portable from one machine to another, and is often difficult to read, regardless of included remarks. The vehicle for developing an algorithm, molded into a neatly structured form, can also be easily readable documentation of the finished product—if that vehicle is a simple, flexible, and restricted form of pseudocode.

A problem should be solved in such a way that it can be presented in a stepwise fashion in order to produce both documentation and a clean final structure. However, I do not believe that programmers who are familiar with stepwise refinement use it exclusively when they attack a problem which they do not know, in essence, how to solve. I, at least, am more likely to work on isolated subproblems, the overall structure, and the communication between modules, in almost any order and then refine the approaches to all three areas as often as the problem requires.

Programs should include pertinent comments, but to my knowledge programs are not truly self-documenting in any language. If a program contains too many comments, then it is difficult to read. I will not read someone else's program until I have understood the structure of it (as presented in pseudocode or an equivalent form).

I believe that there is a difference between techniques for writing programs and techniques that are suitable for teaching people to write programs.

A PHILOSOPHY OF THE TEACHING OF PROGRAMMING

Programming is an age-independent activity, with one restriction—a certain amount of abstraction is required. The required level of abstraction seems to be about that required for algebra and for the finer points of English grammar. Hence, I believe that many people will not be able to write programs with any logical substance in a procedural language like BASIC, prior to the age of 14. There may be more unfamiliar concepts encountered in an introduction to programming than some students have seen in several years outside of it.

Many students seem to approach programming with a latent ability to deal with abstractions, not a practiced skill in doing so; hence that ability must be developed *within* an introduction to programming itself. The major abstraction associated with a program is its logic, and it should be faced very explicitly as a major aspect of program writing. I believe that this abstraction is most effectively faced by teaching students to develop the solution to a problem as a logical structure, expressed in an informal, flexible, but restricted pseudocode. The pseudocode used should be designed to be easy to read and to promote both structured programs and the development of substantial programs by stepwise refinement. The language-independent character of pseudocode helps to separate user interaction with the computing system as such, the solving of a problem, and the details of a computing language. Without such separation, a lot of sympathetic magic and downright confusion are promoted during the early stages of an introductory programming course.

Programming, particularly its problem-solving aspect, should be taught in a spiral manner, just as the writing of English sentences is taught before the construction of paragraphs. This implies a beginning with very simple problems and minimal language constructs, so that problem solutions can be extracted from the students themselves, in class, and easily implemented in a programming language from the logic. The essential logical structures should appear early in the presentation, since they form the bridge between elementary problems and advanced problems. It is comforting for the student to see substantial problems reduced to structures already familiar as the solution to simpler problems. This reduction forms a basis for the tendancy to write modular programs, and to apply stepwise refinement to problem solution. Programming techniques, like stepwise refinement, will sell themselves as the size and complexity of problems are increased, and as their use is repeatedly demonstrated by the instructor. A student who wishes to apply programming to practical problems in almost any area needs to be introduced to topics such as file management, stacks, queues, string handling, linked lists, and trees. An introductory course will often stop short of these topics, but they should be available in abreviated form in a text for students who wish to range beyond the required material. I believe in providing an extremely wide spectrum of problems, from self-review questions and "busy work," to very challenging projects which would not be assigned to a college class because of time constraints.

Specifically with regard to BASIC, some language features like extended names, messages, remarks, and input prompting, may be deferred until program logic has been discussed—a "decorated" program with an ugly skeleton is not beautiful. I believe that INPUT and PRINT should be mastered before READ ... DATA, which is of limited use in an interactive system. Loops as structures should be mastered before the FOR ... NEXT loop is introduced, and the FOR ... NEXT loop should be clearly separated from the concept of the subscripted variable, even though they are natural allies. I believe that the idea of a function may be deferred until all of the other language features of BASIC have been introduced, but should not be omitted altogether, even for students outside of the sciences—it is an essential bridge to other languages, to general forms of modularity, and to a large variety of applications.

A COURSE SYLLABUS

This book is used in an Introduction to Computer Science at Northwest Missouri State University. About 60% of the student body takes the course, and the spectrum of majors represented by the students who take it is broad. The pace of the course is somewhat slower than it would be in a course designed solely for majors in the sciences, but the difference in the two courses would be the amount of material included and the choice of assignments. This three-semester-hour course covers Chapters 1-6. Chapters 7, 8, and 9 are included for use in a course with a faster pace, for enrichment, and for self-study.

Chapter 1

The first five or six class periods cover both Chapter 1 and some details of the use of a PDP11/70 system, such as terminal and debugger availability, account numbers, passwords, the use of DIR, SAVE, OLD, NEW, etc. Students are put on the system immediately, using canned simulations and games, often followed by running a simple program provided by the instructor. When the essential statements have been presented, problems are solved in class. The in-class solutions are extracted from the students and recorded in pseudocode, then translated into BASIC. This activity becomes a personal one when a problem from the program section of Chapter 1 is assigned. The submitted material for this and other program assignments consists of a listing followed by one or more typical runs, and accompanied by the pseudocode description of the logic.

Chapter 2

Roughly three weeks are spent on this chapter, during which many of *programs 1.** which are not assigned as homework are developed by the students in class (as are other examples). This is the most difficult part of the course for many students. The GOSUB ... RETURN and the **case** structure may be deferred until they arise naturally in class examples. Because of their usefulness in interesting applications, RND and INT are introduced at this time. Students are encouraged to run programs developed in class, in addition to their program assignments.

Chapter 3

Perhaps two weeks are spent on this chapter, with GOSUB ...RETURN and **case** picked up if they were not treated earlier. Some of the problems at this stage should have rather natural refinement steps. In particular, nested loops may almost always be approached naturally in this manner. As soon as they have been covered, features such as extended names, prompting of input, instructions to the user, and remarks become *required* in programs submitted during the remainder of the course.

Chapter 4

As much as four weeks are spent on this chapter, since the set of applications widens considerably with the tools treated in it. A lot of in-class problem solving is done with this material and a great deal of tracing. Once the language constructs become familiar, many problems can be solved only in pseudocode, and the translation into BASIC may be left to the student. Students may not request translation by the end of this part of the course—they have come to accept problem solutions and programming ideas as being independent of the *details* of BASIC.

Chapter 5

The amount of time spent on this chapter varies somewhat, because some instructors introduce the material concerning expressions along with example problems of particular interest to them. The idea of a function takes some time to absorb, and more time for those students who are less likely to need to apply it. A week is probably a minimum allocation of time. The emphasis of the course could be easily shifted by introducing this material at any time after Chapter 2, for those with science and engineering interests. This chapter is deliberately written so that it may be used that way.

Chapter 6

The time remaining in the semester is spent on this chapter. (Reviews, exams, discussions of exams, and holidays take their toll.) If time is short, the emphasis is upon sorting, followed by explicit file management.

Most instructors at NWMSU give three one-hour-exams and a two-hour final, and assign ten to twelve programs. The program scores then amount to 25–35% of the total points used to determine grades.

CONTENTS

3.   NAMES AND MESSAGES

4.   THREE DATA STRUCTURES

7.   STRINGS AND LINKED LISTS

8.   STACKS AND QUEUES

9.   TREE-LIKE STRUCTURES

Chapter 1

THE BASIC MACHINE

I.1 BACKGROUND

A computer spins its wheels—very, very rapidly. Its wheels are really electronic circuits which go through a cycle of operations again and again, perhaps several million times a second, as long as the computer is turned on. Each time the computer goes through a cycle it executes some **machine instruction** which tells it what to do during that cycle; and usually where to get the instruction to be executed during the next cycle. What must be done in order to make the computer into a useful tool is to feed it a sequence of instructions so that it will do what the supplier of the instructions has in mind for it to do. A set of instructions for performing one or more tasks is a **program**, a program which must be provided in a form which the computer can use. A computer cannot use the English language directly, partly because English is rich in ambiguities and in multiple meanings—and the better for it; but a machine language needs precision instead of judgement. There is a gap to be filled in between the description of a task to be carried out by a computer and the set of machine instructions which form a procedure for doing that task.

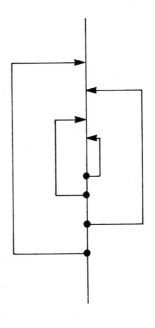

During the early days of computing, programs were written in a form which was very close to the machine instructions. Machine instructions are numbers, and the programs were presented to the machine simply as a sequence of numbers. Of course, people thought up those programs using names and symbols other than simply numbers, because that is how most people think. Gradually methods were developed to write programs symbolically, in an artificial language which people could read and write fairly easily. When programs are written symbolically but executed numerically, it is necessary to *translate* programs from one form to the other. The translation itself is done by a program, and the task of feeding the translation into the cycle is done by a program, as is the task of finding another program to execute when the current one is finished, and so on.

This book is about one of the many languages, BASIC, in which one can write programs to be translated into machine instructions and to then temporarily take control of the computer. (In practice, the program may "take control" only from the viewpoint of the programmer, but that viewpoint will be adopted in this book.) The term BASIC is used to mean both a language in which programs are written, and the large program which translates statements in that language into machine instructions. When a distinction must be made in this book between these two aspects of BASIC, it will be done by referring to either the BASIC *translator* or to the BASIC *language*. The initial approach to BASIC programming taken in this chapter and amplified in the next is:

1. We will examine the kinds of actions that computer instructions determine, and then describe how these actions can be invoked in the BASIC language. BASIC is written in **statements**, which play much the same role as sentences in English. Each statement invokes one or more of the fundamental actions of the machine.

2. When BASIC statements are combined, then the actions which they perform *as a group* has some logical structure. Some common logical patterns will be described, and they in turn can be used to describe an **algorithm**—a set of precise directions for performing some procedure.

3. As the tools of logic and language are developed, they will be applied to the description of procedures which solve problems. However, describing a problem-solving procedure and designing it in the first place are quite different. Solving a problem involves moving from an English description of it to BASIC statements, which often must be done in steps, rather than all at once. The final step to machine instructions is made by the BASIC translator itself.

4. The intermediate steps in deriving an algorithm involve describing the logic of the problem solution as it develops in increasing detail. It is important to present the intermediate steps in such a way that the *logic* of the resulting program can be readily understood by the pro-

grammer and by other people who are interested in the program. In this book, the intermediate steps are described in a form called **pseudocode**, which is designed to describe program logic which can be translated into BASIC as soon as enough detail has been developed to determine all of the logic of the problem solution. Pseudocode is designed for people, not machines, to read, it is flexible, and it is deliberately limited in some ways in order to promote the development of a clean logical program structure.

1.2 THE FUNDAMENTAL ACTIONS OF A COMPUTER

We need to be concerned with only six things that a computer can do with machine instructions: ⟨input⟩, ⟨output⟩, ⟨copy⟩, ⟨branch⟩, ⟨branch on condition⟩, and ⟨arithmetic⟩. The bent brackets ⟨...⟩ are used here because these are *kinds* of instructions, not the instructions themselves. Some machines actually use many small steps to do one of these things, and nearly all allow several variations of each one of them. We will approach these six abilities of a computer one at a time, and look at the way in which BASIC statements are designed to invoke them.

Statements are typed into the computer from a keyboard with a fairly standard set of characters, and numerals, and a few other special symbols. The sets of characters available are not identical in all BASIC systems, but all include:

0123456789ABCDEFGHIJKLMNOPQRSTUVWXYZ*?$%( )−=+",;

There is a program in control of the machine as we type, which collects our statements, keeps them in order, etc. This is the program which we will call BASIC. In fact, BASIC is an entire system of programs, which includes the translation of the user's programs as only one of the functions which it carries out. (For some other programming systems, some of the functions which are carried out by BASIC are done by separate programs.) When a BASIC program is collected, and then translated as a whole, the translator is called a **compiler**. Since not all versions of BASIC work this way, the more general term *translator* will be used in this text. We will be able to type in **commands** as well as statements, and the commands will tell BASIC what to do with the statements. As an example of a command, after a complete program has been input, the command RUN ® will cause control of the computer to be turned over to that program. The ability to react to commands is a third function of BASIC, that of an operating system which provides an environment that supports the translation and execution of a program. The amount of support which the operating system must provide for the other activities of BASIC depends upon the complexity and versatility of the computing system as a whole. The user of a BASIC program only needs to know which commands to use in a given situation in order to call upon the operating system support provided by BASIC.

1.3   INPUT

One of the six things that we might want to do with a program is ⟨input⟩. For example, if a program is to add two numbers together, it must first bring them into the computer. Either numbers or letters are used in any program. These symbols must be in the machine in some form in order to be used, and we need to generate machine instructions with which to fetch them. The input information is called *data*, and the path it takes is indicated by the arrow labeled 1 in the block diagram of a typical computing system, shown in the figure below.

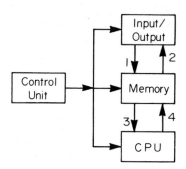

The **CPU** (Central Processing Unit) is where the machine instructions are executed, and **Memory** is where both instructions and data are stored. In the typical system which uses BASIC as its primary language, **Input** is from a keyboard and **Output** is onto a screen, a printer, or the printing part of a typewriter. The general term for a keyboard combined with either a screen or a printer is **terminal**. Hence a terminal provides a means for passing both input and output between the world outside of the computer and the memory of the computer. The **Control Unit** sends out signals which coordinate the other units. One of the important things to note in this diagram is that the lines between boxes are arrows—they indicate the direction of the flow of information. Arrow 1 represents ⟨input⟩, and it ends at memory. This arrow is meant to imply that when symbols of some kind are typed on the keyboard, they will be stored directly in memory. Hence the block diagram above describes what the input statement means in terms of the kind of action which it invokes.

The signal to BASIC that a statement is intended to cause input will be a **keyword**, INPUT. A keyword is a word which has a special meaning to the translator. (In most versions of BASIC, keywords may also be **reserved words**, to appear *only* when used for their special meaning, and so they must be used properly and placed carefully in BASIC statements.) The block diagram above shows that whatever is input must go somewhere in Memory. It does not indicate which *specific* location in Memory, called a **memory cell**, is to receive the input. Even if we were to pick a cell to be used every time, we might want to read in many different things with one program and compare them, add them, and so on. Programs are often used over and over again, with different data supplied for each run of the program. Distinguishing between several input items can be taken care of simply by storing separate items in separate memory cells and giving a name to each one. An item of interest in the program which can take on more than one value is called a **variable**. The value of a variable is stored in some memory cell, and the word "variable" is used because programs can change what is in the cell—the *variable value*. The name of the cell is called a *variable name*, although it is not usually necessary to distinguish between variables and their names.

With the use of variable names to specify storage cells, a decision must be made about which strings of symbols will be used for them. Somehow the BASIC translator must be able to pick a name out of the string of symbols which make up a statement. Special symbols like "+" and "/" need to be reserved for other uses in statements, so most of them are excluded from variable names. In the design of a programming language, a choice must be made between a strict set of rules for forming names and great flexibility. The use of strict rules for deciding which names are valid makes it easier for the translator to pick out names, but makes naming less flexible, makes the names more difficult to remember, and makes the names less meaningful to someone reading a program. There are many different BASIC translators and they do not all have the same rules about variable names. The rule which will be adopted in this chapter and the next will be to use only simple variable names: one letter. Other naming schemes are discussed in Chapter 3. With these considerations, input into variable A is invoked by:

INPUT A

when included properly in a BASIC statement. In fact, input into several variables may be invoked with one INPUT:

INPUT *B, Z*

or even:

INPUT *K, A, M, C*

which has the general form:

INPUT ⟨list of variable names separated by commas⟩

The form of this invocation may vary in some ways, but not in others. For example, may the blank space between "INPUT" and the list of variables be omitted as it is below?

INPUTA

Is the space between *T* and *A* required in order to let the BASIC translator know that the keyword INPUT is finished? To be safe, we will use the space, but most BASICS don't need it—they merely look for the pattern: *I* followed by *N* followed by *P*, etc. When *T* is reached, what follows it is assumed to be a variable name.

Variations like the following are *not* the same as INPUT *A* and may lead to unexpected results, and so they should be avoided:

INNPUT *A*
INPUT   *A*
INPUT, *A*
INPUT *B, C,*
INPUTINPUT

The invocation INPUT *A* will cause a question mark, "?", to be displayed on the screen or printer of the user's terminal. Because of this display, the user of a program will know that the program is prepared to accept input data. With

INPUT *A, B*

a single "?" is displayed, and the expected response is two numbers separated by a comma, for example:

9.3,476®

(Here ® means hitting the terminal key marked CARRIAGE RETURN, or perhaps just RETURN. It is used in BASIC to end a line of type.) If the number of data values entered before the ® is less than the number of variables in the INPUT list, then additional question marks will be generated to prompt the correct number from the user. Extra data values will be ignored.

1.4 OUTPUT

The simplest form for invoking ⟨output⟩ is very similar to that for ⟨input⟩. The following will be sufficient for many programs:

PRINT A

or:

PRINT X, D

or, in general:

PRINT ⟨list of variable names separated by commas or semicolons⟩

There is one option which was not pertinent to INPUT: How close together are the values of the variable list to be displayed? For example, when properly included in a BASIC statement,

PRINT V, W

will print:

7.3   1783

The separating comma causes displays to begin at specified columns in the line or screen. Depending upon the particular computing system involved, displays may begin in the 1st, 15th, 29th, etc. columns or the 1st, 11th, 21st, etc. columns. In some versions of BASIC, a blank is automatically displayed both before and after a number, but not before and after some other kinds of output. In contrast,

PRINT V; W

will print:

7.3   1783

By using a *semicolon* to separate items in the output list instead of a comma, output items are displayed as closely to each other as possible. The spacing of output is an option which affects how many things may be printed on a line, and where.

1.5   STATEMENTS AND THEIR NUMBERS

In order to accomplish a task, a number of invocations like INPUT and PRINT will need to be specified in some order. They are presented to the BASIC translator in the form of **statements**, entered one at a time from a terminal. Statements are *numbered* to give them a relative position within a program. For example,

10 INPUT A ®

is a complete BASIC statement. Statement [10] will not be executed as soon as it is entered, but will be stored away by BASIC as a building block of a program. If very many statements are entered, the programmer will surely make some mistakes. Not only may there be typing errors, but a programmer may wish to correct, delete, or add statements. In an inter-active environment, BASIC must have a fourth function, that of *editor*, to add to its duties as language, translator, and operating system.

The order in which statements are arranged in a program is determined solely by their statement numbers:

1000 INPUT B ®

comes before:

1013 INPUT C ®

and after:

982 INPUT F, G, H ®

These INPUT statements can be *typed* in any order, which is useful because a statement can then be referred to by its number for the purpose of editing:

    85 PRINT Z®
    80 INPUT *XY*®
    80 INPUT *X, Y*®

is a possible sequence of entries. The second statement [80] is taken by BASIC to be a replacement of the previous [80], since two lines of a program cannot have the same number. Because of the replacement, the lines above will result in

    80 INPUT *X, Y*®
    85 PRINT Z®

as a segment of the program being entered. The current set of statements can be determined at any time by typing the command: LIST®. A special statement is used to mark the end of a program:

    32767 END®

Any statement number will do for an END statement, so long as it is the largest one in the program. An END *will* be taken as the last statement in a program, and statements with higher numbers will generally be ignored. The END statement is a message to BASIC, a **non-executable** statement, which does not invoke any of the fundamental actions of the computer, but serves as a marker. The END statement is also an historical artifact from the language FORTRAN from which BASIC was originally derived.

1.6   RUN

The syntax of BASIC statements is defined so that the user and the BASIC translator can agree on their translation and agree on what order they are to appear in a program. If the following are input (into the BASIC translator):

    10 INPUT *A* ®
    20 PRINT *A* ®
    30 END®

nothing will happen, because BASIC is waiting for the programmer to add more statements or edit the ones that have already been entered. In order to execute this program, a command, RUN®, must be given to BASIC, to tell it to turn over control of the machine to the program. Each time this sequence of statements is to be executed, RUN®, must be typed again. Our control of the machine is very limited, but the next few sections will remedy that.

Programs can now be written with BASIC statements which have the general form:

```
[N] INPUT   〈list of variable names separated by commas〉
[N] PRINT   〈list of variable names separated by commas or by
                 semicolons〉
[N] END
```

We also have two commands, LIST and RUN.

1.7   BRANCH

The concept of the order of statements can be split into two orders: the order in which statements appear in the program, and the order in which they are to be executed. The branch capability of the machine forces a separation of these two types of order. Essentially a branch tells the CPU (Central Processing Unit) where to get the next machine instruction. In a BASIC program, a branch determines which statement is to be executed next. To pass control from statement [25] directly to [10], use:

25 GO TO 10®

In general, the syntax is:

```
[N] GO TO [M]
```

If a GO TO statement is put into the program of 1.6 (the change could be made between RUNs), the result is:

10 INPUT A
20 PRINT A

25 GO TO 10
30 END

(The ® has been left off, and for the rest of the book we shall assume that it completes every statement.) Now RUN *really* gives the program control of the computer—forever, in fact, since these statements now form what is called an *infinite loop* with no explicit way to stop their repetition. First [10] is executed, then [20], then [25], and [25] brings control back to [10]. The program above now has a logical structure which is commonly described in two ways:

repeat
  input *A*
  print *A*
forever

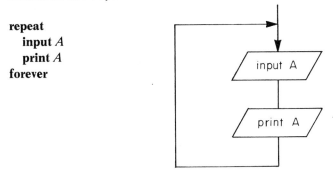

The general form of a program with this structure is described by:

repeat
  S
forever

Here *S* stands for a process to be carried out, whatever it may be, usually many statements in length. The description on the left is an informal one called **pseudocode**. Pseudocode will prove to be useful for developing and documenting the logic of programs. The pictorial description on the right is called a flowchart. Flowcharts are useful for picturing the logic of programs, and we will use both. If the pseudocode had been constructed as a *plan* for writing the program, it would have been clear what the program would do even before the statements themselves were written. Details like statement numbers are distractions when the program *structure* is being considered.

Any description of the logic of the example above brings up a problem that must be faced: How do we get out of the loop? All versions of BASIC have ways of getting out of a program that is caught in an infinite loop like this (since such loops may occur by oversight or error), but the ways vary. On some systems, one breaks out of an infinite loop with a BREAK key or a STOP key or perhaps with two keys depressed simultaneously—the CONTROL and the *C* keys. Of course, it is better to face this problem in the design stage, rather than at the terminal. Some variations of the ways to get out of loops with BASIC statements themselves are described in Chapter 2, and all of them involve the ⟨conditional branch⟩ capability of the machine.

1.8 THE CONDITIONAL BRANCH

We can design our way out of the infinite loop dilemma by using the ⟨branch on condition⟩ facility of the CPU. What the example program needs to do is check to see if some condition is true, and branch back to [10] only if it is. A conditional branch instruction is supplied in BASIC, and it appears in more than one form. One of the simplest forms of syntax for it is:

```
[N] IF ⟨condition⟩ THEN [M]
```

For example:

```
20 . . . .
25 IF A  < 0 THEN 10
30 . . .
```

The IF-statement [25] means that if the value of *A* is less than zero, then [10] is to be executed next instead of [30].

The IF statement raises a host of questions about syntax. The statement number serves for sequencing the statements, and BASIC can determine from the keyword IF that it has received a ⟨conditional branch⟩ statement, but what is allowed for the condition? In the first place, the condition must have the value *true* or *false,* since the IF statement should either cause a branch out of the normal sequence of statements or not cause one. If the condition is true when it is evaluated, control passes to the statement whose number appears after the THEN. If the condition turns out to be false when it is evaluated, control passes to the next statement in sequence.

A true or false condition is arrived at by *comparing* two things. That requires comparison operators, that is, special symbols such as "<" which means "less than". The job of comparison is done in BASIC with six operators put together from keystrokes available on most keyboards:

```
      <     "less than"
     < =    "less than or equal to"
     = >    "equal to or greater than"
      =     "equal to"
      >     "greater than"
     < >    "not equal to"
```

The condition which is to be either true or false lies between the keyword IF and the keyword THEN. The THEN also makes the IF statement read more like English. The logic of the example can now be indicated by:

repeat
   input *A*
   print *A*
until *A* < 14.3

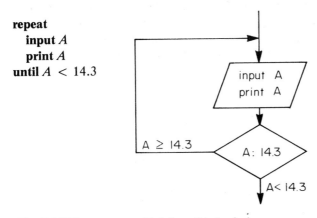

The BASIC program which has this logic is:

```
10 INPUT A
20 PRINT A
25 IF A > = 14.3 THEN 10
30 END
```

This program differs fundamentally from the previous one because the previous program will not stop if a small enough number is the response of the program's user to a "?" generated by [10]. That very limitation is what allows the user to force the program out of the loop. A new level of control has been added with this program—the user controls the program, which in turn can control the computer while it is being executed.

1.9 STOP

The example which we have been developing brings up one more question: What happens with the following sequence?

```
RUN
?72.314
?85
?4
```

The program goes on to the next statement when the condition in [25] is not satisfied, but the next statement is a non-executable one! Remember, END is merely a message to BASIC, which tells the translator that there are no more statements in the program. Because $4 < 14.3$, the program above will fall out of the loop past [25], and probably we would want it to stop. To "stop" means to stop execution of the *program*, not the computer, and hence to return control of the computer to BASIC. The natural statement to use to cause a branch back to BASIC has been adopted:

29 STOP

The difference between STOP and END is:

STOP is the last statement of the program which is *executed during a run*.

END is the last in the *list of statements* of the program.

The STOP may appear *anywhere* in a program, and may appear in more than one place, although as soon as it is executed, the execution of the program is over. The END appears only once in each program. In many versions of BASIC, END will be treated as both a STOP and an END, but in some situations, the distinction is crucial.

EXERCISES

With the INPUT, PRINT, GO TO, IF ... THEN, STOP, and END statements, and the LIST and RUN commands, programs can be written and the translator can be explored a bit. Get on a computer and explore variations of the statements above. In particular:

E1.1 Add statement numbers, a STOP and an END statement to the following to make it into a program, and then run it:

```
INPUT V, W
PRINT V
PRINT W
PRINT V, W
PRINT V; W
```

E1.2 Turn the program in E1.1 into an infinite loop after finding out how to get out of such a loop on your system from your instructor, manual, or other aid.

E1.3 Add a conditional branch to the program, so that it will stop or loop back to the INPUT statement, depending upon the input values.

1.10 FLOWCHARTS

Flowcharts will be used in this text to give a visual form to program logic. For example, the previous program has this structure:

procedure
  repeat
    input A
    print A
  until $A < 14.3$
endproc

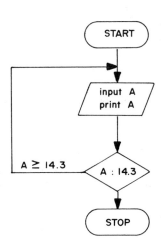

where **procedure** corresponds to the (START) block of the flowchart,

and **endproc** (end procedure) to the (STOP) block. The symbols which we will use for flowcharting are:

terminal block for START and STOP

I/O block for Input or Output

decision block for IF ... THEN

process block for a process of any size

1.11   ASSIGNMENT

The INPUT, PRINT, GO TO, and IF statements don't have the power to carry out interesting tasks in themselves. What is lacking is the power to put arithmetic into programs. A program needs the power of arithmetic even when it is not doing calculations at all, just to keep track of how much of a task it has completed. The next example will show how simple arithmetic makes this possible. The solution that has been devised to put arithmetic into BASIC (and most computer languages) is to combine the two remaining CPU capabilities: ⟨arithmetic⟩ and ⟨copy⟩. The separation of these two capabilities is forced by the syntax of the statement.

⟨arithmetic⟩ and ⟨copy⟩ are combined by first calculating the result of an expression, similar to an algebraic expression, and then assigning the result to some variable (storing the result where it can be retrieved).

In its simplest form, the **assignment** statement (or LET statement), causes no arithmetic to be done, but merely copies data:

10 LET $A = B$

$$A \leftarrow B$$

Statement [10] takes the value of variable B and assigns it to variable A. Values will always be copied from right to left, otherwise the statement would tend to be ambiguous. What [10] does is put a copy of the value of B into A, and leave the value of B unchanged. Whatever was in A before [10] was executed is lost. For example, if B contains -76.85 and A contains 43 before [10] is executed, then after [10] both B and A will contain -76.85.

1.11.1   The Addition Operation

Now we shall add the operations of arithmetic one at a time. Suppose that the number 1 is to be added to the value of the variable A. (A is said to be *incremented* by 1.) This is a common operation to apply to variables used as counters. Then:

15 LET $A = A + 1$

$$A \leftarrow A + 1$$

causes the required change, by adding 1 to the current value of A and then assigning the resulting sum back into A. As a mathematical statement, $A = A + 1$ is false, but [15] is not a mathematical statement. The two actions invoked by statement [15] are carried out in a particular order:

first a value is calculated from the addition of 1 to A,

then the result is stored in memory, in the variable A.

Just the one operation of addition provides some power. For example, suppose that we wish to design a program which will input ten numbers and print their running sum as they are encountered. Such a pattern of action forms part of many applications of programming. The beginning programmer is often faced with a blank wall upon first reading a problem description. This can sometimes be overcome with experience, but with *any* amount of experience, problem descriptions will be encountered which have the same effect. The programmer must fall back upon a systematic approach—that of reducing the problem to parts which *can* be handled, one at a time. The most common error made by beginners is to try to juggle too many things at one time.

A systematic attack on the problem above may begin by describing the kinds of information which will be needed in the program, and naming them as variables:

variable descriptions
   A //a variable to store input values//
   S //the sum of the numbers as they are encountered//
   N //a counter for the number of input values//

A second stage in the attack may be to decide, in a general way, how these variables are related, and how they are to receive their values. For example, A and S are related by the fact that each time a new value of A is entered, it is to be added to the sum S:

   //input A, add it to S, and print S//

is the action to be taken with each input value. When an action like this is repeated, care must be taken with the first time and the last time it is repeated, as well as the general action at the other times. In this case, S will need to be 0 before the first input value of A. It is said to be *initialized* to 0. The only worry about the last time for the action above is that it is to be the 10th time. This can be assured by setting the counter to 1 (another initialization) before the first input, and then each time the input of a value of A occurs, incrementing N by one. A check of the value of N to see if it has yet reached 10, and a repeat of the actions above if it has not, will solve our problem.

A third stage in the attack is to describe the solution, initialization of N and S followed by a loop which performs the indicated actions on each pass through the loop, in pseudocode. The pseudocode description amounts to a rather stylized rendering of the verbal description above (The style will be developed in some detail in Chapter 2.). With an accompanying flowchart it is:

```
procedure ADD__TEN
    S ← 0
    N ← 1
    repeat
        //input A, add it to S,//
        //and print S          //
        N ← N + 1
    until N > 10
endproc
```

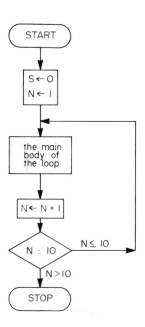

The structure at this stage is the initialization of *A*, followed by a loop which is specified by **repeat ... until**. The number of passes through the loop is controlled by two things: *N* is initialized to 1 before the loop is entered (before the **repeat** is encountered), and *N* is incremented by 1 on each pass through the loop (control is returned to the **repeat** each time the condition of the **until** is checked). Everything between the **repeat** and the **until** is the *body* of the loop. The program could be extended to do a variety of chores in the body of the loop, without changing its overall structure. Now by adding the details of the body, and translating it into flowchart form and BASIC, we have:

procedure ADD__TEN
  $S \leftarrow 0$
  $N \leftarrow 1$
  repeat
    input A
    $S \leftarrow S + A$
    print S
    $N \leftarrow N + 1$
  until $N > 10$
endproc

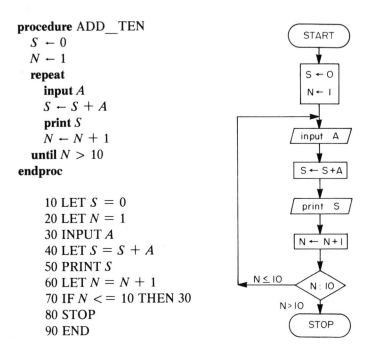

    10 LET $S = 0$
    20 LET $N = 1$
    30 INPUT A
    40 LET $S = S + A$
    50 PRINT S
    60 LET $N = N + 1$
    70 IF $N <= 10$ THEN 30
    80 STOP
    90 END

From the view of the BASIC program itself: the LET and the INPUT statements are used to sum any sequence of input numbers (using [10], [30], [40]). The LET and IF statements are used to count them so that the process will stop after precisely 10 values have been input (using [20], [60], [70]). The PRINT statement in [50] provides a running account of the summation.

1.11.2   Tracing a Program

No problem is easy *before* it has been solved, but many are easy *after* the solution is understood. Techniques for bridging this gap are more important than the specific problems in this book. Such techniques will be developed as they are required by problems of increasing generality and complexity. For example, it is frequently valuable to study the behavior of a possible solution to a problem in some detail in order to understand it better before it is translated into BASIC. One technique which can be used for this purpose is *tracing*.

    The behavior of ADD__TEN can be traced by observing the values of important variables each time [70] is reached. In tracing a program it is important to track the values of variables at the *same point* each time

through a loop in order to avoid confusion. Assuming that the sequence of
input values for A is: 7, 3.5, −1, 2, −10.2, 3, 5, 1, 1, 2:

A	S	N	output
7	7	1	7
3.5	10.5	2	10.5
−1	9.5	3	9.5
2	11.5	4	11.5
−10.2	1.3	5	1.3
3	4.3	6	4.3
5	9.3	7	9.3
1	10.3	8	10.3
1	11.3	9	11.3
2	13.3	10	13.3

The column labeled *output* shows what has *actually* been printed by
execution of the program. For example, given a program segment of the
form:

```
50 LET X = 1.4
60 LET Y = X + X
70 PRINT X; Y
80 STOP
90 END
```

The output is simply:

    1.4   2.8

The output is not 1.4; 2.8 or $X = 1.4$, $Y = 2.8$, or some other indication
of roughly the same information. Determining the output (if any) of example programs as they are presented will sharpen your understanding of
all similar programs.

EXERCISES

You should stop at this point, log onto a computer, and try every one of the
variations below. (Before you do, predict the results by thinking about them,
and tracing the behavior of the resulting program with a pencil and paper to
verify your predictions.)

What happens in procedure ADD_TEN if:

E1.4   [10] is renumbered to be [35]? Note: 10® will delete [10].

E1.5   [20] is renumbered to be [35]?

E1.6   [20] is deleted?

E1.7   [10] is deleted?

E1.8   The condition in [70] is changed from "< =" to "<"?

E1.9   [50] is renumbered [75]?

E1.10   [60] is deleted?

E1.11   We add: 75 GO TO 10

E1.12   We add: 75 GO TO 20

E1.13   [50] is changed to: 50 PRINT $S + A$

E1.14   [40] is changed to: 40 LET $A = S + A$

E1.15   We change the description to the one below:

> **procedure**
> $S \leftarrow 0$
> $N \leftarrow 1$
>   **repeat**
>   **input** A
> $S \leftarrow S + A$
> $N \leftarrow N + 1$
>   **until** $N > 10$
>   **print** S
> **endproc**

1.11.3   More Arithmetic Operations

Subtraction behaves like addition. The statement:

10 LET $X = Y - Z$

will take the value of Y, subtract the value of Z, and assign the result to X. The statement:

20 LET $A = 3*B$

$$A \leftarrow 3^*B$$

will copy three times the value of B into A without changing B. The *multiplication* operator in BASIC is "*". For example, $Z*X$ has the value of the product of the values of X and Z.

The statement:

30 LET $C = 5/2$

$$C \leftarrow 5/2$$

will divide 5 by 2 and assign 2.5 to C. The *division* operator in BASIC is "/". For example, W/B has, as its value, the value of W divided by the value of B. (If $B = 0$ then an error message will be generated by BASIC.)

The statement:

40 LET $D = A \uparrow 3$

$$D \leftarrow A^3$$

will assign $A*A*A$ (the cube of A) to D; for example, if A has the value 1.2 then D will receive 1.728. In some versions of BASIC, one may use (or may need to use) $A**3$ instead of $A \uparrow 3$. The *exponential* operator is "$\uparrow$" (or "**"). For example, $A \uparrow B$ is evaluated to be the value of A raised to the value of B power.

The statement:

50 LET $E = -E$

```
      ┌──────────┐
      │ E ←  -E  │
      └──────────┘
```

will change the *sign* of the value of E, whatever it is.

The general form of the assignment statement is:

[N] LET ⟨variable⟩ = ⟨expression⟩

Here *expression* refers to combinations like $(A + B)*C$, as well as $N + 1$, $Y - Z$, $3*B$, $5/2$, $A \uparrow 3$, and $-E$. The use of expressions is discussed more fully in Chapter 5, but we will not need the full power of expressions in order to solve the problems in the first four chapters.

1.11.4 Constants

A **constant** is some value which explicitly does not change during execution of a program. When both LET $I = 2$ and LET $C = D*2$ appear in a program, I and C are variables, but the number 2 is a constant. There is a single storage cell in that part of memory occupied by the program in which the number 2 is stored. As statements are translated, BASIC generates machine instructions which refer to the cell which contains the constant 2 whenever that constant is required for the translation. There is no way that the programmer can refer to the memory cell containing the constant 2, except by explicitly using the numeral 2 as in statement [30] above.

1.12 AN APPROACH TO PROGRAMMING

The general purpose of a book like this one is to describe how to use a computer to accomplish a task. Doing so involves several stages which will be illustrated in the examples of the chapters which follow:

1. Defining the problem. Most of the suggested problems, programs, and projects at the end of chapters are not *completely* defined as stated. The only complete description of a problem solved by a program is the program itself. Programs written by two people or at two times from the same verbal description may differ. The crucial issue is whether a

program defines a problem solution which adequately matches the intent of the verbal description of the problem. Refining and exploring the verbal description before proceeding to the other stages makes a match more likely.

2. Sorting out the logic of the problem. In effect, this stage determines the **algorithm**, or recipe, for solving the problem, which will be followed by the resulting program. The result of this stage is a description of the algorithm in terms of pseudocode. It may also provide only an *apparent* solution which creates new problems of its own. This pitfall can frequently be avoided by approaching the problem solution in steps, refining the pseudocode more at each step. The pseudocode required at this stage is described in Chapter 2. Such an approach grows in importance as the size of the problems being solved is increased. Tracing the behavior of possible solutions applied to selected data can also be very helpful at this stage.

3. Translating the pseudocode into a computer language—BASIC in this book. A minimum set of statements required for expressing the logic of most, but not all, programs has already been introduced.

4. Trying the code to see if it works. This often involves "debugging"— removing errors. Debugging is an art, but much of it can be prevented by sorting out the logic of the program with the techniques of the first three stages.

5. Using the program. This is the ultimate goal, but using a program is risky unless stage 4 has been carried out carefully, it is painful unless stage 3 has been done properly, it is especially painful if stage 2 has not been done carefully, and it may be a waste of time if stage 1 has not been done thoughtfully.

SELF-REVIEW

1. What are the four meanings of the term BASIC?
2. What are the six fundamental actions of a computer?
3. Give five examples of keywords in BASIC.
4. On a block diagram showing the principle parts of a typical computer label the arrow which corresponds to a PRINT statement with a P. Put double lines around the block in which arithmetic is done. Which block is associated with the storage of variable values?
5. What is the general form of the INPUT, PRINT, IF, and assignment statements?
6. Name two BASIC commands.
7. List the comparison operators used in BASIC, and indicate their meaning.

8. What is the difference between STOP and END?
9. What BASIC statement must be used to translate the **until** part of a **repeat** ... **until** structure?
10. What is an infinite loop? How is it expressed in pseudocode?
11. What is the difference between the way in which pseudocode and flowcharts are used?
12. What are the possible values of a condition in an IF statement?

PROBLEMS

Problems are more involved than exercises and self-review questions, but they do not require the complete programming process. In problems P1.1 and P1.2 below, an algorithm is exhibited in pseudocode and flowchart. You are to study them, answer the accompanying questions, write the corresponding BASIC program, and run it on a computer.

You will need to understand the given procedures in order to answer the questions which accompany them. One way to understand a program which has been written by someone else (or by you!) is to trace it. For example, the following program description may be traced by noting values of I and J at the starred statement on each pass through the loop.

procedure	I	J	output
$I \leftarrow 1$	2	8	8
repeat	4	6	6
$I \leftarrow I + 1$	6	4	4
$J \leftarrow 10 - I$	8	2	2
* print J			
$I \leftarrow I + 1$			
until $I > 8$			
endproc			

The reading of algorithms, which often involves tracing, is an essential part of the education of a programmer. It is sometimes easier to learn how someone else accomplished a task, than to "re-invent the wheel".

P1.1

```
procedure
    I ← 1
    repeat
        J ← I²
        print J
        I ← I + 1
    until I > 10
endproc
```

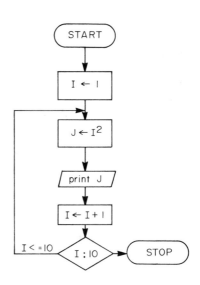

What happens if $J \leftarrow I^2$ is replaced by $I \leftarrow I^2$?
What happens if $I \leftarrow I + 1$ is replaced by $I \leftarrow I + 2$?
What happens if the condition $I > 10$ is replaced with one of the other 5 conditions?

P1.2

```
procedure
    I ← 1
    while I < = 10 do
        J ← I³
        print J
        I ← I + 1
    endwhile
endproc
```

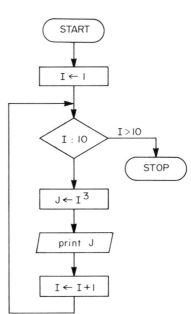

What happens if $I \leftarrow I + 1$ is replaced with $J \leftarrow J + 1$?
What happens if **print** J is moved below **endwhile**?

PROGRAMS

Write programs for the problems below, after developing them with pseudo-code and describing them with a flowchart. You should end up with a program that works, a listing of it in its final form (if you have access to a printer), and some sample runs.

PG1.1   Input a sequence of negative numbers until their sum is less than -250, print the actual sum, and stop.

PG1.2   Input 15 numbers, count how many are less than or equal to zero, and print the count.

PG1.3   Input 15 numbers, sum the negative and positive ones separately, and print both sums on the same line after the last number is in.

PG1.4   Input 15 numbers and find both the largest and the smallest; print them and their average.

PG1.5   The number N-factorial, written $N!$, is defined to be:

$$N! = N(N - 1)(N - 2) \ldots 3 \cdot 2 \cdot 1.$$

Write a program which inputs N and prints $N!$ (Try the program with some fairly small whole numbers after it is written. Then try it with 7.3 and -4 also.)

PG1.6   Input 20 numbers and *then* print the *last* one which is smaller than the one before it.

PG1.7   Input a non-negative integer N and list all of the pairs of non-negative integers which sum to N.

PG1.8   Write a program which will input 20 numbers and count

   I the number of times that an input value is greater than the previous one, and
   J the number of times that an input value is less than the previous one.

Print I and J. (In algebraic terms, input x_1, x_2, ..., x_{20}. The number of k's for which $x_k > x_{k-1}$ is I and the number of k's for which $x_k < x_{k-1}$ is J.) Such counts are used to form non-parametric statistical measures of tendency.

PG1.9 Write a program to input 20 numbers and count the number of non-decreasing runs of input values. For example:

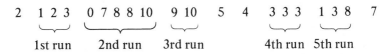

The output would be 5 for the example numbers.

PG1.10 Add the capability to PG1.9 to count the number of non-increasing runs also. Print both counts and the average *length* of both types of runs. In the example of PG1.9, there are 5 non-increasing runs. The average lengths are 3.2 for non-decreasing, and 3.0 for non-increasing.

PG1.11 Write a program to input numbers with values $1 \leq I \leq 15$ and count how many satisfy each of the following:

$$A: 1 \leq I \leq 5 \quad B: 6 \leq I \leq 10 \quad C: 11 \leq I \leq 15$$

Any input value which lies outside of these ranges is to be rejected (not counted): 15 *valid* input values are to be counted. The input values are not necessarily integers.

PG1.12 Write a program which inputs an integer and prints the digits of the integer separately. Hint: $378 - 300 = 78$ but $378 - 400 = -22$.

Chapter 2

LOOPS AND STRUCTURES

2.1 TECHNIQUE

We now have tools with which to work, but in order to apply them, we also need technique, and something to apply it to. The statements which were developed in Chapter 1 can be used to solve many problems in Mathematics, Physics, Chemistry, Biology, Economics, Finance, Accounting, and so on, but most readers of this book, or any book, do not have the knowledge to deal with problems in all of these areas. Fortunately there are many problems which do not require a great deal of background, including some games and some general problems in the area of computing itself. This leaves us with the need for practice and for technique, and in fact, solving most interesting problems of any kind demand both.

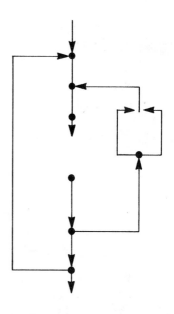

The technique which is covered in this chapter is concerned with designing a clear structure for a program. It is possible to solve a major problem that has a flowchart which looks like a spaghetti monster, but the time spent in debugging it is excessive (and painful). Such a solution is never *clearly* correct, so who should trust it? Programmers who use good technique to create programs are *much* more effective than those who try to solve a problem by following one thread at a time until they create a tangle which (hopefully) has no loose ends. The use of pseudocode throughout the design process *forces* the resulting algorithm into readable structures. The structures which are suitable for describing a program solution to a problem can then be translated into any available version of BASIC.

2.2 THE repeat ... forever STRUCTURE

Some structures which help to straighten out the logic of a program have already been used in the examples in Chapter 1. Some are built into the language. For example, the placing of statements causes the flow of logic to be like this:

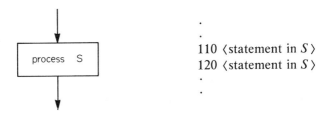

110 ⟨statement in S⟩
120 ⟨statement in S⟩

The branch statement, which in BASIC is a GO TO, allows statements to be reused many times in a loop. The reuse of statements takes advantage of the speed of the computer, but the only loops which can be created with it have the following structure:

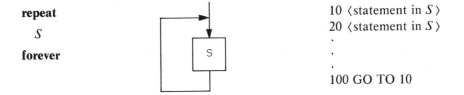

repeat
  S
forever

10 ⟨statement in S⟩
20 ⟨statement in S⟩
.
.
.
100 GO TO 10

Here S may be any block of statements, which itself may have a complex structure. The conditional branch capability of BASIC provides an escape from the **repeat** ... **forever** loop:

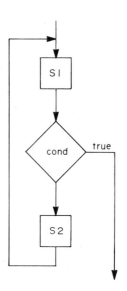

repeat
  *S*1
  if cond **then exit**
  *S*2
forever

  10 ⟨first statement of *S*1⟩
     .
     .
     .
  40 ⟨last statement of *S*1⟩
  50 IF ⟨cond⟩ THEN 110
  60 ⟨first statement of *S*2⟩
     .
     .
     .
  90 ⟨last statement of *S*2⟩
100 GO TO 10
110 ⟨statement which follows the loop⟩

Here *S*1 and *S*2 are *blocks* of one or more statements. This is the structure which can be used for the input of variable values that are to be processed before a new value is entered. In such an input loop, we may check to see what input values occur, and branch out of the loop if the values satisfy some condition. The same structure may be used in a variety of other situations also, of course.

2.3 THE CONDITIONAL BRANCH STRUCTURE

The conditional branch itself is a structure which occurs in two varieties. One of them is:

if cond **then** S

which may also be displayed by:

if cond
   then S
   endif

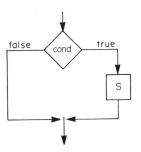

The **endif** is often left off when it is *clear* which statement in the pseudo-code is the last one in the block of statements indicated by S above. When in doubt about clarity, include it.

The **if** ... **then** structure appears in three forms in many versions of BASIC, although some versions support only one of them:

general form	example
[N] IF ⟨cond⟩ THEN [M]	10 IF $A < 0$ THEN 100
[N] IF ⟨cond⟩ GO TO [M]	20 IF $A > 0$ GO TO 200
[N] IF ⟨cond⟩ THEN ⟨statement⟩	30 IF $B < A$ THEN PRINT S

In [10] and [20], S is a branch, and in [30] it is a single statement. The pseudocode is more general than this, however. It allows more than one statement for process S, and that can be very useful because it arises naturally in the logic of a program solution. In order to express this more general structure in BASIC while leaving the program structure obvious to the reader of a program, the program may branch around S if the condition is *false,* and leave S placed physically after the IF statement. For example, suppose that a value in the variable A is to be added to a total in the variable T, but only if it is less than the value in the variable B. Suppose further that the running total is to be printed whenever it changes —which is also when $A < B$. These two events can be treated with separate conditional statements:

if $A < B$ **then** $T \leftarrow T + A$ 100 IF $A < B$ THEN $T = T + A$
if $A < B$ **then print** T 110 IF $A < B$ THEN PRINT T

They can also be collected as a block of statements which are to be executed if the condition $A < B$ is true:

if $A < B$
    then
        $T \leftarrow T + A$
        print T
    endif
$C \leftarrow C + 1$

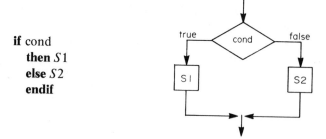

        100 IF $A >= B$ THEN 130
        110 LET $T = T + A$
        120 PRINT T
        130 LET $C = C + 1$

With a larger block of statements to be executed when the condition is true, this more general form becomes even more attractive as a suitable description for the logic of a program.

Not all of the variations of the IF ... THEN shown in this section are available in all versions of BASIC, but some versions do include the general form of the **if** ... **then** and allow multiple statements in process S. In all versions of BASIC, the general form can be implemented by branching around a block of statements.

There is an even more general form of the conditional branch:

if cond
    then $S1$
    else $S2$
    endif

The **if** ... **then** ... **else** can be realized in simple BASIC as shown below, where [20] − [100] acts as $S2$ and [110] − [200] as $S1$.

```
 10  IF ⟨cond⟩ THEN 110
 20  ⟨first statement of S2⟩
  .
  .
  .
 90  ⟨last statement of S2⟩
100  GO TO 210
110  ⟨first statement of S1⟩
  .
  .
  .
200  ⟨last statement of S1⟩
210  ⟨statement which logically follows the endif⟩
  .
  .
  .
```

The difference between the **if** ... **then** and the **if** ... **then** ... **else** structures shows up in the example below:

.
.
.

if $A < 0$ **then** $N \leftarrow N + A$
      else $P \leftarrow P + A$
       endif
$C \leftarrow C + 1$
.
.
.

If A is less than zero then A is added to N, whereas if A is greater than or equal to zero, then A is added to P, and in *either* case, C is incremented. Compare this with:

.
.
.

if $A < 0$ **then** $N \leftarrow N + A$
$P \leftarrow P + A$
$C \leftarrow C + 1$
.
.
.

In this second structure, when A is less than zero, then A is added to N, but whether it *is or not,* A is added to P and then C is incremented.

A program segment that is equivalent to the **if** ... **then** ... **else** example may be constructed with only the simple **if** ... **then** structure like this:

.
.
.

if $A < 0$ **then** $N \leftarrow N + A$
if $A \geq 0$ **then** $P \leftarrow P + A$
$C \leftarrow C + 1$
.
.
.

We already have the bare minimum of structure required to do all of the things we might wish to do:

> It has been shown that the logical structure of BASIC programs can be written using only the assignment, branch, and the conditional branch statements.

In this book, we wish to approach the overall structure of problems more effectively than these minimal logical structures will allow. We will do that by introducing a few more structures that express some logical patterns which arise rather naturally when problems are analyzed.

2.4   THE repeat ... until AND while ... do LOOPS

A conditional branch was inserted as an exit in the middle of a loop in Section 2.2. One can also be inserted at either end. If a conditional branch is inserted at the bottom, then the resulting loop is:

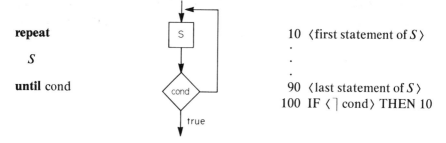

repeat

   S

until cond

10 ⟨first statement of S⟩
.
.
.
90 ⟨last statement of S⟩
100 IF ⟨ ⌐ cond⟩ THEN 10

The symbol ⌐ means "not", hence ⟨ ⌐ cond⟩ is true when ⟨cond⟩ is false, whence ⟨ ⌐ cond⟩ is false when ⟨cond⟩ is true.

With the conditional branch at the other end of the loop we get:

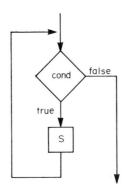

while cond **do**
  S
endwhile

```
 10 IF ⟨⌐ cond⟩ THEN 110
 20 ⟨first statement of S⟩
    .
    .
    .
 90 ⟨last statement of S⟩
100 GO TO 10
110 ⟨statement which follows the loop⟩
```

This form of loop has the advantage that if the condition is not true, then the process *S* will not be executed at all. A number of languages, including BASIC, incorporate statements which form a specialized but common type of **while** ... **do** structure within a program.

A program can be designed with either the **repeat** ... **until** structure or the **while** ... **do** structure. As an example, suppose that we wish to input a number of days, and output the corresponding number of weeks and days. Two variables will certainly be involved:

D //the number of days//
W //the number of weeks//

An algorithm for making the transformation can be derived by noting that all of the following represent the same number of days:

W	D
(weeks)	(days)
0	27
1	20
2	13
3	6

The usual description of this many days is 3 weeks and 6 days, and so that should be the output of the program when the input is 27 days. This result can be derived by forming a loop which repeatedly decrements D by 7 and increments W by 1 as long as D is greater than 7. Expressed in pseudo-code, this is:

```
procedure WEEKS__AND__DAYS        10 INPUT D
    input D                       20 LET W = 0
    W ← 0                         30 If D < 7 THEN 70
    while D ≥ 7 do                40 LET D = D - 7
        D ← D - 7                 50 LET W = W + 1
        W ← W + 1                 60 GO TO 30
    endwhile                      70 PRINT W, D
    print W, D                    80 STOP
endproc                           90 END
```

Here is an apparent solution with a **repeat** ... **until** loop:

```
input D
W ← 0
repeat
    D ← D - 7
    W ← W + 1
until D < 7
print W, D
```

Actually, this is not equivalent to the **while** ... **do** solution for *all* input data. The difference occurs when the input for D is less than 7. The **repeat** ... **until** structure will output:

1   −1

when the input value of D is 6.

The **repeat** . . . **until** is a very natural and useful structure, but the body of the loop is *always* executed at least once because the test is at the bottom of the loop. Having the test at the bottom of a loop can lead to problems if, for some data, it is not desirable to make a pass through the loop at all. A valid **repeat** . . . **until** structure for this problem is:

input D	10 INPUT D
$W \leftarrow 0$	20 LET $W = 0$
if $D \geq 7$	30 IF $D < 7$ THEN 70
then repeat	40 LET $D = D - 7$
$D \leftarrow D - 7$	50 LET $W = W + 1$
$W \leftarrow W + 1$	60 IF $D > = 7$ THEN 40
until $D < 7$	70 PRINT W, D
endif	80 STOP
print W, D	90 END

The reader should note that the forms of these loops are explicit:

1. The body of a **repeat** . . . **forever** loop lies between the **repeat** at the top and the **forever** at the bottom. That block of pseudocode is precisely what is included on each pass.
2. The body of a **repeat** . . . **until** loop lies between the **repeat** and the **until**. That block of pseudocode is precisely what is included on each pass, and the loop is controlled by the condition. The test for exit from a **repeat** . . . **until** loop is at the bottom. If the test controlling the loop is at the top or in the middle, then the structure is not a **repeat** . . . **until**.
3. The body of a **while** . . . **do** loop lies between the **while** . . . **do** and the **endwhile**. That block of pseudocode is precisely what is included on each pass. The test for exit from a **while** . . . **do** is at the top, and the loop is controlled by the condition. If the test controlling the loop is at the bottom or the middle, then the structure is not a **while** . . . **do**.
4. An exit may be made from any of these loops at any point by: **if** cond2 **then exit**. (The condition here is usually distinct from the condition which controls the loop.) There are no statement numbers or labels in pseudocode, and the *only* other way out of a loop is by satisfying the condition which controls its repetitions. On exit of either kind, control passes to the pseudocode immediately following the **forever, until,** or **endwhile**.
5. There are *no* other loop forms in pseudocode.

One result of these restrictions is that in the pseudocode description of an algorithm, control enters a loop, the loop repeatedly executes (iterates) until the control condition is satisfied, and then control passes to the pseudocode which follows the loop. Hence the loop forms a unit and may be designed, and read, as a package. It may then be translated into any version of BASIC and retain the logical structure designed into the algorithm.

2.4.1 A Comparison of Loop Structures

The logic of a **while** ... **do** loop may also be expressed in terms of the **repeat** ... **until** and the **repeat** ... **forever** structures. The following are equivalent:

while cond **do**	**if** cond	**repeat**
S	**then repeat**	**if** cond
endwhile	S	**then** S
	until $\rceil$ cond	**else exit**
	endif	**endif**
		forever

For the special cases in which the initial value of the condition is determined by the logic itself, the equivalence may take on a simpler form. For example, the following are equivalent:

$I \leftarrow 1$	$I \leftarrow 1$	$I \leftarrow 1$
while $I \leq 10$ **do**	**repeat**	**repeat**
S	S	**if** $I > 10$ **then exit**
$I \leftarrow I + 1$	$I \leftarrow I + 1$	S
endwhile	**until** $I > 10$	$I \leftarrow I + 1$
		forever

However, if the condition $I \leq N$ replaces $I \leq 10$ in the **while** ... **do** structure, the equivalence of the **repeat** ... **until** with condition $I > N$ depends upon the initial value of N. (If $N < 1$ then S will not be executed in the **while** ... **do**.) The **repeat** ... **forever** form with condition $I > N$ will still be equivalent when the **if** $I > N$ **then exit** is placed before the block of statements S. It may not be equivalent when the **if** follows S. The difference in the forms in all cases depends upon whether or not the statement block S is executed at least one time.

As a more specific example, consider the following loop:

```
Z ← 0
repeat
  input X, Y
  if X ≤ Y then exit
  Z ← X + Y + Z
forever
print Z
```

This is *equivalent* to the two loops immediately below in the sense that for *all* possible sequences of input data, the output will be precisely the same for all three programs:

```
Z ← 0
input X, Y
while X > Y do
  Z ← X + Y + Z
  input X, Y
endwhile
print Z
```

```
Z ← 0
X ← 0
Y ← 0
repeat
  Z ← X + Y + Z
  input X, Y
until X ≤ Y
print Z
```

In contrast, the loops below are *not* equivalent to the three above:

```
Z ← 0
repeat
  input X, Y
  Z ← X + Y + Z
until X ≤ Y
print Z
```

If the initial pair of input values of X, Y is 1, 2 then this routine will print 3 and stop, whereas the original three routines will print 0 and stop.

```
Z ← 0
while X > Y do
  Z ← X + Y + Z
  input X, Y
endwhile
print Z
```

If $X ← 0$ and $Y ← 0$ by the BASIC translator at the start of a run, then a BASIC version of this loop will never input any data. If BASIC does not pre-determine the values of X and Y, then the results will vary from one run to another. The pseudocode is not equivalent because X and Y are undetermined in this routine when they are first used, but they are determined in the original routines at that point.

$Z \leftarrow 0$
$X \leftarrow 0$
$Y \leftarrow 0$
repeat
  input X, Y
  $Z \leftarrow X + Y + Z$
until $X \leq Y$
print Z

If the initial pair of input values of X, Y is 1, 2 then this routine will print 3 and stop. The original three would print 0 and stop. (This routine will have the same output as the original three only when $X + Y$ is the same for both the next-to-last and the last pair of input values.)

$Z \leftarrow 0$
input X, Y
repeat
  $Z \leftarrow X + Y + Z$
  input X, Y
until $X \leq Y$
print Z

If the initial pair of input values of X, Y is 1, 2 then this routine will *not* stop, like the original three: it will call for more data.

For *most* sequences of input pairs, the four alternate routines will behave just like the original three. In fact, they will do so for the kind of data for which they seem to be intended: a sequence of data pairs for which the X-value is larger than the Y-value, followed by one pair for which this is reversed, and which acts as a signal to stop. Program logic, and programs, need to be tested for a variety of possibilities.

The BASIC translation of the original three routines is as follows:

```
10 LET Z = 0
20 INPUT X, Y
30 IF X < = Y THEN 60
40 LET Z = X + Y + Z
50 GO TO 20
60 PRINT Z
70 STOP
80 END
```
The **repeat** ... **forever** form.

```
10 LET Z = 0
20 INPUT X, Y
30 IF X < = Y THEN 70
40 LET Z = X + Y + Z
50 INPUT X, Y
60 GO TO 30
70 PRINT Z
80 STOP
90 END
```
The **while** ... **do** form.

```
10 LET Z = 0
20 LET X = 0
30 LET Y = 0
40 LET Z = X + Y + Z          The repeat ... until form.
50 INPUT X, Y
60 IF X > Y THEN 40
70 PRINT Z
80 STOP
90 END
```

2.5 AN IF-LOOP EXAMPLE

The **while** ... **do** form of a loop is so useful that it is built into the BASIC language, although in a restricted form. We shall display that form as an IF-loop in this section before we introduce it as a language feature in the following section. Quite often the number of times a program execution passes through a loop needs to be counted. For this, a *counter* can be used to control the looping process: a variable in which to keep the count of the number of passes. A counter must be initialized to a starting value, incremented each time through the loop, and checked to see if it has yet reached some limit. When the limit has been reached, an exit from the loop has to be made. A **while** ... **do** loop which is controlled by a counter that runs from 1 to 10, and exits by way of an IF statement, has the form:

```
I ← 1                          10 LET I = 1
while I < = 10 do              20 IF I > 10 THEN 110
   S                           30 ⟨first statement of S⟩
   I ← I + 1                    .
endwhile                        .
                                .
                               80 ⟨last statement of S⟩
                               90 LET I = I + 1
                               100 GO TO 20
                               110 ⟨statement which follows the loop⟩
```

In the loop above, the counter is initialized to 1 in [10], incremented by 1 each time through the loop in [90], and is compared to the limit 10 to generate an exit at [20]. Consider the problem of producing a table of the squares and cubes of the first 20 integers. This can be done by forming a loop which prints the squares and cubes of the value of a counter, I, on each pass through the loop. Hence I must be initialized to 1 before the loop is entered, incremented by one on each pass, and the loop should terminate after the 20th value has been processed. The variable I may then be used as the loop control counter also. Expressed in pseudocode and translated into BASIC this process is:

procedure TABLE	10 LET $I = 1$
$I \leftarrow 1$	20 IF $I > 20$ THEN 80
while $I \leq 20$ **do**	30 LET $S = I \uparrow 2$
print I, I^2, I^3	40 LET $C = S*I$
$I \leftarrow I + 1$	50 PRINT I, S, C
endwhile	60 LET $I = I + 1$
endproc	70 GO TO 20
	80 STOP
	90 END

The counter I in the loop above is also called the **control variable** of the loop. Like many slight changes in terminology or notation, this term indicates a different view of the matter at hand. The term control variable actually implies a generalization of the idea of a counter. The use of a loop can be controlled by starting the control variable at any value, not just 1, changing it by any value, not just $+1$, and checking it against any limit value.

It is important to understand the IF-loop before reading the next section. The exercises which follow should help.

EXERCISES

In the program derived from procedure TABLE, what happens if:

E2.1   [70] is replaced by:

70 GO TO 10

E2.2   [60] is replaced by:

60 LET $I = I + 2$

or by:

60 LET $I = I*1$

(how many times does control pass through the loop?)

E2.3   [20] is replaced by:

20 IF $I >= 20$ THEN 80

or by:

20 IF $I < 20$ THEN 80

E2.4   We include the statement:

55 LET $I = 3$

E2.5   [10], [20], and [60] become:

10 LET $I = 20$
20 IF $I < 1$ THEN 80
.
.
.
60 LET $I = I - 1$

You should get on a computer and try these variations of an IF-loop.

2.6   FOR ... NEXT LOOPS

Some IF-loops, controlled by counters like the following one, can be expressed in a neat way in BASIC:

procedure SUM__OF__SQUARES   10 LET $S = 0$
    $S \leftarrow 0$
    $I \leftarrow 1$ 20 LET $I = 1$
    while $I <= 10$ **do**   30 IF $I > 10$ THEN 70
        $S \leftarrow S + I^2$
        $I \leftarrow I + 1$ 40   LET $S = S + I \uparrow 2$
    endwhile
    print S 50 LET $I = I + 1$
endproc

                                        60 GO TO 30

                                        70 PRINT S
                                        80 STOP
                                        90 END

The program which follows generates the *same* results as the one above:

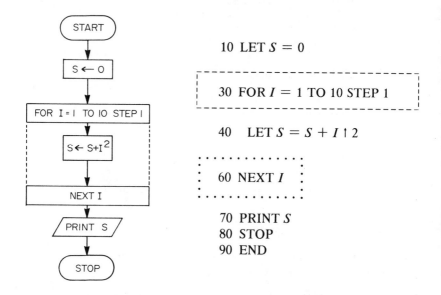

10 LET $S = 0$

30 FOR $I = 1$ TO 10 STEP 1

40 LET $S = S + I \uparrow 2$

60 NEXT I

70 PRINT S
80 STOP
90 END

The changes that occurred are:

1. The control information in the statements [20], [30], and [50] are all combined in the FOR statement, which determines the control variable I, its initial value 1, its limit 10, and the amount by which the value of I is to be stepped up each time through the loop (when [60] is executed).
2. Statements [50] and [60] are replaced by the NEXT statement, which explicitly determines the location of the end of the loop which was initialized by the FOR statement. It also causes the step to occur. The connection between the FOR and the NEXT statements is made by the translator because of two things: the NEXT comes *after* the FOR, and both refer to the *same control variable*.

The FOR ... NEXT loop above is merely a shorthand notation for the corresponding IF-loop. The information within the dashed lines, and the information within the dotted lines are contained within the FOR statement and the NEXT statement. The crucial information is:

1. The name, I, of the control variable.
2. The initial value, 1, of I.

3. The limiting value, 10, of *I*.
4. The step value, 1, of *I*.
5. The position of the top of the loop.
6. The position of the bottom of the loop.

Note that the loop *will* be executed when *I* is 1 and when it is 10, just as the IF-loop will be.

The SUM_OF_SQUARES example can be generalized somewhat. If [30] were:

30 FOR *I* = 3 TO 10 STEP 1

then the loop would be executed 8 times instead of 10 because it would be equivalent to the corresponding IF-loop with:

20 LET *I* = 3

If [30] were changed to:

30 FOR *I* = 1 TO 10 STEP 3

then the loop would be executed with *I* equal to 1, 4, 7, and then 10—four times. This change would be equivalent to the corresponding IF-loop with [50] replaced by:

50 LET *I* = *I* + 3

Most versions of BASIC include a still more generalized form of the FOR statement: the initial value, the limit value, and the STEP value of the control variable may be specified by variables, as in this example:

JKL program

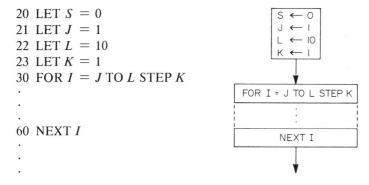

20 LET *S* = 0
21 LET *J* = 1
22 LET *L* = 10
23 LET *K* = 1
30 FOR *I* = *J* TO *L* STEP *K*
.
.
.
60 NEXT *I*
.
.
.

Of course, the values of the variables *J, K,* and *L* may be determined in some other part of the program or acquired with an INPUT statement, but they do need to be determined before [30] is executed. It is their values *only at the entry to* [30] which are used for loop control. No statements within the loop can change the *control* values, although the values of *I, J,* and *K* as variables may be changed, and then affect other aspects of the program. For example:

```
10 LET K = 3
20 FOR A = 1 TO K STEP 1
30    PRINT A;
40    LET K = 6
50 NEXT A
60 PRINT K
70 STOP
80 END
```

has the output:

```
1  2  3  6
```

not the output:

```
1  2  3  4  5  6  6
```

The BASIC translator needs only the *value* of *J, K,* and *L* at the time of execution in order to translate the loop structure.

Although a FOR ... NEXT loop is a **while** ... **do** loop, the converse is not necessarily true. The following cannot be written as a FOR ... NEXT loop because the number of passes to be made through the loop are not determined at the time the loop is entered during execution.

procedure CONTROL
  input *A*
  while *A* ≥ 0 **do**
    print *A* ↑ 7
    input *A*
  endwhile
endproc

EXERCISE E2.6

Rewrite the loop above as an IF-loop, and run it on a computer.

2.6.1   The Nesting of Loops

A programming error that must be avoided when using FOR ... NEXT loops (and IF-loops also) is the transfer of control into the middle of one without going through the initialization at the top of it. The following is forbidden:

100 FOR $L = $ ...
.
.
.
150 ⟨statement within the L-loop⟩
.
.
.
200 NEXT L
.
.
.
300 GO TO 150
.
.
.

In the IF-loop of the previous section, the initialization was [10]. In a FOR ... NEXT loop, it is the FOR statement itself. Jumping into a loop from outside generally leads to disaster, or at the least, to an error message and the unplanned stopping of execution. Loops can be *nested,* one inside of the other, but not overlapped.

This *will* work:

while cond1 **do**
  *S*1
  while cond2 **do**
    *S*2
  endwhile
  *S*3
endwhile

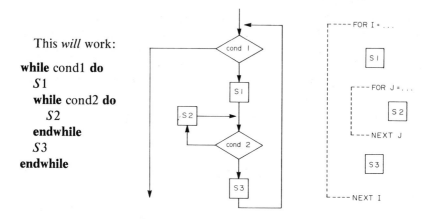

This will *not* work.

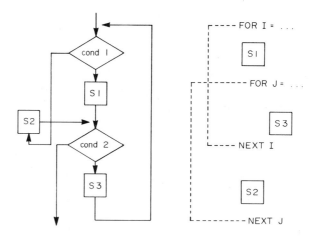

The advantage of pseudocode over BASIC or flowcharting is very clear in this example. Try to construct pseudocode with overlapping loops! (An **endwhile** is the bottom of the loop begun by the *previous* **while**.) That is one reason why some languages are designed to be written very much like pseudocode.

2.6.2 No STEP

Most versions of BASIC allow the STEP ⟨variable⟩ part of the FOR statement to be omitted. Of course, there must be a step in value of the control variable somewhere in the loop, else the procedure will be a **loop ... forever**. What the BASIC translator does is to always assume a **default value** of 1 for the step if it is not explicitly specified. The programmer leaves the choice of step value to the translator by default. This:

FOR $W = 9$ TO 870 STEP 1

and this:

FOR $W = 9$ TO 870

are equivalent.

Most versions of BASIC will also allow the step value to be negative. When it is, the control variable will be **decremented** (go down) by the step value each time. In that case, the control variable should start high and be checked to see if it has fallen below the limit. For example:

```
.
.
.
R ← 1                  10 LET R = 1
Z ← 9                  20 FOR Z = 9 TO 3 STEP − 2
while Z > = 3 do       30    LET R = R + 5
  R ← R + 5            40    PRINT R
  print R              50 NEXT Z
  Z ← Z − 2            .
endwhile               .
.                      .
.
.
```

Some versions of BASIC will also allow the initial value, limit, and step to be *any* numbers, such as −0.0012, but most will not.

EXERCISE E2.7

Rewrite the loop above as an IF-loop, and try it on a computer, but trace it first.

2.7   THE case STRUCTURE

There is still another useful structure built of the conditional branch. At times, we may want a program to do one of several things, and which one is to be done depends upon a set of conditions, or perhaps upon several possible values of a variable. One way to reflect this natural logic is with the **case** structure:

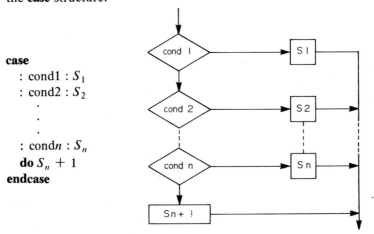

case
   : cond1 : S_1
   : cond2 : S_2
     .
     .
   : cond$n$: S_n
   do S_n + 1
endcase

The case structure can be constructed in BASIC like this:

```
   10  IF ⟨⌐ cond1⟩ THEN 100
        .                        ⎫
        .                        ⎬ ⟨statements of S1⟩
        .                        ⎭
   90  GO TO 1000
  100  IF ⟨⌐ cond2⟩ THEN 200
        .                        ⎫
        .                        ⎬ ⟨statements of S2⟩
        .                        ⎭
  190  GO TO 1000
  200  IF ...
        .

        .

        .
  890  GO TO 1000
  900  IF ⟨⌐ cond10⟩ THEN 1000
        .

        .

        .
 1000  statement
```

The case structure is especially useful for breaking up large tasks into smaller ones. Each case may represent a major subtask, and be developed as a procedure itself. The conditions should be written so that they *do not overlap* (they are mutually exclusive).

The **case** structure is a *sequence* of **if** statements, but it differs from a *nest* of **if** statements. For example, contrast these two procedures:

```
procedure LEFT                    procedure RIGHT
   case of X                         if X < 0
      : X < 0  : procedure XNEG      then
      : Y > 10 : procedure YBIG         procedure XNEG
      procedure SMALL                   if Y > 10
   endcase                                then procedure YBIG
endproc                                endif
                                     endif
                                     procedure SMALL
                                  endproc
```

If $X < 0$ and $Y \leq 10$ then both LEFT and RIGHT will execute procedures XNEG and SMALL. If, on the other hand, $X \geq 0$ and $Y > 10$, then LEFT will execute procedures YBIG and SMALL, but RIGHT will execute only procedure SMALL because it never checks Y. LEFT may be written as a sequence of **if** ... **then** structures like this:

```
procedure LEFT
   if X < 0 then procedure XNEG
   if Y > 10 then procedure YBIG
   procedure SMALL
endproc
```

The student should be aware that the transformation of procedure LEFT into procedure RIGHT is fairly likely to happen accidentally during the translation of pseudocode into BASIC, but it can be avoided by the careful placement of GO TO in the BASIC. It is also worth noting that *some* data will give the expected results ($X = 3$, $Y = 10$), and some will not ($X = 11$, $Y = 11$). The next section presents a program which uses the **case** structure. The program of the next section is more difficult than one which the reader would be expected to produce at this point because of some features which have not yet been introduced—but the **case** part of its structure is quite straightforward.

2.8   THE GAME OF CRAPS

The ancient game of Craps is a game in which a crowd of onlookers and participants may bet for or against the luck of one player who rolls a pair of dice. The roller begins with a single throw. If the dice show 7 or 11 on this first round, then s/he wins. If they show 2 (snake-eyes), 3 (craps), or 12 (boxcars), then the roller loses. If, however, the dice show some other number (4, 5, 6, 8, 9, or 10) then that number becomes the *point*. If the first roll establishes a point instead of determining a win or a loss, then the dice are repeatedly thrown until they show one of:

> 7—a loss for the roller
> the point again—a win for the roller

A game of Craps is a sequence of rolls which ends with either a win or a loss for the roller.

Each of the nine sequences of rolls below would determine a game—4 are wins for the roller, and 5 are losses for the roller:

wins: 7
        11
        5, 3, 11, 4, 5
        9, 6, 8, 9
losses: 2
        3
        12
        5, 3, 11, 4, 7
        9, 6, 8, 7

We shall write a program which is a **simulation** of Craps: the program will pretend to be a roller, carrying out 100 games. The output will be the number of first-round wins, the number of first-round losses, and the number of times the point is made.

In order to simulate a roll of the dice, it is necessary to choose an integer from 1 to 6 for each die, all with equal probability, to represent the face value of the die. The two face values can then be added together to form the value of the roll. BASIC provides a way, called the RND function, to choose numbers with equal probability.

2.8.1   The RND Function

Many games and simulations involve choosing items at random, rather than in a predetermined pattern. A number RND is said to be *randomly chosen between 0 and 1* if any fraction in that range is equally likely to be chosen as the value of RND. BASIC provides a way to approximate a random choice in the range 0 to 1 (no way is available to make all such fractions precisely equal in their probability of being chosen). The resulting choice is called a **pseudorandom** number, and it is invoked in a BASIC expression by use of RND in place of a variable. For example,

```
100 LET X = RND
110 PRINT X
```

will display numbers like .765243516, or .001465938. Each time [100] and [110] are executed during a run, a different choice is made by RND. When [100] and [110] are placed in a loop, the output might look like this:

```
.587907766
.176195373
.894661129
.391726293
.
.
.
```

(as it actually did on a personal computer.) Quite often, the value that is to be chosen is to be within some range of numbers other than $0 < X < 1$. This can be done with statements like this:

```
100 LET X = 6*RND
110 PRINT X
```

which will yield the following from the same sequence of numbers which were displayed above:

```
3.52254466
1.05717224
5.36796677
2.35035776
.
.
.
```

These numbers are in the range $0 < X < 6$, but may be shifted to the range $7 < X < 13$ by:

```
100 LET X = 7 + 6*RND
110 PRINT X
```

The numbers may be shifted to any range, with the use of an appropriate multiplier and addend. In particular, to obtain $A < X < B$, use:

100 LET $X = A + (B - A)*$RND

The utility of pseudorandom numbers is enhanced even more by the ability to restrict the chosen values to be integers. This can be done in BASIC with a *function*, INT. (Functions are discussed in Chapter 5, and only the *use* of INT will be illustrated here.) INT(A) will take on the value of the largest integer less than or equal to the value of A. For example, if $X = 3.41$, then INT(A) has the value 3. If $X = 11.956$, then INT(A) has the value 11. When combined with RND, INT(6*RND) will take on the values 0, 1, 2, 3, 4, 5 with equal probability, and

100 LET $X = $ INT(6*RND $+ 1$)

will assign 1, 2, 3, 4, 5, 6 to X with equal probability. This is the result that is needed for a simulation of Craps.

In most versions of BASIC, the same *sequence* of pseudorandom numbers will be produced each time a program is run, unless a special statement is added to the beginning of the program, either

[N] RANDOM

or perhaps

[N] RANDOMIZE

In other systems:

RND(-1) will produce the same number with each use in a run
RND(0) will produce the same sequence of values for each run
RND(1) will produce a different sequence of values with every run

2.8.2   An Approach to Craps

The problem of simulating Craps is substantial enough to be approached with caution, and we begin with some variable descriptions, in order to develop an understanding of the information with which the program must deal. We certainly will need counters for the number of games and the three results to be tabulated. We will also need a variable for the current show of the dice and the value of the current point:

variable descriptions
>   W //the number of first-round wins//
>   L //the number of first-round losses//
>   P //the number of point wins//
>   C //the show value of the pair of dice//
>   V //the value of the current point//
>   N //the count of the number of games played//

An initial description of the process that is to be carried out in one game, in terms of these variables, is:

> Roll the dice (using RND) to obtain the face value *C*. If *C* is 7 or 11 then *W* should be incremented, and this game is finished. If *C* is 2, 3, or 12 then *L* should be incremented, and this game is finished. If *C* is not 7, 11, 2, 3, or 12 then it becomes the point and is assigned to *V*. The game can then only be finished by repeatedly rolling the dice until either 7 or the value of *V* occurs. The rolls may be done with a loop which continues until there is a win and *W* is incremented (the dice show the value *V*), or a loss and *L* is incremented (the dice show the value 7). As soon as either occurs, the game is finished.

The three possible results of the first roll fit nicely into a **case** structure, since they are all initiated by the first roll, and when any one of them is completed, the game being simulated is over. If the process above is in terms of the **case** structure we have:

I. If $N \leq 100$ then roll the dice and determine *C*.

II. Choose between three cases of *C*:

   a. *C* is 7 or 11. Increment *W* and go to III.
   b. *C* is 2, 3, or 12. Increment *L* and go to III.
   c. *C* is 4, 5, 6, 8, 9, or 10. Begin a loop of the form:

      1. Roll the dice to determine *C* again.
      2. If *C* is 7 then go to III.
      3. If *C* is the point then increment *P* and go to III.
      4. Go back to 1.

III. Increment *N* and go back to I.

One problem with this algorithm may not be immediately obvious: the loop in II.c *may* be an infinite loop. It is less and less probable that the number of passes will be *X* as *X* gets larger and larger, however, and so we shall ignore this problem, just as it is ignored by human players of Craps. It would be possible to put in a counter which allows the program to detect and hence limit the number of rolls involved in trying to make a point. A more complete program would print an error message if a point try were cut off by such a limit, because the resulting counts of wins and losses would no longer be unbiased statistics. (The printing of messages is discussed in Chapter 3.) It would also be possible to determine more statistics, such as the average number of tries before a point is made, but that has not been done in order to keep the logic of the example program relatively simple. It is not unusual for a programmer to develop a simplified version of a program and try it out before one with all of the possible bells, lights, and whistles is written. This is just one aspect of a general philosophy of focusing upon a few aspects of a problem at one time, rather than trying to juggle more than is comfortable.

The initial description of the Craps solution may be turned into a pseudo-code description as the next step in the process of the step-wise refinement of the algorithm:

procedure CRAPS
    $W \leftarrow 0 : L \leftarrow 0 : P \leftarrow 0$
    $N \leftarrow 1$
    while $N \leq 100$ **do**
        procedure ROLL   //randomly determine the show of the dice for//
                         //one throw, C//
       case of C //do one of the following, depending upon the value of C//
         : 7, 11 : $W \leftarrow W + 1$
         : 2, 3, 12 : $L \leftarrow L + 1$
         : 4, 5, 6, 8, 9, 10 : $V \leftarrow C$
                    repeat
                      procedure ROLL   //determine C//
                      if $C = 7$ **then exit**
                      if $C = V$ **then** $P \leftarrow P + 1$
                                  exit
                          endif
                  forever
      endcase
      $N \leftarrow N + 1$
    endwhile
    print W, L, P
endproc

The remaining refinement required for the pseudocode description of CRAPS is the design of procedure ROLL.

2.8.3   Procedure ROLL

Procedure ROLL is the simulation of the throw of a pair of dice, and RND provides a way to do that:

procedure ROLL
$\quad C \leftarrow$ INT(6*RND + 1)
$\quad A \leftarrow$ INT(6*RND + 1)
$\quad C \leftarrow C + A$
endproc

The reader should beware that:

$C \leftarrow$ INT(11*RND + 2)

will give different (and erroneous) results, for reasons which would be encountered in a study of probability. (Briefly, with the technique of procedure ROLL, there is only one way for C to acquire a value of 2 but there are 6 ways for it to acquire a value of 7. The other code yields both 2 and 7 with equal probability.)

Procedure ROLL appears in *two* places in the program, and may be inserted into both of them.

2.8.4   The CRAPS Program

With the details in hand, we may now translate CRAPS into BASIC. With the BASIC language features which we have described, CRAPS is somewhat stark. It is always much more difficult to understand the *logic* of the program from the BASIC listing than it is to follow it in the pseudocode description. In Chapter 3 we will describe features of BASIC which will make such a program more readable, and CRAPS will be relisted to demonstrate the difference. Even with careful use of all available BASIC features, the best way to follow the logic of a program is to read the pseudocode. At this point, you should carefully compare the pseudocode for CRAPS with the listing, in order to better understand the correspondence between a program and its logic.

```
  10 LET W = 0
  20 LET L = 0
  30 LET P = 0
  40 FOR N = 1 TO 100
  50    LET C = INT(6*RND + 1)
  51    LET A = INT(6*RND + 1)
  52    LET C = C + A
  60    IF C = 7 THEN 80
  70    IF C < > 11 THEN 100
  80    LET W = W + 1
  90    GO TO 220
 100    IF C = 2 THEN 130
 110    IF C = 3 THEN 130
 120    IF C < > 12 THEN 150
 130    LET L = L + 1
 140    GO TO 220
 150    LET V = C
 160    LET C = INT(6*RND + 1)
 161    LET A = INT(6*RND + 1)
 162    LET C = C + A
 170    IF C = 7 THEN 220
 180    IF C < > V THEN 210
 190    LET P = P + 1
 200    GO TO 220
 210    GO TO 160
 220 NEXT N
 230 PRINT W, L, P
 240 STOP
1040 END
```

2.9   THE GOSUB ... RETURN STRUCTURE

With GO TO statements, it is possible to place a block of code, like procedure ROLL in CRAPS, anywhere in a program, transfer to it, and transfer back again. For example, ROLL could have been put in [1000], [1010], and [1020] and then [50], [51], [52] replaced by 50 GO TO 1000. With the addition of 1030 GO TO 60 to the program, control will still pass from [40] to ROLL and back to [60]. With the changes just indicated, it would be tempting to also replace [160], [161], and [162] with 160 GO TO 1000. However, in that case we would need for [1030] to be 1030 GO TO 170. If ROLL is to be used from more than one position within the program, then a scheme is needed which will remember the position from which ROLL is entered, and return accordingly. BASIC provides for such an unforgetting entry to a program segment with the GOSUB ... RETURN structure. As an example, the body of procedure ROLL may be translated into BASIC as:

```
1000 LET C = INT(6*RND + 1)
1010 LET A = INT(6*RND + 1)
1020 LET C = C + A
```

Then in order to use procedure ROLL from [50], we may write:

```
50 GOSUB 1000
60 ...
```

and:

```
1000 LET C = INT(6*RND + 1)
1010 LET A = INT(6*RND + 1)
1020 LET C = C + A
```

If we then add:

```
1030 RETURN
```

to the program, control will return from [1030] to [60], triggered by the execution of [50], which is "remembered" by the RETURN. If the same program also contains:

```
160 GOSUB 1000
170 ...
```

then the execution of [160] will cause the execution of:

[1000], [1010], [1020], [1030], and then [170].

The RETURN keeps track of the previous GOSUB execution, and returns control accordingly. A program segment like [1000] − [1030] may be used by any number of GOSUB 1000 statements. There is nothing special about the number 1000: any sequence of statements which ends in RETURN will behave in the same way. (The remembering technique that is used for the GOSUB ... RETURN structure is discussed in Chapter 8.)

A major advantage of the GOSUB ... RETURN structure is that it promotes *modularity* in a program. A programmer may break up a programming task into GOSUB ... RETURN modules, each of which handles some distinct part of the problem. They may be called upon in any sequence, from any position in the program, as they are needed. It is essential to split a complex problem into parts which can be solved separately, and this technique will be applied with increasing frequency in later chapters. A modular program is easier to understand and to debug than one that is developed and presented as a whole.

With the use of the GOSUB ... RETURN structure, the CRAPS code becomes the version listed below. (It is this version of CRAPS which will be properly annotated and displayed in Chapter 3.)

```
  10 LET W = 0
  20 LET L = 0
  30 LET P = 0
  40 FOR N = 1 TO 100
  50    GOSUB 1000
  60    IF C = 7 THEN 80
  70    IF C < > 11 THEN 100
  80    LET W = W + 1
  90    GO TO 220
 100    IF C = 2 THEN 130
 110    IF C = 3 THEN 130
 120    IF C < > 12 THEN 150
 130    LET L = L + 1
 140    GO TO 220
 150    LET V = C
 160    GOSUB 1000
 170    IF C = 7 THEN 220
 180    IF C < > V THEN 210
 190    LET P = P + 1
 200    GO TO 220
 210    GO TO 160
 220 NEXT N
 230 PRINT W, L, P
 240 STOP
1000 LET C = INT(6*RND + 1)
1010 LET A = INT(6*RND + 1)
1020 LET C = C + A
1030 RETURN
1040 END
```

2.10   A SUMMARY OF PSEUDOCODE STRUCTURES

variable ← expression

input variable list   **print** variable list

if cond **then** *S* **endif**   **if** cond
 then *S*1
 else *S*2
 endif

case
  cond1 : *S*1
  cond2 : *S*2
    .
    .
    .
  cond*n* : *Sn*
  S_{n+1}
endcase

repeat   **repeat**   **while** cond **do**
  S   *S*   *S*
forever   **until** cond   **endwhile**

Finally we allow **exit** from a loop, and comments between double slashes anywhere.

SELF-REVIEW

1. Is it possible for a **repeat** ... **forever** structure to execute only a finite number of passes?

2. Convert the loop structure in procedure ADD__TEN (1.11.1,), in procedure TABLE (Section 2.5), and in procedure CONTROL (Section 2.6) into the other two equivalent forms.

3. Which conditional branch structures in pseudocode cannot be converted directly into the IF ... THEN statement of Chapter 1?

4. Determine the *minimum* number of GO TO statements required to translate the following into BASIC.

   if $A > 1$
     then $A \leftarrow A - 1$
     else $A \leftarrow A^2$
       print A^2
   endif

(and what is to be printed if $A = 0.6$?)

5. What is the difference between a counter and a control variable?

6. Why is it not possible to translate every **while** ... **do** into a FOR ... NEXT loop?

7. What is the difference between increment and decrement?

8. What happens in a **case** structure if S_{n+1} is omitted, and then none of the conditions are satisfied during an execution?

9. What is the difference between 50 GO TO 450 and 50 GOSUB 450?

PROBLEMS

For problems P2.1 to P2.3, trace the program execution, then produce the other ways of expressing the same routine: pseudocode, flowchart, IF-loop, FOR ... NEXT loop; then answer the accompanying questions:

P2.1

$B \leftarrow 10$ Q: What happens if $C \leftarrow C - 1$
$A \leftarrow 2$ is replaced by $B \leftarrow B - 1$?
$C \leftarrow 2$
while $A < B$ **do**
$\quad C \leftarrow C - 1$ Q: What would be the output of
$\quad A \leftarrow A + 3$ the corresponding program?
endwhile

P2.2

```
10 FOR L = 1 TO 7 STEP 2      Q: What is the output of this
20     LET K = L - 1                program?
30     FOR M = K TO 5
40        PRINT K;
50     NEXT M
55     PRINT
60 NEXT L
70 STOP
80 END
```

P2.3

```
10 LET D = 1
20 IF D < − 8 THEN 120
30 LET E = − D
40 IF E > = 0 THEN 60
50 LET E = − E
60 IF E > 0 THEN 80
70 LET E = 0
80 PRINT E;
90 LET D = D − 1
100 GO TO 20
120 STOP
130 END
```

Q: What is the output of this program?

Q: Can it be simplified and still produce exactly the same output?

P2.4 Convert the following loop into a **repeat** ... **until** loop which has exactly the same output:

$I \leftarrow 7$
while $I < 11$ **do**
  print $I + 1$;
  $I \leftarrow I + 1$
endwhile
print I

Now convert this into a FOR ... NEXT loop and run it.

Note: If $I \leftarrow 7$ is replaced by **input** I, the translation into a **repeat** ... **until** loop is more difficult.

P2.5 How many times is the **print** I; executed in each of the loops below? What is the output of the BASIC translation of the algorithms? (Find out by tracing.)

procedure
  $J \leftarrow 4$
  while $J \leq 9$ **do**
    $I \leftarrow J + J/2$
    $J \leftarrow J + 1$
    print I;
  endwhile
endproc

procedure
  $X \leftarrow 7$
  repeat
    $X \leftarrow X - 1$
    if $X < 3$ **then** $X \leftarrow X - 1$
    $I \leftarrow X \uparrow 2$
    print I;
  until $X < -2$
endproc

P2.6 Convert the procedure at right into pseudocode which uses *only* simple **if** ... **then** structures in place of the **if** ... **then** ... **else** structure. Translate the procedure into BASIC.

procedure
  $K \leftarrow 1$
  repeat
    input A, B, C
    if $A > B$
      then $C \leftarrow A*C$
        print B, C
      else $C \leftarrow - C$
        print A, B, C
    endif
    $K \leftarrow K + 1$
  until $B < 0$
  print K
endproc

PROGRAMS

For the problems posed below: define the variables needed, write the pseudocode (in stages where necessary), then make a flowchart, then code the algorithm in BASIC, and finally run it on a computer.

PG2.1 The average topsoil depth in this country has dropped from 9 inches to 6 inches since 1620. Topsoil is now eroding away at a rate of 1% each year. When the depth is down to 3 inches, growing crops will be very difficult. At the present rate of erosion, when will the depth be 3 inches or less?

PG2.2 Write a program which finds the minimum value of

$$\frac{A + B - 2C}{A*B*C}$$

where A, B, and C can each be any of the digits 1, 2, 3, 4, 5, 6, 7, 8, 9.

PG2.3 Suppose that there are three billion people on earth at the present time, and that the population increases by 2% each year. Write a program which inputs a date, (say 2050), and calculates the population for that year if the rate of increase does not change.

PG2.4 Consider a sequence of numbers which has the property that beginning with the 4th one, each number is the sum of the previous one and twice the one before that minus the one before that. For example, the 8th one is (the 7th one) plus twice (the 6th one) minus (the 5th one). Suppose that the first three numbers in the sequence are 1, 2, 3. Write a program which finds the 15th one.

PG2.5   On the planet Arcturus IV lives the creature Nevrhungri who eats precisely ½ of its available food supply every day. Write a program which inputs an initial food-supply tonnage and calculates how many days will pass before the Nevrhungri eats that supply down to one ounce or less.

PG2.6   The Nevrhungri always adjusts its weight to be the weight of its food supply of two days before. Each morning it is weighed, its food supply is adjusted, and then it eats. If the food supply of the Nevrhungri is kept constant at 100 pounds for three days, and then the creature is only resupplied with 3 times its own weight every 4 days, what will it weigh after 50 days?

PG2.7   The Euclidean algorithm for finding the GCD (Greatest Common Divisor) of two positive numbers is to repeatedly replace the larger with their difference until that difference is zero, at which point they *are* the GCD of the original pair. Write a program which inputs two numbers and prints their GCD.

PG2.8   Write a program which inputs STATUS (with value 1 for unmarried, and 2 for married), and INCOME, and prints TAXPER. The marginal tax percentage TAXPER for the married STATUS is to be 32% if INCOME ≥ 20000 and 28% otherwise. For unmarried STATUS, TAXPER is to be 34% if INCOME ≥ 12000 and 30% otherwise. Repeat this process until a STATUS and INCOME pair is encountered for which INCOME < 0.

PG2.9   Input a sequence of numbers until one is encountered which is less than the first. Print the sum of the squares of all but the last one. (Try this with your own data, then with the input sequence 5, 4.)

PG2.10   Generate a sequence of (pseudo-)random numbers with RND and print only the first five values which are larger than the previous ones that have been printed. Then print the number of rejects. Repeat the process four times before stopping the run.

PG2.11   Generate a sequence of 30 (pseudo-)random numbers. Use the

case structure to separate them into three groups:

Group 1 $0 < X < .3$
Group 2 $.3 \leq X < .7$
Group 3 $.7 \leq X < 1.0$

Group 1 is to be summed and averaged, Group 2 is to have its squares summed and averaged, and Group 3 is to have its cubes summed and averaged. At the end of the run print the count, the sum, and the average of each group on a separate line.

PG2.12 Write a program which inputs two numbers, $0 \leq R \leq 10$ and $0 \leq T \leq 10$. These determine a rectangle within a 10 by 10 square in the plane. Use a GOSUB ... RETURN structure to generate ten pairs of X values and Y values at random, and count the number of pairs (X, Y) for which *both* $0 \leq X \leq R$ *and* $0 \leq Y \leq T$. Repeat this process 15 times, and average the results. The average should be a *rough* estimate of the area of the rectangle. Better estimates by this technique (called Monte Carlo Integration) require larger numbers of trials, and more pairs of points per trial. The general technique is heavily used in the design of Nuclear Reactors.

Chapter 3

NAMES AND MESSAGES

3.1 PORTABILITY

Most BASIC translators allow some features in statements which are not essential to the logic of a program, but which make programs more pleasant to use and read. The price that is paid for extra features is that they make the translator larger and more complicated, and so it can take up so much of the memory of a very small system that there is not much room for the user's

```
W O R D S T A G S N
A M E S M O N I K E
R S H A N D L E S L
O V E C H E R I E P
E T A P P E L A T I
O N T I T L E E P I
T H E T D E S I G N
```

programs. Even so, some personal computers costing under $1000 have quite a few non-essential features in their BASIC, and most of the systems used in schools have even more. Each choice of possible features creates a different version of BASIC. A problem with having many variations of BASIC available is that programs are not **portable**—a program which runs on one machine may need to be altered if it is to be used on another. We will introduce some of the features which are commonly encountered, and encourage the reader to explore the limits of the BASIC that s/he is using.

It is the pseudocode (or flowcharts) of the procedures in this book, and in other publications, which are portable in the broadest sense. A program copied onto a storage medium such as magnetic tape or a magnetic disk can be transferred to an identical computing system. The transfer can sometimes be made if the target system differs from the source system, but the adjustments may be impractical or unavailable. Program listings are prone to error (typographical or otherwise) during transmission. The major difficulty with the transfer of a program from one system or programmer to another via a listing is that the logic of the program is difficult to extract from it. If there are differences in the versions of BASIC being used in the source and target systems, or if the receiving programmer wishes to make changes or discovers a bug in the program, then it becomes essential to understand the program logic. It is much quicker to translate pseudocode into BASIC than it is to extract the logic of a program from its listing. Pseudocode is deliberately independent of particular versions of BASIC, deliberately readable, and deliberately designed to promote clean logic.

A BASIC listing lacks some of the attributes of pseudocode, but then pseudocode is not executable. A BASIC program can be much closer to the ideal in readability and kindness to the user with the features which will be explored in this chapter than was possible with the simple BASIC of Chapters 1 and 2.

3.2   VARIABLE NAMES

It is nice to have variable names which have more meaning than single letters of the alphabet. Almost all BASICs allow variable names to be an alphabetic character followed by one of the numerals 0, 1, ..., 9; for example $A1$ and $Z3$ are accepted. An even better feature which is available in many BASICs is to allow longer names which must begin with an alphabetic, but may be followed by either numerals or alphabetics. For example: SUM, or MAXIMUM, or INDEX3. However, most of the special characters cannot be used in such an identifier. If the BASIC translator encounters WAGE + TAX, then it naturally assumes that the value of TAX is to be added to the value of WAGE, rather than assuming that the whole string of characters "WAGE + TAX" is a name.

3.3   MESSAGES

It can be very valuable for a program and a user of it to be able to communicate with each other. The programmer is the user of the BASIC (translator) program, the program s/he inputs is data for BASIC, and that program has a (possibly) different user when it is in control of the machine. The attitude that should be taken by a programmer is that programs are written for someone else to use. One capability which makes programs more pleasant to use is the explanation of output. When the user types RUN, the programs which have been exhibited in the first two chapters respond with either a "?" or a sequence of numbers. How is the user of such a program to know what s/he is supposed to input, or what the results mean? This problem can be easily avoided in BASIC as follows:

    50 PRINT "THIS IS A MESSAGE"
    60 PRINT "THE SUM IS ..."; SUM

Character strings inside of the quotation marks are literally printed as they appear. An item which has the value of its appearance is called a **literal**. In the example above, if SUM contains 103.4, then execution of [50] and [60] will cause the following to be printed:

    THIS IS A MESSAGE
    THE SUM IS ... 103.4

One character which must be treated as a special case is the ". When it is encountered in a literal, it marks the end of the literal, rather than being only another character. Sometimes the problem can be avoided by using single quotes, ', and sometimes repeating a quote symbol will work. On a computer try:

    PRINT "JOE" "HALL"
    PRINT 'THE "QUOTE" IS HERE'

3.4 THE PROMPTING OF INPUT

Character strings may be placed in an INPUT statement, and they then appear as **prompting** to the user. For example:

    10 INPUT "WHAT IS THE NEXT GUESS"; VALUE

will return the following when it is executed:

    WHAT IS THE NEXT GUESS?

Note that the question mark is still generated by the INPUT statement, in order to request the user's response. The prompting message provided by the programmer is used for explanation of the prompting provided by the "?".

The INPUT statement will perform the output of literals while in the process of requesting input data, but it cannot serve to display variable values.

3.5 THE REMARK

A statement which is included in a program only to make its listing more readable is the **remark**. As listings get longer and programs get to be more complicated, remarks included in programs get to be more important. Remarks are recognized by the keyword REM following the statement number, and they are not executed, so they do not affect the program logic determined by the executable statements in a program. Examples of REM (remark) statements are:

```
10  REM PROGRAMMER: LISA STRANGEWAY
20  REM CLASS ASSIGNMENT 3
    .
    .
    .
100  REM STATEMENTS 110 − 300 FIND THE TOTAL WAGE
    .
    .
    .
```

Remarks should *not* simply echo the code (state the obvious). For example:

```
179  REM ADD ONE TO A
180  LET A = A + 1
```

As a more positive example, the CRAPS program in Chapter 2 might reasonably contain:

```
49  REM   CHOOSE A NEW VALUE FOR C
```

3.6   DOCUMENTATION

Associated with a program may be: a variable description, one or more stages of pseudocode description, a flowchart, a listing (which may include remarks), extended names, and the information which is printed during execution. These sorts of thing are called **documentation**. With these features, programs can be written as a guide to their own use, as well as being more understandable. They can print instructions, tell the user what input is expected at each stage, and explain what the output means. To put it bluntly, programs which are to be used on an interactive system that do not include this type of documentation are low quality programs. **Interactive** means that the user sits at a terminal, types something, and the system responds directly to whatever s/he has done. That differs from batch processing, in which a batch of programs are (usually), read from punched cards or tape and some time later the output from the entire batch is available for the users. Most BASIC programs are run in an interactive environment, and they should be designed to suit it. The use of meaningful names, remarks, and the pseudocode description of programs should be applied in *any* environment.

3.6.1 An Annotated Version of the CRAPS Program

The CRAPS program of Chapter 2 may be written with the documentation features of BASIC to be much more readable. Such a program *needs* to be self-documenting it its pseudocode is not available. Compare the version of CRAPS which follows with the original version.

```
 10 PRINT "THIS PROGRAM IS A SIMULATION OF THE"
 20 PRINT "GAME OF CRAPS. IT CHOOSES RANDOM"
 30 PRINT "VALUES FOR A DICE PAIR UNTIL 100 GAMES"
 40 PRINT "HAVE BEEN SIMULATED. IT THEN REPORTS"
 50 PRINT "THE NUMBER OF FIRST-ROUND WINS, THE"
 60 PRINT "NUMBER OF FIRST-ROUND LOSSES, AND"
 70 PRINT "THE NUMBER OF POINT WINS."
 80 PRINT
 90 REM
100 LET FIRSTWIN = 0
110 LET FIRSTLOSS = 0
120 LET POINTWIN = 0
130 REM
140 FOR GAMECOUNT = 1 TO 100
150 REM
160 REM ... THROW THE DICE AND CHECK THEIR VALUE
170    GOSUB 1000
180    IF VALUE = 7 THEN 220
190    IF VALUE < > 11 THEN 260
200 REM
210 REM ... FIRST-ROUND WIN
220    LET FIRSTWIN = FIRSTWIN + 1
230    GO TO 530
240 REM
250 REM ... CHECK FOR FIRST-ROUND LOSS
260    IF VALUE = 2 THEN 310
270    IF VALUE = 3 THEN 310
280    IF VALUE < > 12 THEN 350
290 REM
300 REM ... FIRST-ROUND LOSS
310    LET FIRSTLOSS = FIRSTLOSS + 1
```

```
320    GO TO 530
330 REM
340 REM ... THE POINT IS ESTABLISHED.
350    LET POINT = VALUE
360 REM ... A LOOP FROM 410 TO 520
370 REM ... REPEATS UNTIL THERE IS A
380 REM ... WIN OR A LOSS.
390 REM
400 REM ... ROLL THE DICE
410    GOSUB 1000
420 REM
430 REM ... CHECK FOR A LOSS
440    IF VALUE = 7 THEN 530
450 REM
460 REM ... CHECK FOR A WIN
470    IF VALUE < > POINT THEN 520
480    LET POINTWIN = POINTWIN + 1
490    GO TO 530
500 REM
510 REM ... TRY AGAIN
520    GO TO 410
530 NEXT GAMECOUNT
540 PRINT "THERE WERE"; FIRSTWIN;
550 PRINT "FIRST-ROUND WINS."
560 PRINT "THERE WERE"; FIRSTLOSS;
570 PRINT "FIRST-ROUND LOSSES."
580 PRINT "THERE WERE"; POINTWIN;
590 PRINT "POINT WINS."
600 STOP
990 REM ... 1000-1030 SIMULATE A DICE ROLL
991 REM
1000 LET DIE1 = INT(6*RND + 1)
1010 LET DIE2 = INT(6*RND + 1)
1020 LET VALUE = DIE1 + DIE2
1030 RETURN
1040 END
```

3.7 STRING VARIABLES

Strings of characters, as well as numbers, can be stored and retrieved with variables in BASIC. The names of the variables involved are different from the names of numerical variables. The standard naming scheme for **string variables** is simply to add a $ to the end of the variable name:

```
10 INPUT "WHAT IS YOUR NAME"; TAG$
20 PRINT "HELLO "; TAG$;", HOW ARE YOU?"
```

when run by Wilma will look like this:

```
WHAT IS YOUR NAME? WILMA
HELLO WILMA, HOW ARE YOU?
```

String variables store data in a different way than numerical variables, and it does not make sense to apply the operations of arithmetic to them. TWO$/4 is meaningless in BASIC, although

```
50 LET JUNK$ = "GOBBLEDYGOOK"
```

is a perfectly valid BASIC statement. On the other hand, it is not legal to assign "GOBBLEDYGOOK" to the variable JUNK, because JUNK is not a string variable name.

It should be kept in mind that the variable TWO$ has no connection with the variable TWO. One of these names has three characters, and the other has four characters, the last one of which is $. That is all that BASIC needs in order to tell the two names apart. Neither of these variables is assumed by the translator to have any connection with the number 2.

It is possible to compare character strings with each other. For example,

$$\text{``}A\text{''} < \text{``}B\text{''}, \quad \text{``}B\text{''} < \text{``}C\text{''}, \ldots, \quad \text{``}Y\text{''} < \text{``}Z\text{''}$$

Similarly,

$$\text{``TOM''} < \text{``TOMMY''}$$

The order involved here is called **lexicographic order**, the order of words in a dictionary and of the call letters in the Dewey Decimal System used by libraries. In this system, not only is "AX" < "C", but "10" < "9" because "1" < "9" and the characters of the string are compared one by one until there is a difference. Such comparisons are quite important in many data processing applications, since they allow alphabetic sorting. The fundamental statement required for such sorting is of the form:

```
320 IF A$ < B$ THEN C$ = A$
```

Note that the condition $A\$ < B\$$ is either true or false, as required for any condition.

The comparison of strings arises in the problem of writing a program which inputs ten names and prints the one which is last in alphabetic order. One way to approach this task is to input the names one at a time, and remember the "largest" one encountered so far. This approach will work on a list of 1000 names read over the telephone, as well as serving as a program model. If the largest name so far is called LAST$, then the very first input name should be LAST$, since it is the largest entry at that point in the process. As the other nine names are entered into TAG$, say, they can be compared to LAST$. If TAG$ > LAST$, then TAG$ should become the new LAST$ and the old value of LAST$ can be discarded, otherwise the name in TAG$ can be discarded. After the tenth entry, LAST$ can be displayed as the result. With the choice of COUNTER to control the loop, this scheme will work like this:

COUNTER	TAG$	LAST$
1	—	"AMY"
2	"JOE"	"JOE"
3	"BOYD"	"JOE"
4	"JANE"	"JOE"
5	"JUNE"	"JUNE"
6	"SALLY"	"SALLY"
7	"BILL"	"SALLY"
8	"SUE"	"SUE"
9	"RALPH"	"SUE"
10	"KEVIN"	"SUE"

The pseudocode is a fairly direct translation of the process outlined above:

```
procedure ROLL__END
  input LAST$
  COUNTER ← 1
  while COUNTER ≤ 9 do
    input TAG$
    if TAG$ > LAST$ then LAST$ ← TAG$
    COUNTER ← COUNTER + 1
  endwhile
  print LAST$
endproc
```

Procedure ROLL__END can form the basis of an alphabetic sorting program. Sorting programs are discussed in the programs and projects at the end of Chapter 4. Applications of sorting play an important role in Chapters 6, 7, 8, and 9.

Two more features associated with strings are used in the program example DIRECTION later in this chapter, and in Chapter 7. They are not available in all versions of BASIC:

1. $A\$ + B\$$ is the **catenation** (or concatenation) of the strings $A\$$ and $B\$$. (In some versions of BASIC, the syntax is: $A\$\&B\$$.) It causes the second string to be attached to the first: $B\$$ becomes the tail of a new string with $A\$$ as its head. For example, "X" + "YES" becomes "XYES".
2. $A\$ = $ "" forms a **null string** with storage facilities provided for a string, but with no characters placed in it.

3.8 INTEGER VARIABLES

Another type of variable that is useful is the **integer variable**. Integers are whole numbers; they have no fractional part. They are used for counting and for tagging things which fit into discrete categories. One scheme used in BASIC to distinguish integer variables is to append a "%" to the end of the name:

    10 LET X = 3.765
    20 LET A% = X
    30 PRINT A%

will print 3 when executed. The reason is that the fraction, .765, is truncated. (For the positive number 3.765 this has the same effect as INT(3.765) —where INT is the function discussed in 2.8.1 and in 5.4.3). To find the *nearest* positive whole number (to round), the following could have been substituted for [20]:

    20 LET A% = X + 0.5

With this substitution the program segment would have printed 4 instead of 3. If a positive number is of the form $w.d$, and $d < 0.5$, then $w.d + 0.5$ is still less than the next integer $w + 1$, and truncating the fraction will produce w. If $d \geq 0.5$, however, then $w.d + 0.5$ will be as large as $w + 1$, and truncating the fraction will produce $w + 1$.

The action of the INT function differs from assignment to an integer variable:

    500 LET CHOP% = −17.9
    501 LET HACK = INT(−17.9)
    503 PRINT CHOP%, HACK

will yield:

   −17   −18

as output.

One of the applications where an integer variable is valuable is when converting calculations to dollars and cents:

```
10 LET PRINCIPLE = 137.50
20 LET INTEREST = 0.085*PRINCIPLE
30 LET I% = INTEREST*100 + 0.5
40 PRINT "$"; I%/100.0
```

The program segment above will calculate:

   INTEREST as 11.6875 in [20], and
             as 1169.25 in [30],

and it will store the truncated number 1169 in $I\%$ in the assignment statement [30]. Then in [40], 1169/100.0 returns 11.69, which causes $11.69 to be printed. What is to be remembered here is that *only* an integer can be stored (even temporarily) with assignment to a variable name which ends in %. For the same reason, if a user responds to INPUT $A\%$ with 11.3Ⓡ, the result will be an error message from the translator. That is as it should be, since the question and the answer are not in agreement about the subject.

> The effect of the operations of arithmetic involving variables that are specifically *integer* is not the same in all versions of BASIC. The discussion in the remainder of this section assumes that integer arithmetic differs from real arithmetic, as it does in some versions of BASIC, and in the machine instructions of most computers.

Whenever two integer variables are combined with an operation in an expression, a *temporary* result is generated as an *integer,* and then used to complete the statement in which it occurs. For example:

```
10 LET I% = 3
20 LET J% = 2
30 LET X = I%/J%
40 PRINT X
```

will have 1 as its output, not 1.5, even though the values of X are not restricted to integers. The temporary result will be truncated before it is stored in X. (In a version of BASIC in which *all* arithmetic is real, the result *will* be 1.5.) On the other hand, in any BASIC, if we add:

```
50 LET Y = I%/2.5
60 PRINT Y
```

the output will be 1.2, not 1. The fraction is retained in the temporary result because one of the items involved in the operation is a *real number* instead of an integer, and the translator treats the numbers as real. The combining of an integer variable and a real variable with an arithmetic operator is called **mixed-mode arithmetic**, and it is actually carried out by converting the numbers involved to the same type before performing the operation.

The difference between integer variables and real variables is dramatized by the following pair of programs:

```
10 FOR I = 1 TO 3            10 FOR I% = 1 TO 3
20    FOR J = 1 TO 3         20    FOR J% = 1 TO 3
30       X = (I/J)*(J/I)     30       X = (I%/J%)*(J%/I%)
40       PRINT X;            40       PRINT X;
50    NEXT J                 50    NEXT J%
60    PRINT                  60    PRINT
70 NEXT I                    70 NEXT I%
80 STOP                      80 STOP
90 END                       90 END
```

output   *output*

```
1   1   1                    1   0   0
1   1   1                    0   1   0
1   1   1                    0   0   1
```

Note: The output values of the left program may only be *close* to 1, because numbers like $1/3$ may only be approximated in memory. Hence some of them may appear as .999999 or as .999998, but the essential difference in the two programs is displayed above. (Again, not all versions of BASIC which provide integer variables also provide integer arithmetic, and this scheme will not work in such a case.)

3.9 A MAP EXAMPLE

In many small towns in the Midwest it is possible to think of a street map as a table. The streets run north and south or east and west. They are often named First Street, Second Street, etc. beginning one block over from Maple, and First Avenue, Second Avenue, etc. beginning one block over from Main. A corner is the junction of an avenue and a street. We may shorten the way we indicate a corner as (ROW, COLUMN). For example the corner of Third Avenue and Fourth Street is located by (3, 4). A corner, then, can be specified with just two integers, as in Figure 3.2.

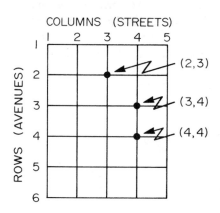

We are going to develop a procedure which will tell the user the *direction* of one corner from a previously given one. Since it is preferable to indicate directions by a character string, like "SOUTH", the string manipulations indicated in 3.7 are helpful. With these tools, it is technically possible to solve the problem, but in themselves the tools do not provide an algorithm. The professional approach to program design is to juggle only a comfortable part of the logic at a time. One way to do this is to describe the major tasks to be done, and the way in which these tasks go together to form a solution of the problem. The major tasks are then broken into cooperating subtasks, and the process of refinement is repeated. When the subtasks at some stage are detailed enough to be directly translated into BASIC statements, then it is time to stop. An organized attack of this sort is called step-wise refinement, and the first step is to describe in English the things which must be done. For the street map problem the first step might be:

1. Input an initial position, indicated by row (Avenue) and column (Street) numbers, say ROWNOW, COLNOW.
2. Form a loop within which a new position, say ROWTO, COLTO, will be input and used to determine a message indicating the direction of the new position from the old. At the end of each pass through the

loop, the new position will become the old position for the next pass. Hence the user may "walk around the town".

3. Provide an exit from the loop so that the user may quit when finished. Since avenues are seldom negative, input of a negative value for ROWTO will provide such a message from the user to the program. With a user-controlled exit provided, the loop structure may be a **loop** . . . **forever**.

The structure of this algorithm looks like this:

procedure DIRECTION
   input ROWNOW, COLNOW
   repeat
      input ROWTO, COLTO
      if ROWTO < 0 **then exit**
      //determine the direction of the change of position from//
      //ROWNOW, COLNOW to ROWTO, COLTO and print//
      //the direction message//
      ROWNOW ← ROWTO
      COLNOW ← COLTO
   forever
endproc

The next stage is to develop the description between the slashes into a detailed description. It is straightforward, in some sense, to determine direction by comparing pairs of numbers, such as COLTO and COLNOW. The *result* of the comparisons, however, is to be a character string, so that the output can be a direction like "SOUTH". The determination of a move East or West is independent of the determination of North or South, since one comes from comparing columns, and the other from comparing rows. In the printed direction, "NORTHEAST" is a standard form, but "EASTNORTH" is not, hence the north-south part of the direction should be placed before the east-west part. This can be done by catenating the direction, say DIR$, from two string variables: DIR$ ← NS$ + EW$, where NS$ will contain one of "", "NORTH", "SOUTH" and EW$ will contain one of "", "EAST", "WEST". This will produce strings of the desired type, like "WEST" or "SOUTHWEST". The value of EW$ is determined by comparing the input COLTO with COLNOW. For example, if COLTO < COLNOW, then there has been a move to the west, and so "WEST" is assigned to EW$. The values of NS$ are similarly determined by ROWTO and ROWNOW. Finally, both EW$ and NS$ may be null. In that case, DIR$ will be null, and a "not moved" message should be generated.

When these comments are written in pseudocode we have:

```
procedure DIRECTION
  input ROWNOW, COLNOW
  repeat
    input ROWTO, COLTO
    if ROWTO < 0 then exit
    NS$ ← ""
    EW$ ← ""
    if COLTO < COLNOW then EW$ ← "WEST"
    if COLTO > COLNOW then EW$ ← "EAST"
    if ROWTO < ROWNOW then NS$ ← "NORTH"
    if ROWTO > ROWNOW then NS$ ← "SOUTH"
    DIR$ ← NS$ + EW$
    if DIR$ = "" then print "YOU HAVE NOT MOVED."
              else  print "THE DIRECTION OF THE NEXT
                          POINT IS "; DIR$;"."
              endif
    ROWNOW ← ROWTO
    COLNOW ← COLTO
  forever
endproc
```

If this procedure is initialized with ROWNOW ← 3 and COLNOW ← 2 and the input is 4, 4 then the printed message will be:

THE DIRECTION OF THE NEXT POINT IS SOUTHEAST.

The listing which follows contains some of the documentation required to make this a useable program:

```
10 REM ... STREET DIRECTION PROGRAM
20 REM ... BY WAYNE AMSBURY
30 PRINT "THIS PROGRAM WILL ACCEPT A SEQUENCE"
40 PRINT "OF CORNER POSITIONS ON A STREET GRID."
50 PRINT "THE CORNERS ARE INPUT AS AN AVENUE"
60 PRINT "NUMBER FOLLOWED BY A STREET NUMBER."
70 PRINT "THE OUTPUT IS THE DIRECTION OF AN"
80 PRINT "POSITION FROM THE PREVIOUS CORNER."
90 PRINT "A NEGATIVE AVENUE NUMBER WILL STOP"
100 PRINT "THE EXECUTION OF THE PROGRAM."
110 PRINT
```

```
120 INPUT "THE INITIAL CORNER IS";ROWNOW,COLNOW
130 PRINT
140 REM ... NEW CORNER LOOP BEGINS HERE
150 REM
160 INPUT "THE NEW CORNER IS";ROWTO,COLTO
170   IF ROWTO < 0 THEN 450
180 REM
190 REM ... INITIALIZE THE OUTPUT DIRECTION
200   LET NS$=""
210   LET EW$=""
220 REM
230 REM ... DETERMINE THE EAST-WEST, THEN
240 REM ... THE NORTH-SOUTH PARTS OF THE
250 REM ... DIRECTION, AND CATENATE THEM.
260 REM
270 IF COLTO < COLNOW THEN EW$= "WEST"
280 IF COLTO > COLNOW THEN EW$= "EAST"
290 IF ROWTO < ROWNOW THEN NS$= "NORTH"
300 IF ROWTO > ROWNOW THEN NS$= "SOUTH"
310 LET DIR$ = NS$ + EW$
320 REM
330 REM ... THE DIRECTION MAY STILL BE NULL:
340   IF DIR$ <>"" THEN 370
350   PRINT "YOU HAVE NOT MOVED."
360   GO TO 420
370 PRINT "THE DIRECTION OF THIS CORNER FROM"
380 PRINT "THE PREVIOUS ONE IS ";DIR$
390 PRINT
400 REM ... THE NEW CORNER BECOMES THE
410 REM ... OLD CORNER.
420   LET ROWNOW = ROWTO
430   LET COLNOW = COLTO
440 GO TO 160
450 STOP
460 END
```

A typical run for this program would be:

RUN
THIS PROGRAM WILL ACCEPT A SEQUENCE
OF CORNER POSITIONS ON A STREET GRID.
THE CORNERS ARE INPUT AS AN AVENUE
NUMBER FOLLOWED BY A STREET NUMBER.
THE OUTPUT IS THE DIRECTION OF A
POSITION FROM THE PREVIOUS CORNER.
A NEGATIVE AVENUE NUMBER WILL STOP
THE EXECUTION OF THE PROGRAM.

THE INITIAL CORNER IS?2,3
THE NEW CORNER IS?3,4
THE DIRECTION OF THIS CORNER FROM
THE PREVIOUS ONE IS SOUTHEAST

THE NEW CORNER IS?3,1
THE DIRECTION OF THIS CORNER FROM
THE PREVIOUS ONE IS NORTH

THE NEW CORNER IS? $-1,1$

3.10   TAB

The purpose of many programs is to develop a *report*—a summary of results. Such a report should be neat and well-organized. One feature which is common to almost all versions of BASIC is quite helpful in creating well-organized output. It is called TAB, it appears in a PRINT statement, and TAB(N) refers to the Nth column of a print line or a display line. For example, TAB(5) refers to column 5, and TAB(10) indicates column 10. On a typewriter, TAB(N) has the effect of moving the carriage over N columns. On a screen, it moves the **cursor** (position marker) to the Nth column. (In some versions of BASIC, the column is shifted by one to the left or right. In particular, most versions of BASIC display numbers surrounded by a leading and a trailing blank.) For example:

```
10 LET A = 17.3
20 PRINT TAB(2); A
```

will result in:

17.3

with the 1 in column 3. On the other hand,

TAB   85

    10 LET A = 17.3
    20 PRINT A; TAB(12); A

will result in:

    17.3   17.3

with the first 1 in column 2 and the second 1 in column 13. The TAB may be mixed into the list in any position, but on many terminals it cannot be used to back up the carriage or cursor.

TAB(N); in a PRINT statement locates the column of the next character to be output.

The value within the parentheses which follow TAB may be any variable or expression. For example, the output of

    5 LET X = 2
    10 FOR I = 1 TO 6
    20   PRINT TAB(I); "X"
    30 NEXT I
    40 STOP
    50 END

will be:

    X
     X
      X
       X
        X
         X

Note that the variable X and the literal "X" are not related. If [20] is replaced by

    20   PRINT TAB(I); X

then the output will be:

    2
     2
      2
       2
        2
         2

because the value of the variable X does not change from its assigned value of 2.

3.11   PRINT USING

For some reports, the PRINT statement, even with the TAB, does not provide sufficient control of the output. For example, if an account ledger is being printed, part of the output might be credits to an account of 197.63, 85.00, and 0.84 dollars. With a statement of the form:

   10 PRINT TAB(5); CREDIT

the values of credit would be printed beginning in column 6 as:

   197.63
   85
   .84

A much preferred format for this output would be:

   197.63
   85.00
    0.84

   A statement which is available in many versions of BASIC can be used to get this second result. It is the PRINT USING instruction. This state- ·
ment uses a **format**, a formal description of what is to be printed in which columns. The syntax of this statement varies a great deal, but it always refers to a format description which is defined as a string of characters. Perhaps the simplest form of PRINT USING is one which uses a string variable for the format description. For example:

   10 LET $A\$$ = "###.##"

defines a format, and the three values of CREDIT, above, can be printed by referring to it with a statement like the following:

   110 PRINT USING $A\$$, CREDIT

The resulting output will be:

   197.63
   85.00
    0.84

The # signs are replaced by digits (and, if necessary, by minus signs or blanks). The positions of the printed digits are strictly determined by the # signs, which occur in **fields**. The first variable listed in the PRINT statement is printed in the position of the first field of #'s, the second variable in the second field, etc.

In order to print the numbers above beginning in column 5 we could use:

10 LET $A\$$ = "   ###.##"
.
.
.
110 PRINT USING $A\$$, CREDIT

Other characters may be added, such as "$" to the format. They are **literals,** characters literally printed as given. In fact, the "." in the above examples is a literal. For example:

10 LET $A\$$ = " $###.##"
.
.
.
110 PRINT USING $A\$$, CREDIT

will produce:

$197.63
$ 85.00
$ 0.84

In some versions of BASIC the format may be included directly into the PRINT statement:

110 PRINT USING " $###.##", CREDIT

will produce the same result as the last example.

In some versions the format is put into a separate statement. For example:

100:    $###.##
110 PRINT USING 100, CREDIT

will produce the same result as the last example. In this case, the colon ":" is required by the translator in order for it to recognize [100] as a nonexecutable **format statement**.

The treatment of string variables, of trailing and leading minus signs, and of leading blanks, must be determined from the manual describing the particular version of BASIC that is being used. In all cases, however, the PRINT USING is not required for most programs, but when it is needed, it is essential.

3.12   DEBUGGING

We have enough tools now to write some interesting interactive programs, and you are asked to do that in the problems at the end of the chapter. They will need to be **debugged**, that is, the errors in syntax and logic must be removed. The ideal method of debugging would be to try variations that will use a program in all of the logical paths through it that could possibly be followed by some user on purpose or by accident. If that were done, and everything that went amiss were corrected, then the behavior of the program would be known. In practice, there are often too many paths through the program to be tried in any reasonable amount of time, and finding all of the errors is impractical. If a program is intended for use in a general situation, and if it is tried out only in special cases, then it is fair to assume that the program will *not* work in all cases. A compromise must be made between trying all possible paths, and too few. Pseudocode, step-wise refinement, and full documentation all make debugging easier and more effective.

3.13   BASIC VARIATIONS

In some versions of BASIC the LET keyword in an assignment statement may be left off, since it is the "=" which determines assignment.

In some versions, both capital letters and lower-case letters may be used. The use of lower-case letters is particularly nice for prompting and instructions, and it is crucial for most practical applications of the word-processing techniques discussed in Chapter 7.

In some versions of BASIC, more than one statement may be placed between a statement number and a ®. For example, [110] and [120] of procedure DIRECTION may be combined on one line:

> 115 NS$ = "" : EW$ = ""®

or, in some versions:

> 115 N#$ = ""\EW$ = ""®

For this reason the "statement numbers" are often called "line numbers". In small systems, the packing of more than one statement into a line may make a difference in the size of program which can be used on the machine.

SELF-REVIEW

1.   What is portability? Suppose that each of 500 installations use essen-

tially the same utility algorithms, which require a total of 8000 lines of code (statements). Suppose that the programming cost is $20/line. What is the total cost of "re-inventing the wheel" by reprogramming the utility algorithms at each installation?

2. What is the distinction between a literal and a string variable: Can their values be altered by the user of a program?

3. From the user's viewpoint, what is the distinction between requesting input with an INPUT and a PRINT statement, and prompting with an INPUT statement?

4. Name all of the types of documentation discussed so far in this book.

5. Name three types of data (or types of variable values), and explain how the translator matches them with variable names.

6. What does the following statement assign to $A\%$?

    50 $A\% = -9.7$

7. Why is TAB an inadequate tool for book-keeping reports?

8. In business data processing, it is necessary to do the following things with output:

    a. Snuggle a "$" up to the first significant digit.
    b. Replace leading zeroes with "*" (in checks).
    c. Print a trailing "$-$" with negative values, and omit it with positive values.
    d. Print values of string variables in specific columns.

    If the version of BASIC which you are using provides these features, (with PRINT USING), then find out how they are done.

PROGRAMS

When you write the following programs and projects, you should develop the logic of the program in pseudocode, in steps if necessary. No coding should be done until the algorithm is satisfactory, since the computer will not solve logical problems by itself. Each program should include instructions to the user, with prompting for input and labelling of output. You should end up with a listing (if your system includes a printer), and with several sample runs which exercise the options in the program. Use the REM statement to explain what is done by important parts of your program.

PG3.1 Write a program which will input 15 names and count how many of them are out of alphabetic order in one of the following senses:

1. They would come before the preceding name, or
2. they would come after the succeeding name,

if the input list were in alphabetic order. For example, in the sequence (JOE, ANN, BILL), ANN would be counted as being out of place in the first sense, and JOE would be counted as being out of place in the second sense, but BILL would not be counted as being out of place in either sense.

PG3.2 Input a list of words and punctuation marks one at a time, catenate them with blanks between (in a single variable), and print them on one line. The input process is to terminate when the input is a period. Commas, periods, question marks, colons, and semicolons are to be treated as words, but special handling is required in order to omit blanks where appropriate.

PG3.3 Write a program which prints a 10 by 10 square full of randomly chosen integers 0, 1, 2, . . . , 9. One of the integers may be chosen by

$I \leftarrow \text{INT(RND*10)}$

Display the table in the center of the screen (or page) on your terminal.

PG3.4 Input an initial integer and a final integer, and print the 1st, 2nd, 3rd, and 4th powers of all of the integers between (and including) the initial and final integers. Print the powers in four columns, with a heading for each column. Part of an example run:

What is the initial integer?3
What is the final integer?5

BASE NUMBER	SQUARE	CUBE	FOURTH POWER
3	9	27	81
4	16	64	256
5	25	125	625

PG3.5 Print a "graph" of 12 numbers chosen at random, to be between 1 and 9. The numbers may be chosen with:

$X \leftarrow \text{INT(RND*9 + 1)}$

As each number is chosen, use the TAB function to print the symbol *R* in the print column of 6 times that value minus 3. Print the appropriate heading above the graph, and print a separator between columns. For example, the first five numbers might appear like this:

```
1  *  2  *  3  *  4  *  5  *  6  *  7  *  8  *  9
      *     *     *     *     *     *     *     *
-----------------------------------------------------
      *     *     *     *     *     *     *     *
      *     *     * R   *     *     *     *     *
      *     *     *     *     * R   *     *     *
      *     *     *     *     *     *     *     *
      *     * R   *     *     *     *     *     *
      *     *     *     *     *     *     *     *
      *     *     *     *     *     *     * R   *
      *     *     *     *     *     *     *     *
      *     *     *     * R   *     *     *     *
```

Note: There are two more plotting problems in Chapter 5: PG5.6 and PG5.7.

PG3.6 Print a table of 30 random numbers $(0 < N < 1)$ in three columns, beginning in print columns 2, 17, and 33. For example:

```
.778926        .407312        .829837
.838105        .530783        .115780
.606286 .         .              .
   .              .              .
   .              .
   .
```

PG3.7 Plot the values of $X = Y^2 - 2*Y - 5$ for values of $Y = 1, 2, 3,$ ..., 10 with the TAB function. Label the appropriate print columns (See PG3.5). Example output might be:

A PLOT OF THE FUNCTION X = Y**2 − 2*Y − 5

```
X-VALUES     −5* 0* 5*10*15*20*25*30*35*45*50*55*60*65*70* 75
--------------*--*--*--*--*--*--*--*--*--*--*--*--*--*--*--
Y-VALUES  1  Y*  *  *  *  *  *  *  *  *  *  *  *  *  *  *
             *  *  *  *  *  *  *  *  *  *  *  *  *  *  *
          2  Y*  *  *  *  *  *  *  *  *  *  *  *  *  *  *
             *  *  *  *  *  *  *  *  *  *  *  *  *  *  *
          3  * Y*  *  *  *  *  *  *  *  *  *  *  *  *  *
             *  *  *  *  *  *  *  *  *  *  *  *  *  *  *
          4  * Y*  *  *  *  *  *  *  *  *  *  *  *  *  *
             *  *  *  *  *  *  *  *  *  *  *  *  *  *  *
          5  *  *  * Y*  *  *  *  *  *  *  *  *  *  *  *
             .
             .
             .
```

PROJECTS

Projects are not intended to be ordinary programming problems. They are time consuming and they require more thought and effort to develop and debug than program assignments. However, they give more insight into possible applications of the text material and they can be more easily personalized. They should not be attempted by a student who has not yet worked some of the program problems in this chapter.

One approach to projects is to program a simplified version of the problem, examine it to see how it may be restructured to include more features, and then rewrite it. The introduction of new features into a program may lead to a quite different structure than the one developed for the original version. Do not hesitate to rewrite, instead of "patching" a program. It will save much time spent in debugging.

A second approach is to plan for all of the features of interest from the beginning. All features of the program do not need to be implemented during the initial, exploratory runs, however. The code which would provide some feature, such as nicely arranged output or instructions to the user, may be bypassed or replaced with simplified versions at first.

Both approaches are greatly eased by the judicious use of the GOSUB ... RETURN structure.

PJ3.1 Write a guessing game program. The simplest games could be placed in the program section, but there are interesting variations to be explored:

a. The program is to pick a random integer between 1 and, say, 64 with the following:

LET SECRET = INT(RND*64 + 1)

The player guesses a number, and the program responds with a message which indicates that the guess is too high, too low, or correct. Q: How many guesses should be enough to guarantee success?

b. You may want to give information about how close the guess of the player is to the correct number. Example: COLD, COOL, LUKEWARM, WARM, HOT. If your output is a display, then you may want to use stars or shrinking squares. If you have color graphics, you might change the "NEXT GUESS?" from cool to warm colors with no explanation, and let the player learn what that means by playing the game.

c. You may want to return, at the player's option, for another game (with a new SECRET).

d. You may use letters instead of numbers.

e. Use a SECRET point somewhere within a square, and let the player guess its coordinates. The feedback to the player after a guess could be the sum of the differences, or perhaps just which coordinate is closer.

f. Ask for a pair of numbers (or letters) and respond with whether the pair catches SECRET in between. The strategy that is used to do this effectively is worth knowing, even if you do not program this option.

PJ3.2 For the next set of problems, you will need to know about monetary interest. What follows is only intended to be a reminder of definitions with which it is hoped you are already familiar!

A yearly rate of interest, or *rate*, is usually given as a percentage but is used as a fraction for calculations. Sometimes rates are given in the form 1% per month (on the *unpaid balance*), and sometimes in the form 12% per year.

The *principal* of a loan or account is the amount on which interest is paid or collected.

The interest is the amount paid by one party to another for the use of money. It can be *simple* or *compound*. For simple interest, the interest at the end of one time period changes hands, but for compound interest it is added to the account and gains interest itself during the next time period.

1. Write a program which accepts a principal, a rate, and a number of years and then calculates the interest accumulated for that period of time, either simple interest or compound interest, at the user's request. In the case of compound interest, the number of times per year it is to be compounded must also be input data. Break the program up into GOSUB ... RETURN structures.

2. Write a program which accepts an initial value of the principal, a final value of the principal, a time span, and a time span between the times at which interest is compounded. The program is to determine the interest rate (by iteration—successive approximation) that would generate the final value of principal from the given data.

3. Write a program which accepts a principal, an interest rate, an initial unpaid balance for a loan or mortgage, and a length of time such as 24 months, or 20 years. The program is to determine the uniform monthly payments required to pay the loan back in the given time.

4. To problem 1 add the capability to make additional withdrawals or deposits to the loan account. In particular, what happens with double payments?

PJ3.3 Reverse the roles of player and program in the options in PJ3.1. To do that, you need to develop a strategy for the program to use when it is solving the puzzle posed by the player. You probably also need to try to detect misleading information provided by the player.

PJ3.4 Write a program which generates Arithmetic Drill and Practice problems for the user to do, and checks the answers. For example:

$3 + 7 = ?$
or $8 * 5 = ?$

you can pick numbers randomly from 0 to some value LIMIT by:

LET $N = $ INT(LIMIT*RND $+ 0.5$)

There are many variations of the basic program. For example:

a. Keep track of the number of correct responses, print encouraging remarks for correct answers, give the correct response after a few tries, summarize the results with a grade when the user is finished (at the user's option).

b. Let the user pick a level of problems from several choices.

c. Keep track of the mix of problems: if the user is doing very well with addition problems but having trouble with multiplication, start giving a higher percentage of (easier?) multiplication problems. If the user is doing well in all phases, give harder problems.

Chapter 4

THREE DATA STRUCTURES

4.1 A PROBLEM OF AVERAGES

There are problems for which the BASIC language constructs developed in the first three chapters are not adequate. An example of a problem of that sort is the one of comparing a set of numbers to their average value. Many teachers use such a comparison as part of the analysis of the test scores of their classes. Rather than solve this problem for a particular class of students, we may develop a program which will deal with test scores for any class of 50 or less students. Such a program is of 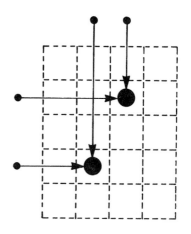 more general use than one designed for just one particular class, and it requires little more effort to write. One difficulty in programming this problem is that *all* of the scores must be input before their average score can be calculated. All of the scores need to be *retained* in Memory so that they will not need to be input a second time after the average has been calculated. Another difficulty with this problem is that if there are more than a few numbers to compare with their average, then it is awkward to give them all distinct names. As many as 50 names are needed, but they are all values which fit under the general heading: "the name of a student in the class." We shall describe a scheme which treats the names as a group, and the scores as a group, but which distinguishes them from each other just the same.

4.2 SUBSCRIPTED VARIABLES

Suppose that scores could be stored into memory in a sequence, that is, the first score first, the second score second, and so on, with the last score being last in sequence. We say that the **index** of the fifth score is 5, since it is in the fifth memory cell, and the index of the 17th score is 17. A way is needed to tell BASIC to store them in a sequence of cells, yet allow them to be retrieved in any order—we may want to use the 4th one before the 2nd, for example. In our example, we will have SCORE(1), SCORE(2), ... SCORE(N), where $N \leq 50$, represent the first score, second score, ... up to the Nth score. This is clearly a different naming scheme from those used in the previous chapters. The set of things called SCORE(I) for some range of values of I is a **subscripted variable**, or one-dimensional array, or linear array. If a subscripted variable is to be used, its use must be consistent: SCORE then refers to all or none; the index must be attached to the name in order to access a particular score.

In the subscripted variable naming scheme of BASIC, the index itself may be a variable: When I has the value 14, then:

60 SCORE(I) = 17.4

is equivalent to

60 SCORE(14) = 17.4

A particular position in the array may be chosen from outside of the program by the user:

70 INPUT L
80 PRINT $X(L)$

Most versions of BASIC will even allow the subscript to be calculated as an integer derived from an expression: SCORE($7*J$ + 3.4) will refer to SCORE(24) when the value of J is 3. Any index must be reduced to an integer, since the index acts as a selector of one of a set of things—the "2.5th item in the set" is meaningless.

4.3 DIMENSION

With the first use of a variable name in a BASIC program, the translator chooses a memory cell to associate with that name. The connection between variables and memory cells must be made before the program can be turned into machine instructions. When SCORE(7) or SCORE(19) is used, more than one memory cell must be reserved, since these names refer to the seventh SCORE or the nineteenth SCORE. This implies that there are at least eighteen other cells in SCORE. The cells in SCORE may be thought of as being arranged as shown below. Then SCORE(7) is six places below SCORE(1). Similarly, SCORE(19) is 18 places further along in the memory cell sequence than SCORE (1). Hence

100 LET SCORE(7) = X

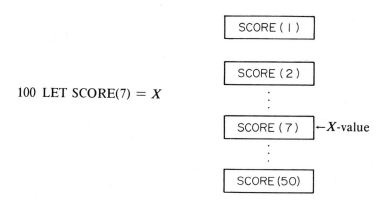

will change the contents of the 7th memory cell of those reserved for the array SCORE. The storage for SCORE needs to be allocated in advance, so that SCORE(7) does not coincide in memory with some other variable, or with instructions, or with some other program. This means that the programmer must decide in advance what *maximum* index for a variable will occur in the program, because BASIC needs to know the amount of storage to set aside for a variable, and this amount remains fixed during execution of the program. The programmer informs BASIC of the storage requirements with, for example:

10 DIM SCORE(50)

This statement has the general form:

[*N*] DIM ⟨list of subscripted variable names, separated by commas⟩

This non-executable statement is called the **dimension** statement. The integer in parentheses is the maximum index value that the programmer believes will be needed during execution. BASIC then sets aside the requested storage, and if the maximum index is exceeded during execution, an error message will result. The smallest allowed index is zero, not one, in most BASICS, so the **subscript range** is from zero to the number indicated in the parentheses which follow a variable name in the DIM statement.

4.4 A SCORE DEVIATION PROGRAM

With the help of subscripted variables, a program can be written which will allow up to 50 student names with a test score for each name, and output the list of names along with the test score for each name as well as the difference between each test score and the average of the scores. This problem has a natural division into three parts:

1. Input all of the name-score pairs, and count them.
2. Calculate the average score value.
3. Print the names, scores, and difference from the average score, one triplet at a time.

The first part involves reading a name and a score, and then repeating that process until all of the data has been acquired, hence it is naturally done with a loop structure. Some way must be provided to exit the loop with less than 50 names and scores. One way to do this is to allow the user to input a *negative* score to indicate that s/he is finished with input. An initial description of this part is:

//Input STUDENT$(1) and SCORE(1), STUDENT$(2)//
//and SCORE(2), ..., STUDENT$(I) and SCORE(I), ... until//
//SCORE(I) < 0, then exit. Add the non-negative SCORE values//
//to SUM as they are input.//

The second part of the problem involves only the number of input name-score pairs, N. If I is the input loop counter, then at the time of exit from the input loop, N should have the value $I - 1$, since the final negative score is not to be counted. The average is then calculated by:

$$AVERAGE \leftarrow SUM/N.$$

The third part of the problem is a loop which runs through the N name-score pairs, calculates:

$$DIFF \leftarrow SCORE(I) - AVERAGE$$

for $I = 1, 2, ..., N$ and prints STUDENT$(I), SCORE(I), and DIFF.

With this division of the problem into parts, an initial pseudocode description of the algorithm is:

procedure DEVIATE
  print (instructions to the user)
  SUM ← 0
  //Input STUDENT\$(I), SCORE(I), for I = 1, 2, ... //
  //If SCORE(I) < 0 then exit, otherwise add SCORE(I) to SUM//
  N ← I − 1
  AVERAGE ← SUM/N
  print (headings)
  //calculate DIFF as SCORE(I) − AVERAGE and print STUDENT\$(I),//
  //SCORE(I), and DIFF for I = 1, 2, ..., N//
endproc

The final step in developing the pseudocode is to fill in the details of the input loop and the print loop, which are similar to others in previous examples:

procedure DEVIATE
  print (instructions to the user)
  SUM ← 0 : I ← 1
  while I ≤ 50 **do**
    input STUDENT\$(I), SCORE(I)
    if SCORE(I) < 0 **then exit**
    SUM ← SUM + SCORE(I)
    I ← I + 1
  endwhile
  N ← I − 1
  AVERAGE ← SUM/N
  print (headings)
  I ← 1
  while I ≤ N **do**
    DIFF ← SCORE(I) − AVERAGE
    print STUDENT\$(I), SCORE(I), DIFF
    I ← I + 1
  endwhile
endproc

In the listing of this procedure, given below, some of the features mentioned in the last chapter that are not universally available are used. In particular the LET is omitted from assignment statements, and there are multiple statements on some lines.

```
 10 REM ... PROGRAM DEVIATE
 20 PRINT "THIS PROGRAM WILL ACCEPT UP TO 50"
 30 PRINT "NAMES AND SCORES, AND CALCULATE"
 40 PRINT "THE DIFFERENCE BETWEEN THE SCORES"
 50 PRINT "AND THEIR AVERAGE. ENTER A NAME"
 60 PRINT "AND A NEGATIVE SCORE AFTER THE"
 70 PRINT "LAST VALID SCORE AS A SIGNAL THAT"
 80 PRINT "THE INPUT DATA IS COMPLETE."
 90 PRINT
100 PRINT "RESPOND TO EACH ? WITH ENTRIES OF"
110 PRINT "THE FORM: NAME,SCORE"
120 PRINT
130 REM ... 170-220 INPUTS DATA AND SUMS
140 REM ... THE SCORES.
150 REM
160     DIM STUDENT$(50),SCORE(50)
170 SUM = 0 : I = 1
180 IF I>50 THEN 160
190     INPUT STUDENT$(I),SCORE(I)
200     IF SCORE(I)<0 THEN 260
210     SUM = SUM + SCORE(I)
220 I = I+1 : GO TO 180
230 REM
240 REM ... THE NEGATIVE SCORE ENTRY
250 REM ... HAS BEEN COUNTED.
260     N = I−1
270 AVERAGE = SUM/N
280 REM
290 REM ... 360-410 CALCULATES THE
300 REM ... DIFFERENCES AND DISPLAYS
310 REM ... THEM UNDER A HEADING.
320 PRINT
330 PRINT TAB(5);"NAME";TAB(20);"SCORE";
340 PRINT TAB(27);"DIFFERENCE"
350 PRINT : PRINT
360 I = 1
370 IF I>N THEN 420
380     DIFF = SCORE(I) − AVERAGE
390     PRINT STUDENT$(I);TAB(21);SCORE(I);
400     PRINT TAB(29);DIFF
410 I = I+1 : GO TO 370
420 STOP
430 END
```

Procedure DEVIATE can also be written with FOR ... NEXT loops. Omitting some remarks and the instructions, here it is:

.

.

.

```
160    DIM STUDENT$(50),SCORE(50)
170 SUM = 0
180 FOR I = 1 TO 50
190    INPUT STUDENT$(I),SCORE(I)
200    IF SCORE(I) 0 THEN 260
210    SUM = SUM + SCORE(I)
220 NEXT I
230 REM
240 REM ... THE NEGATIVE SCORE ENTRY
250 REM ... HAS BEEN COUNTED.
260    N = I−1
270 AVERAGE = SUM/N
280 REM
290 REM ... 360-410 CALCULATES THE
300 REM ... DIFFERENCES AND DISPLAYS
310 REM ... THEM UNDER A HEADING.
320 PRINT
330 PRINT TAB(5);"NAME";TAB(20);"SCORE";
340 PRINT TAB(27);"DIFFERENCE"
350 PRINT : PRINT
360 FOR I = 1 TO N
380    DIFF = SCORE(I) − AVERAGE
390    PRINT STUDENT$(I);TAB(21);SCORE(I);
400    PRINT TAB(29);DIFF
410 NEXT I
420 STOP
430 END
```

A typical run for program DEVIATE will produce:

THIS PROGRAM WILL ACCEPT UP TO 50
NAMES AND SCORES, AND CALCULATE
THE DIFFERENCE BETWEEN THE SCORES
AND THEIR AVERAGE. ENTER A NAME
AND A NEGATIVE SCORE AFTER THE
LAST VALID SCORE AS A SIGNAL THAT
THE INPUT DATA IS COMPLETE.

RESPOND TO EACH ? WITH ENTRIES OF
THE FORM: NAME,SCORE

?WHISTLER,67
?SOMBER,46
?WILLING,82
?SPACEY,41
?FLASH,97
?ACEHIGH,86
?QUEEN,73
?MIDDLING,72
?OVER, −1

NAME	SCORE	DIFFERENCE
WHISTLER	67	−3.5
SOMBER	46	−26.5
WILLING	82	11.5
SPACEY	41	−29.5
FLASH	97	26.5
ACEHIGH	86	15.5
QUEEN	73	2.5
MIDDLING	72	1.5

4.5   THE READ ... DATA STRUCTURE

At times, it is useful to reference constants, and to assign them to variables in parts of the program. If constants are needed in a game program, for example, the player cannot be expected to supply them through an INPUT—they may be secret, or many. As another example, the information in a tax table is not something one would want to enter into a tax calculation program each time it is used. There is a way to provide constants which are more accessible to programmer control than those that we have used so far—with the DATA statement. It is used in conjunction with a partner statement which provides a way to copy constants from their storage locations into variables. In BASIC the copying is done with a

READ statement. Here is an example:

       10 READ FROST, SNOW, MUD
         .
         .
         .
       100 DATA 7.3, −14.8, 0.3

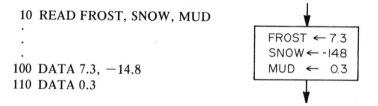

The general forms of these statements are:

```
[N] READ    ⟨list of variable names separated by commas⟩
[N] DATA    ⟨list of values separated by commas⟩
```

DATA constants can be placed in more than one DATA statement, in which case the DATA statements may be thought of as being strung together as a unit in the order determined by their statement numbers:

       10 READ FROST, SNOW, MUD
         .
         .
       100 DATA 7.3, −14.8
       110 DATA 0.3

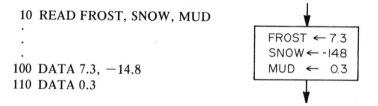

The very same assignments will occur if [10] is replaced by:

       10 READ FROST
       11 READ SNOW, MUD

Notice what happens if the DATA statements are switched:

       10 READ FROST, SNOW, MUD
         .
         .
       100 DATA 0.3
       110 DATA 7.3, −14.8

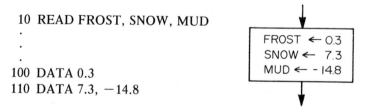

4.6   RESTORE

Suppose that:

20 READ NEXT

is added to the program segment above. With this addition, an error will occur during execution of the program because the data in the DATA statements is "used up" and yet more is requested. What actually happens is that BASIC generates instructions which save the *location* of the next available constant in the set of DATA statements of the program. If DATA constants are to be used more than once, then a way is needed to reset that **pointer** to the next available constant. The term pointer is often restricted to apply to address variables, (a variable which has a memory address as its value), but there are none in BASIC, and the term is used in this text in the sense of "locator". The pointer may be reset to the first constant in that DATA statement which has lowest statement number. This can be done by the execution of:

[*N*] RESTORE

Here is an example of the effect of RESTORE:

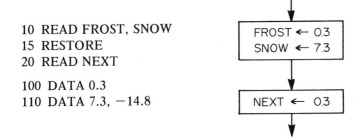

```
10  READ FROST, SNOW
15  RESTORE
20  READ NEXT

100  DATA 0.3
110  DATA 7.3, −14.8
```

In summary, the BASIC system keeps track of three addresses related to the collection of DATA statements in the program taken as a whole, in sequence:

   a—pointer to the first data item.
   b—pointer to the next data item to be used by a READ.
   c—pointer to the last data item in the DATA statements.

When a READ is executed, its variable list is assigned values determined by the pointer b. If a RESTORE is executed, then $b \leftarrow a$, and if $b > c$, then an error message is generated. One may think of the DATA items as being in a subscripted variable, for which b acts as an index.

4.7 STRING CONSTANTS

There are constants other than numbers. We have used some of them already, when literal strings like "HEADING" were used in INPUT and PRINT statements. String constants can be placed in DATA statements and can be copied into variables also:

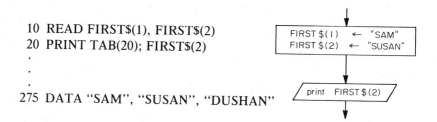

```
 10  READ FIRST$(1), FIRST$(2)
 20  PRINT TAB(20); FIRST$(2)
  .
  .
  .
275  DATA "SAM", "SUSAN", "DUSHAN"
```

This program segment will print SUSAN in columns 20-24.

Most versions of BASIC will allow the quotes to be omitted in DATA statements, but they are necessary if the constant contains a blank or a comma. The statement must contain constants, not variable names, and so there is no confusion to be resolved. For example:

```
275  DATA SAM, SUSAN, DUSHAN
```

There must be a match between the type of DATA constant and the type of the variable into which it is copied by a READ statement, just as there must be in an assignment or an INPUT.

4.8 A SQUARE GENERATOR EXAMPLE

The major use of the READ ... DATA structure is to provide initial values of variables. Stored in DATA statements, values can be assigned to variables with READ statements at the beginning of a program execution, and again when re-initialization is required. The structure plays the role of a permanent storage facility, and is particularly effective when other such storage is not available.

As an example of the use of the READ ... DATA for initialization, consider the problem of generating a pattern of squares for a game program. Three rows and five columns may be generated with asterisks like this:

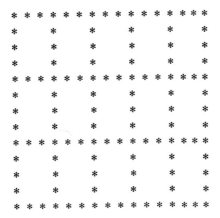

A GOSUB ... RETURN structure which will print such a grid with any (reasonable) number of rows and columns can be derived from a small amount of data. What is required is to loop through the rows of the grid (ROWS of them), and for the *I*th row print a solid line of asterisks followed by three lines of asterisks spaced four blanks apart. These lines themselves can be generated with a loop in which the *J*th column (COLS of them), are constructed from either "*****" or "* ". Generation of the solid line is separated as a procedure itself, since it must be done again after exit from the row loop in order to form the bottom line of the grid. Here is procedure BOX:

```
procedure BOX
   I ← 1
   while I ≤ ROWS do
      procedure STARLINE
      print (three lines of "* ", with an end "*")
      I ← I + 1
   endwhile
   procedure STARLINE
return
```

The solid line of asterisks can be generated with:

procedure STARLINE
  $J \leftarrow 1$
  while $J \leq$ COLS **do**
    print "*****";
    $J \leftarrow J + 1$
  endwhile
return

The GOSUB ... RETURN structure has been handled above by introducing **procedure** "NAME" at a point in the pseudocode at which a GOSUB would occur in the corresponding BASIC code.

If we assume that BOX is itself a GOSUB ... RETURN structure built within a main routine, then the code for these procedures is:

```
 90 REM ... PROCEDURE BOX
100 RESTORE
110 READ STAR1$, STAR5$
120 FOR I = 1 TO ROWS
130    GOSUB 500
140    FOR L = 1 TO 3
150      FOR J = 1 TO COLS
160        PRINT STAR1$;
170      NEXT J
180      PRINT "*"
190    NEXT L
200 NEXT I
210 GOSUB 500
220 RETURN
230 DATA "* ", "*****"
  .
  .
  .
500 REM ... PROCEDURE STARLINE
510 FOR J = 1 TO COLS
520    PRINT STAR5$;
530 NEXT J
540 PRINT "*"
550 RETURN
```

4.9 TABLES

One data structure which plays an important role in programming is the **table**, or two-dimensional array. This is again a subscripted variable, but with two subscripts instead of one. The reason that it is so useful is that people tend to arrange things into tables with rows and columns. For example, it is natural to deal with the payroll of a business, or with allowances and chore payments to children in a family, by using a table with a row for each person, and columns for items associated with them. Not all versions of BASIC allow tables of character strings, and none allow a mixture of strings and numbers in a table, so we will deal only with tables of numbers in this chapter.

Consider the problem of calculating a simplified payroll for a business. (A more realistic payroll problem involves a great many details that are best incorporated after the logic of this example is understood.) The payroll information can be arranged in three rows and five columns in a table in which:

ROW 1 is (information) for JACK SPRAT
     2 is   for LIANNE LUMP
     3 is   for BEN HECHT

COLUMN 1 is for hourly wages
           2 is for hours worked this week
           3 is for medical insurance deductions
           4 is for social security deductions
           5 is for tax deductions

In geometrical form, the table would appear as:

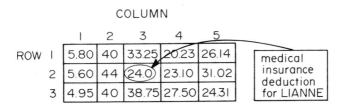

This is called a "3 × 5" or a "3 by 5" table. Any *meaning* that is attached to the rows and columns is attached by the programmer, not by the program. (However, the program can print headings when a table is displayed!)

An interesting thing about a table is that only two pieces of information are needed in order to find a value in it: a row and a column. Furthermore, only one value can be in both a given row and a given column. A row and a column uniquely determine a position in a table, so an index for the row, together with an index for the column, should locate a memory cell of the table. For example, the pair of indices (2, 3) should point to row 2 and column 3. That position in the table above is the medical insurance deduction of LIANNE.

4.9.1   Rows and Columns

In order for BASIC to **allocate** (set aside) the correct block of storage for a table, it needs to know the number of rows and the number of columns in the table. In order to know how to locate a memory cell in the array, BASIC also needs to know which index is for rows and which is for columns. The information in the table above could also have been put in a 5 by 3 table like this:

COLUMN

	1	2	3
ROW 1	5.80	5.60	4.95
2	40	44	40
3	33.25	0	38.75
4	20.23	23.10	27.80
5	26.14	31.02	24.31

In this new table, the columns are associated with the three people and the rows contain the information which was in the columns of the previous table. The pair (2, 3) again points to row 2, column 3, but that location now contains the hours worked for BEN. The medical insurance for LIANNE is in (3, 2) in the second table. One of the two arrangements can be specified and storage allocated for it at the same time like this:

    10 DIM DEDUC(3, 5)

Values can be stored into a particular cell in the array DEDUC, or retrieved from it by referring to DEDUC(I, J), where I is the row index and J is the column index. The naming scheme for tables is very much like the one for one-dimensional arrays, except that the name has three parts: the subscripted variable name, the first (row) index, and the second (column) index.

4.9.2   A Payroll Example

Consider the problem of printing the net wage for JACK, LIANNE, and BEN from the 3 by 5 payroll table. A program which does this must loop through the rows, each of which contains all of the pertinent information for one of the employees, and for the *I*th row do three things:

1. Calculate the gross wage from DEDUC(*I*, 1)*DEDUC(*I*, 2).
2. Loop through the deductions, subtracting DEDUC(*I*, *J*) from the wage for *J* equal to 3, 4, and 5.
3. Print the net wage (identified with the worker's name, WORKER$(*I*)).

Here is that procedure in pseudocode:

procedure DEDUCTION
   I ← 1
  while *I* ≤ 3 **do**
    WAGE ← DEDUC(*I*, 1)*DEDUC(*I*, 2)
    //subtract deductions from the gross wage//
    print WORKER$(*I*), WAGE
    I ← *I* + 1
  endwhile
endproc

After refining the subtraction of deductions we have:

procedure DEDUCTION
   I ← 1
  while *I* ≤ 3 **do**
    WAGE ← DEDUC(*I*, 1)*DEDUC(*I*, 2)
    J ← 3
    while *J* ≤ 5 **do**
      WAGE ← WAGE − DEDUC(*I*, *J*)
      J ← *J* + 1
    endwhile
    print WORKER$(*I*), WAGE
    I ← *I* + 1
  endwhile
endproc

A BASIC program which obtains the required values from DATA statements and then follows the procedure above to calculate the wages looks like this:

```
 10 REM ... WAGE DEDUCTION EXAMPLE
 20 PRINT "THIS PROGRAM CALCULATES THE"
 30 PRINT "WAGE FOR EMPLOYEES, USING"
 40 PRINT "HOURLY WAGES, HOURS WORKED"
 50 PRINT "THIS WEEK, AND DEDUCTIONS FOR"
 60 PRINT "MEDICAL INSURANCE, SOCIAL"
 70 PRINT "SECURITY, AND TAX. THE DATA"
 80 PRINT "IS INTERNAL TO THE PROGRAM."
 90 PRINT
100    DIM DEDUC(3,5),WORKER$(3)
110 REM
120 REM ... RETRIEVE DATA, ONE ROW PER
130 REM ... EMPLOYEE.
140    FOR I = 1 TO 3
150      FOR J = 1 TO 5
160        READ DEDUC(I,J)
170      NEXT J
180      READ WORKER$(I)
190    NEXT I
200 REM ... WAGE IS (HOURLY WAGE)*HOURS
210 REM ... DEDUCTIONS OCCUPY THE LAST
220 REM ... THREE ROWS OF THE EMPLOYEE
230 REM ... ROW. THE RESULTS ARE
240 REM ... DISPLAYED AS SOON AS THEY
250 REM ... ARE CALCULATED.
260 REM
270 FOR I = 1 TO 3
280    LET WAGE = DEDUC(I,1)*DEDUC(I,2)
290      FOR J = 3 TO 5
300        LET WAGE = WAGE − DEDUC(I,J)
310      NEXT J
320    PRINT WORKER$(I),WAGE
330 NEXT I
340 STOP
350 REM ... DATA IS IN THE ORDER LISTED
360 REM ... IN THE INSTRUCTIONS, ONE
370 REM ... DATA STATEMENT PER EMPLOYEE
```

```
380 REM
390 DATA 5.80,40,33.25,20.23,26.14,"JACK SPRATT"
400 DATA 5.60,44,00.00,23.10,31.02,"LIANNE LUMP"
410 DATA 4.95,40,38.75,27.50,24.31,"BEN HECHT"
420 END
```

The output would be:

THIS PROGRAM CALCULATES THE
WAGE FOR EMPLOYEES, USING
HOURLY WAGES, HOURS WORKED
THIS WEEK, AND DEDUCTIONS FOR
MEDICAL INSURANCE, SOCIAL
SECURITY, AND TAX. THE DATA
IS INTERNAL TO THE PROGRAM.

JACK SPRATT	152.38
LIANNE LUMP	192.28
BEN HECHT	107.44

4.9.3 Table Storage

One thing that is not apparent is how BASIC actually arranges the rows and columns of an array in memory. They are seldom, if ever, stored in rows and columns of memory cells, and in a sense, there are no such rows and columns in memory anyway. What is usually done is to store them in a sequence of cells just as the one-dimensional arrays are stored. Usually the first row is followed by the second, and so on. This is called **row-major** order of storage.

Consider the array A which has its storage allocated by:

10 DIM $A(2, 2)$

Since BASIC uses row-major storage, and since BASIC begins each subscript range with index 0, storage cells will be allocated for A in the order:

$A(0, 0), A(0, 1) A(0, 2), A(1, 0), A(1, 1), A(1, 2) A(2, 0), A(2, 1) A(2, 2)$

If the columns of an array are stored one after the other, the allocation is said to be in **column-major** order. In some circumstances the entire array can be returned with one statement from storage, and then it matters which is used. An even more likely event is that the programmer will need to think of an array in terms or its rows and columns. In a program which stores an array, containing many crossword puzzles, for example, three indices are needed: One for each puzzle, one for puzzle rows, and one for puzzle columns. Many versions of BASIC allow only two dimensions, and in that case, two of the indices which would be natural for such a problem must be combined into one. Problems which involve the "folding" of indices appear in the exercises.

4.10   MATRICES

One of the things which makes the use of tables so common and so powerful in applications of mathematics to the real world is that they have an *algebra* associated with them. This means that operations, such as "addition" and "multiplication" can be performed on them. Quotes have been used for the operations above because they are not the same operations which are performed on numbers—numbers and their operations form a different algebraic system. The table operations *are* defined in terms of those of ordinary arithmetic, however. Tables together with their algebra are called **matrices**. Matrix algebra and its applications are not covered in this book, but for the reader who wishes to use matrices, pseudocode descriptions of procedures which carry out some matrix operations follow. *The reader who is unfamiliar with matrix operations may skip this section and the next one, since the material in them is not used in the remainder of the book.*

To add two N by M matrices A and B to form C:

```
I ← 1
while I ≤ N do
   J ← 1
   while J ≤ M do
      C(I, J) ← A(I, J) + B(I, J)
      J ← J + 1
   endwhile
   I ← I + 1
endwhile
```

To multiply an N by M matrix A times an M by P matrix B to get an N by P product matrix C:

```
I ← 1
while I ≤ N do
  J ← 1
  while J ≤ P do
    K ← 1 : SUM ← 0
    while K ≤ M do
      SUM ← SUM + A(I, K)*B(K, J)
      K ← K + 1
    endwhile
    C(I, J) ← SUM
    J ← J + 1
  endwhile
  I ← I + 1
endwhile
```

A useful matrix which can be derived from a given one is its **transpose**. The transpose A^T of A is obtained by switching the rows and columns of A. The procedure for finding $B = A^T$ for an N by M matrix A is:

```
I ← 1
while I ≤ M do
  J ← 1
  while J ≤ N do
    B(I, J) ← A(J, I)
    J ← J + 1
  endwhile
  I ← I + 1
endwhile
```

However, to do this *in place* for a *square* matrix (N by N) requires some care:

```
I ← 1
while I ≤ N do
  J ← 1
  while J < I do
    TEMP ← A(I, J)
    A(I, J) ← A(J, I)
    A(J, I) ← TEMP
    J ← J + 1
  endwhile
  I ← I + 1
endwhile
```

The clue needed to generate the **identity** matrix, which has 1's where the row index is equal to the column index and 0's everywhere else, is to be found in problem PG4.10.

The most useful matrix to be derived from another is the **inverse**. The process of finding the inverse is such a rich topic that it forms a fairly extensive area within applied matrix algebra. We shall leave it at that.

4.10.1   Mat

(Note: this section, like the previous one, is intended for readers already familiar with matrix calculations.) Some versions of BASIC will do matrix arithmetic for the programmer. Since the operations involve the *entire* matrix, the subscripts can be left off in such statements. Leaving them off requires that the statements be distinguished by a keyword. The chosen keyword is MAT. For example:

    10 MAT $C = A + B$

has the same effect as the addition procedure of the previous section. The transpose of A is found with TRN(A), and the inverse with INV(A). For example:

    20 MAT B = TRN(A)
    30 MAT C = INV(A)

There is a difference between matrix multiplication and the multiplication of a matrix by a constant (our third kind of "multiplication" in this book!). If A and B are matrices for which multiplication makes sense, and D is an unsubscripted variable, then:

    40 MAT RSLT $= S*B$

multiplies the two matrices, but:

    50 MAT $C = (D)*A$

requires the parentheses.

SELF-REVIEW

1. How many memory cells are reserved by:

        10 DIM A(11), B(2, 5)

    or by:

10 DIM $C(K)$

2. What are the subscript ranges of the variables A and B in (1) above?

3. Why is it unnecessary to subscript the variable DIFF in procedure DEVIATE?

4. Why is the following an illegal statement in BASIC?

50 INPUT 2

5. What is the major use of the READ ... DATA structure?

6. What are the three pointers which BASIC uses to keep track of the use of a READ ... DATA structure?

7. Suppose that a table is printed, one entry at a time, in row-major order, using nested FOR ... NEXT loops. Does the inner loop leave the first index fixed, or the second?

8. What is the difference between a table and a matrix?

9. Does the system which you are using permit tables of strings?

10. Suppose that the inventory of a supply business is arranged in rows (for items) and columns (for warehouses). How would you do the following things within a program written to manage this data:

    a. Locate an item in a specific warehouse?
    b. Locate a warehouse from which a specific item may be shipped?
    c. Indicate in the inventory that a shipment of some item has been stored at a given warehouse?
    d. Indicate in the inventory that a shipment of a specific item had been made from a specific warehouse?
    e. Locate the warehouse which contains the largest inventory of a given item?
    f. Find the total inventory of a given item?
    g. Find the total number of items in a given warehouse?
    h. Locate items which require reorder? How could you provide re-order levels to prevent searches for low inventories?
    i. Deal with a request for shipment of an item from a warehouse which does not contain a sufficient inventory of the item to fill the order? How may back orders be dealt with?
    j. Locate a warehouse from which a *large* order of a specific item can be made? What if a single warehouse cannot fill the order?
    k. Keep track of costs and prices?

l.   Deal with costs which are different for different orders of the same item?

m.   Determine the *value* of the total inventory for tax purposes?

PROBLEMS

P4.1   What is the output of the BASIC translation of the following algorithms? (Trace them.)

$X(1) \leftarrow 1$
$X(2) \leftarrow 1$
$I \leftarrow 3$
while $I \leq 7$ **do**
   $X(I) \leftarrow X(I - 1) + X(I - 2)$
   print $X(I)$;
   $I \leftarrow I + 1$
endwhile

$I \leftarrow 1$
while $I \leq 10$ **do**
   $X(I) \leftarrow I$
   $I \leftarrow I + 1$
endwhile
$J \leftarrow 5 : K \leftarrow 10$
while $J \leq 10$ **do**
   $X(K) \leftarrow X(J) \uparrow 2$
   $J \leftarrow J + 1$
   $K \leftarrow K - 2$
endwhile
$L \leftarrow 1$
while $L \leq 10$ **do**
   print $X(L)$;
   $L \leftarrow L + 1$
endwhile

P4.2   Suppose that an array X is initialized by $X(I) \leftarrow I$. What is the output of the following program segment:

```
 50 FOR I = 1 TO 3
 60    FOR J = 1 TO 3
 70       K = 3*(I - 1) + J
 80       PRINT X(K);
 90    NEXT J : PRINT
100 NEXT I
```

P4.3   Write the pseudocode for a program which will input the values of a one-dimensional array, and then print them in *reverse* order.

P4.4   Consider the program segment at right:
What is the output of this program segment?

```
40 DIM X(12)
50 FOR I = 1 TO 8
60    X(I) = I + 2
70    GOSUB 100
```

After it is executed,	80 NEXT *I*
What are the values of	90 STOP
$X(1), X(2), \ldots, X(9)$?	100 $X(I + 1) = X(I) - I$
	110 PRINT $X(I + 1)$;
	120 RETURN
	130 END

P4.5 Write the pseudocode for a program segment which will input a column number for a 5 by 4 array, then list the entries in that column and print the sum of them.

P4.6 What is the output of each of the program segments below? Hint: Trace the programs one step at a time, by keeping track of *I, J, M, N,* and *L,* and filling in the table *A* just as the program would.

```
50 FOR I = 1 TO 3            49 RESTORE
60    FOR J = 1 TO 3         50 FOR I = 1 TO 3
70       A(J, I) = I + J ↑ 2 60    FOR L = 3 TO 1 STEP −1
80    NEXT J                 70       READ A(L, I)
90 NEXT I                    80    NEXT L
100 FOR I = 3 TO 1 STEP −1   90 NEXT I
110    FOR J = 1 TO 3        100 FOR M = 1 TO 3
120       PRINT A(I, J);     110    FOR N = 1 TO 3
130    NEXT J                120       PRINT A(M, N);
140    PRINT                 130    NEXT N
150 NEXT I                   140    PRINT
                             150 NEXT M
                             160 DATA 1, 2, 3, 4, 5, 6, 7, 8, 9
```

PROGRAMS

PG4.1 Input a 4 by 5 array, bringing in one row each time with an INPUT statement. Input the entire array by looping through the *same* INPUT statement. Print the array, one *column* per line.

PG4.2 The power made available by having as many subscripts as desired is made clear by doing the following: Rewrite the wage-calculation program of this chapter using a linear array for DEDUC instead of a table.

PG4.3 Write a program which initializes a 4 by 3 array from DATA statements, and then allows a user to **update** it (change some of the values), by inputting a row index, a column index, and the corresponding value. The user must have a way to indicate that s/he is finished with updating and would like a print-out (display) of the current (updated) array. Label the rows and the columns with their correct index, for example:

COLUMNS

		1	2	3
ROWS	1	14.7	−85.0	171.6
	2	0	27.2	−5
	3	3.8	16.9	−0.08
	4	−7	2.3	1

You may want to add *'s to create a grid for the values, with a version of procedure BOX.

PG4.4   Write a program which will input the values of a 4 by 5 table, then search the table for negative entries and print a list of them together with their row and column indices.

PG4.5   Write a program which will input the values of a 4 by 4 table, search it for its minimum entry, and then print the minimum entry together with the *indices* of the row and column in which it is found.

PG4.6   Input twelve names and numbers into arrays $A\$$ and X, then create new arrays $B\$$ and Y from them as follows: Y is created by: $Y(1) \leftarrow X(12)$, $Y(2) \leftarrow X(11)$, ..., $Y(12) \leftarrow X(1)$. The corresponding names are switched similarly. Print the old and the new arrays side by side. Typical output might look like this:

JOE	17	71	KIM
JANE	83	68	JUDY
.	.	.	.
.	.	.	.
.	.	.	.
JUDY	68	83	JANE
KIM	71	17	JOE

PG4.7   Write a program which selects items at random from a noun array, a verb array, and an adjective array (and perhaps an adverb array and a connective array), and prints twenty nonsense(?) sentences.

PG4.8   Input 15 numbers into array X and then move the largest one of them into $X(15)$ by the process of making exchanges:

1. If $X(1) > X(2)$, then switch them.
3. If (the new) $X(2) > X(3)$ then switch them.
3. Continue this process by switching when $X(I) > X(I + 1)$ for $I = 3, 4, \ldots, 14$.
4. Print the resulting array.

Repeat steps 1–4 twice more. Note: If steps 1, 2, and 3 are repeated a sufficient number of times, the numbers in X will all be sorted in ascending order.

PG4.9 The location of a word in a book involves three pieces of information—the page, the number of the line on that page, and the number of the word in that line, i.e., "The fourth word on the 19th line on page 247." Many versions of BASIC provide only two indices. A data structure which would naturally use three indices, like the word location above, must have two indices folded into one. (See problem P4.2.) Write a program which will accept 3-dimensional tick-tack-toe positions (indicated by row, column, and level), store the information in a *single* 2-dimensional table, and print the game position as tables, each of which represents a level.

PG4.10 Write a program which forms a 4 by 4 array which has 1's on the main diagonal (row index = column index) and 0's elsewhere. Such arrays are very useful when solving equations simultaneously or calculating the effect of the national budget on the economy. Hint: For various values of $I\%$ and $J\%$ what is the value of $(I\%/J\%)$ and of $(J\%/I\%)$? (In versions of BASIC without integer arithmetic, this hint will not help, but the program is still a reasonable exercise.)

PG4.11 Many versions of BASIC allow string variables to be subscripted, although some do not. Most will allow comparison of strings in an IF statement, using "A" < "B" is true, and so on. You will need to experiment with your translator to see how it treats special characters. Here is the problem: Input a sequence of names in the form:

MCLUTZ, SEAN J.

Which will input as two variables. Sort them into alphabetical order, using the last name and then for matching last names, the first name. Then print the names as a list. Do not expect to come up with a good method of sorting in a few minutes. (See PG4.8.)

PROJECTS

The comments at the beginning of the projects section in Chapter 3 also apply to the following:

PJ4.1   A deck of cards may be represented with a 4 by 13 array. Each row is one of the suits: spades, hearts, diamonds, clubs. The columns represent values 2, 3, . . . , 10, jack, queen, king, ace. Write a program which initializes the deck array to zeroes, inputs a 13-card hand, assigns a value to the hand, and prints it. The presence of a card in the input is to be reflected by marking the position in the deck array with a non-zero value. (Check for redundant input!) A simple valuation is to count 4 points for an ace, 3 for a king, 2 for a queen, and 1 for a jack. A void suit (no cards of that suit in the hand) is worth 2, a singleton suit (only one card of that suit in the hand) is worth 1 point. The usual valuation schemes are more complex, but may be investigated and included in the program. A more challenging variation is to randomly split the deck into four hands, and display them, together with their values. (The four hands are usually called North, South, East, and West.)

PJ4.2   One may use the card deck representation developed in PJ4.1 to study poker hands also. Write a program which inputs four poker hands and determines the best hand. Poker hands, listed in decreasing value are as follows:

1.   Royal flush: ace, king, queen, jack, ten in the same suit.
2.   Straight flush: five cards in sequence, in the same suit, but not a Royal flush.
3.   Four of a kind.
4.   Full house: Three of a kind together with a pair.
5.   Flush: Five cards in a suit which are not in sequence.
6.   Straight: Five cards in sequence but not of the same suit.
7.   Three of a kind.
8.   Two pairs.
9.   One pair.
10.   None of the above.

Variations on this theme include generating the hands at random. If many hands are generated at random, and types of hands are counted, then one may generate statistics which tend to indicate the relative probability of dealing each of them. It is also possible to write poker *playing* programs of various sorts with the tools available in the first few chapters of this book. They are quite challenging projects.

PJ4.3   Write a program which inputs 15 numbers into a linear array X and sorts them into a linear array Y in increasing order. One technique for doing this is as follows:

1. $Y(1) \leftarrow X(1)$
2.   If $X(2) > X(1)$ then $Y(2) \leftarrow X(2)$, otherwise $Y(1) \leftarrow X(2)$ and $Y(2) \leftarrow X(1)$.
3.   Insert $X(3)$ into $Y(1)$ if it is smaller than both $Y(1)$ and $Y(2)$ (after moving them down), or into $Y(2)$ if it lies between $Y(1)$ and $Y(2)$ in value (after moving $Y(2)$ down), or into $Y(3)$ if it is not smaller than $Y(2)$.
4.   Continue inserting $X(I)$ into its correct position in Y for $I = 4, 5, \ldots, 15$.
5.   Print the sorted (and the unsorted) array.

You may be able to think of improved variations of this scheme.

PJ4.4   Write a program which inputs 15 numbers into the linear array X and sorts them in place into ascending order. One technique for doing this is:

1.   Select the smallest element of X, and exchange it with $X(1)$.
2.   Select the smallest of the remaining 14 items, $X(2)$, $X(3)$, $\ldots, X(15)$, and exchange it with the first of them, $X(2)$.
3.   Continue this process, using the last 13 items, then the last 12, then 11, $\ldots$
4.   Print the resulting array.

You may be able to think of improved variations of this scheme.

PJ4.5   A point can be randomly located in a table by choosing both a row index and a column index at random. Write a program which picks such a point in an 8 by 8 table. Let the user of the program guess where it is as follows: First s/he picks a row and gets feedback as to whether the guess is too high, too low, or just right.

Second, s/he picks a column and gets similar feedback. This cycle is repeated until the point is found.

PJ4.6   The squares of a checkerboard (chessboard) can be strung together to make paths. A sequence q_1, q_2, ..., q_n of squares forms a path if q_k has a side in common with both q_{k-1} and q_{k+1} for $k = 2, 3, ..., (n - 1)$. For example:

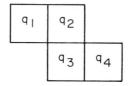

is a path, but it would not be if q_3 were removed. A *simple path* from q_i to q_j is a path which is minimal, that is, if any square is removed it is no longer a path between q_i and q_j. The path above is not a simple path from q_2 to q_4 because if q_1 were removed it would still be a path from q_2 to q_4. It *is* a simple path from q_1 to q_4. For an 8 by 8 (or 10 by 10 or 20 by 20) chessboard, write a program which will connect any two squares with a simple path of squares. The user should supply two end squares, and the program should print an array which displays a simple path joining them. For example, it may use 1's at path-square positions, 2's at end-square positions, and 0's everywhere else. If (2, 3) and (5, 6) are input, then the program might print:

```
0  0  0  0  0  0  0  0           0  0  0  0  0  0  0  0
0  0  2  1  0  0  0  0           0  0  2  0  0  0  0  0
0  0  0  1  1  0  0  0           0  0  1  0  0  0  0  0
0  0  0  0  1  0  0  0   OR:     0  0  1  0  0  0  0  0
0  0  0  0  1  2  0  0           0  0  1  1  1  2  0  0
0  0  0  0  0  0  0  0           0  0  0  0  0  0  0  0
0  0  0  0  0  0  0  0           0  0  0  0  0  0  0  0
0  0  0  0  0  0  0  0           0  0  0  0  0  0  0  0
```

PJ4.7   Reverse the roles of the user and the program in PJ4.5.

PJ4.8   Alter PJ4.6 by allowing the user to put 1, 2, . . . *blocking squares* into the board, which cannot be included in the path. Note: One blocking square is one project, two is another, and three or more is another. If it is not *possible* to create a simple path for some input, then the program should say so, and not loop forever.

PJ4.9   Invent a game in which one searches for treasure (at some randomly chosen point in a 10 by 10 array). The user needs to be able to move from an entrance (say $A(1, 1)$) along either rows or columns, and must get some feedback about the progress s/he is making (For example: hot, warm, etc.) with respect to both trap and treasure. More interesting feedback is generated by having "adventures", both good and bad, at various other randomly chosen points. One can add more treasures and traps of various worths and dangers. The game can be a multiple player game with scores. It can also be a lifetime project.

PJ4.10   The board project PJ4.6 may be altered so that the input is three or more points, and the program finds a network of simple paths (spiderweb?) between them which is minimal in one of two senses:

1. No square can be removed without disconnecting two of the points.
2. No network of fewer squares will do the job.

PJ4.11   A variation of PJ4.9 can be created in which the illusion is that the trap (monster?) is *hunting* for the player. It *can* be if it always moves a step *toward* the player each time the player moves two steps, or even one step! The trap can even move randomly and perhaps capture the treasure for itself.

PJ4.12   Combine PJ4.8 and PJ4.10.

PJ4.13   Write an inventory program which solves a combination of *several* of the items mentioned in **self-review** item 10.

Comment: Programs which would involve changing the *structure* of an inventory, and related applications in business, are best left until the techniques of Chapter 6 have been developed.

Chapter 5

EXPRESSIONS AND FUNCTIONS

This chapter was written to be used by readers with a mathematical bent at any time after Chapter 2. Because of that, some of the features of BASIC which were introduced in earlier chapters are missing from this one.

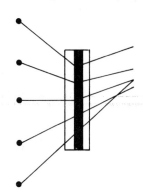

5.1 EXPRESSIONS

Restricting arithmetic to one operation per assignment statement may produce a string of statements which looked like this:

40 LET $N = X/G$
50 LET $N = N + G$
60 LET $N = N/2$

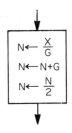

The effect of these statements is really to do the following:

$$N \leftarrow \frac{X/G + G}{2}$$

It would be convenient to put the entire expression in one assignment statement, but of course, the dividing bars cannot easily be arranged at

126

the keyboard. Even if they could, how would BASIC interpret the resulting display? It would need to determine what things are to be done, and in what order as well. When we look at the display above, we *assume* that X/G is formed before the addition is done. The translator, however, needs some other means of deciding on the order of operations. One way in which the order of the operations can be dealt with is by the use of parentheses. Statements [40], [50], and [60] above can be replaced by:

40 LET $N = ((X/G) + G)/2$

The BASIC translator can decipher this by treating everything within a pair of matching parentheses as an expression to be evaluated before the result is combined with other values. BASIC locates the innermost pair of values to be operated on, evaluates that combination, and works its way out until the last pair of values is combined with an operation. In the example above, the translation will cause (X/G) to be calculated first, then the sum of that value with G, then the result of that to be divided by 2, and finally the assignment is made to N. The only difficulty with this scheme is that if the expression is very complex, the many parentheses in it make a visual mess. That does not bother BASIC, but it is difficult for a person to understand. The visual difficulties can be alleviated, as we shall see.

5.1.1   Precedence

Consider the simple expression "A plus B times C." This expression seems to require parentheses, since it could mean either $(A + B)*C$ or $A + (B*C)$. With $A \leftarrow 2$, $B \leftarrow 4$, and $C \leftarrow 3$, the two interpretations yield two answers, 14 and 18, for the value of the expression. The only way to resolve this difference is to adopt a convention that determines which operation comes first. This convention is called a **precedence of operations**. Before it is stated, one other confusion must be resolved: $-A$ and $+B$ do not involve subtraction and addition. The "$-$" and the "$+$" in the previous sentence are **unary** operations: the value of a variable is changed by "$-$" or left alone by "$+$". The precedence which is adopted for BASIC is:

first	$-$, $+$	unary operations
second	$\uparrow$ or $**$	exponentiation
third	$*$, $/$	multiplication and division
fourth	$-$, $+$	subtraction and addition

This precedence *will* be followed by BASIC, and so it *should* be followed by the programmer. The precedence can be overridden by parentheses. $A + B*C$ yields the same result as $A + (B*C)$, which has the value 14 with the example values chosen above. The expression $(A + B)*C$ has the value 18 because the parentheses cause the addition operation to be done first.

Even with the precedence, it is still possible to do unexpected things. For example, $2 - 4 - 3$ could be either $(2 - 4) - 3 = -5$ or $2 - (4 - 3) = 1$. In some circumstances the difference between $(X*Y)/Z$ and $X*(Y/Z)$ is also important. The convention that is followed is that operations on the same level of precedence are done *left-to-right*. With that convention,

$$2 - 4 - 3 = (2 - 4) - 3 = -5, \text{ and}$$
$$2 \uparrow 2 \uparrow 3 = (2 \uparrow 2) \uparrow 3 = 64, \text{ not } 256$$

When expressions are rather complicated, it may still be best to break them up into pieces in order to make the program readable.

5.1.2   Included Expressions

A BASIC translator must have a part of itself, a **subroutine**, or **subprogram**, or **module** or **procedure**, or whatever it is called, which has the job of translating expressions. (In BASIC, programs are broken up with the GOSUB ... RETURN structure discussed at the end of Chapter 2). Since that procedure must exist, it can be called upon by the parts of the translator which have other tasks, such as the translation of PRINT statements. This means that the possibility of statements like:

265 PRINT $A + B*C$

not only exists, but is actually available in many versions of BASIC. If $A \leftarrow 2$, $B \leftarrow 3$, and $C \leftarrow 1.7$ then the result of execution of the statement above will be the display of 7.1. On the other hand, "INPUT $A + B$" is nonsense, and so is "LET $A + B = C$". In both cases, an expression "$A + B$" appears where the syntax of a statement requires the name of a variable and "$A + B$" is not a legal variable name.

5.2   SCIENTIFIC NOTATION

Many programs which are designed specifically to do calculations cannot deal only with integers or with fractions confined to a range which can be displaced compactly. For example, a chemistry program might need to use

Avogadro's Number, which is the number of molecules in one mole of gas. It is approximately 6.023×10^{23}. This notation means that 6.023 is to be multiplied by 10^{23} (1 followed by 23 zeroes). Some similar notation must be used for both input and output by BASIC. It is: $+6.023E+23$ (both of the $+$'s may usually be omitted). For input the key letter E tells BASIC that this number is expressed in scientific notation. A number calculated by a program to be either very small or very large will be automatically displayed in scientific notation. The values at which the switches occur vary from one version of BASIC to another.

5.3 BOOLEAN EXPRESSIONS

Many versions of BASIC will allow statements of the following type:

927 IF $A > B$ AND $B <= C$ THEN 980

Recall that $A > B$ is a condition which is either true or false. Logical connectives like AND, OR, and NOT apply to things which are true or false, and so [927] makes sense as an English sentence.

The power of Boolean expressions is that:

1. Most things which can be expressed with logic can be expressed with AND, OR, and NOT, and
2. anything which can be expressed with AND, OR, and NOT can be modeled with a digital circuit and vice versa, and
3. a computer language which includes AND, OR, and NOT can be used to write programs which model both the logic and the circuits.

The precedence of operations needs to be extended in order to deal with the three Boolean operators:

fifth	NOT	negation
sixth	AND	conjunction
seventh	OR	disjunction

Here are their definitions, using T for true and F for false:

cond1	cond2	cond1 AND cond2	cond1 OR cond2	NOT cond1
T	T	T	T	F
T	F	F	T	F
F	T	F	T	T
F	F	F	F	T

The Boolean operators can be used to make a program more readable:

```
100 IF A >= 0 AND A < R THEN R = A
110 IF A < 0 AND A > L THEN L = A
120 PRINT L, R
```

has the same effect as:

```
100 IF A < 0 THEN 110
102 IF A < R THEN R = A
104 GO TO 120
110 IF A > L THEN L = A
120 PRINT L, R
```

but it is easier to understand.

The following is also allowed:

```
401 IF A OR B >= C THEN 500
```

In order to make sense of [401], the value of the variable A must be treated as either true or false. The standard solution is fairly natural (but not logical!): a variable is "false" if 0, and "true" otherwise.

5.4 THE FUNCTION CONCEPT

Expressions, scientific notation, Boolean expressions, and precedence are refinements and sophistications of the BASIC language. Functions are an even more fundamental extension of elementary BASIC, and they will be introduced by considering an application in which they arise naturally.

5.4.1   A Collision Course Example

Let us suppose that a comet is traveling in the plane of Earth's orbit, is farther away from the sun than Earth is at the moment, but is clearly going to move inside Earth's orbit at some later time. It would be worthwhile to calculate the radial distance of Earth from the sun, and the distance of the comet from the sun, and find out at what time they coincide. Suppose that the distance of Earth from the sun is of the form:

$$E3*T^3 + E2*T^2 + E1*T + E0 = E$$

where T is the time from now, and $E3$, $D2$, $E1$, and $E0$ are constants. Suppose also, that the distance of the comet from the sun is of the form:

$$C3*T^3 + C2*T^2 + C1*T + C0 = C$$

where $C3$, $C2$, $C1$, and $C0$ are constants. As astronomers watch the comet, they refine the values of the constants in the second expression, and so they would like to have a program into which they can feed the current values of $C3$, $C2$, $C1$, and $C0$ and have it calculate the time at which the distances are equal: $C = E$.

Such a program may be constructed by repeatedly calculating both C and E for increasing values of T. At some time T, either $C = E$, or there will be an overshoot of the value of C, at which time $C < E$. If large steps in T values are taken, then the magnitude of the overshoot $C - E$ may be quite large. The solution to the problem of overshooting the mark is to simply reverse direction, and take smaller steps back in time until there is an overshoot in the other direction. This process is repeated until the steps make only small changes in $|C - E|$ (the absolute value of $C - E$). A simplified picture of this scheme can be made by assuming that E is constant, and C is larger. First choose a step value for T, say DT, and calculate new values of C until there is an overshoot:

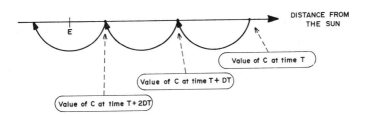

Now choose a smaller value of DT and calculate values of C until there is an overshoot in the opposite direction:

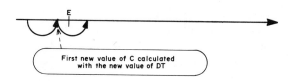

First new value of C calculated
with the new value of DT

Choose an even smaller value of DT and repeat this process until $|C - E|$ is small enough for acceptable precision.

The process described above may be outlined in three steps:

1. Input the constants required to calculate C and E, and initialize the time T. Choose a stepsize DT for changing T, and a value for a **flag** F which will indicate the *direction* of the time steps.

2. Form a loop which, on each pass, flips F to $-F$ and decreases DT, then calculates value of E and C with T, $T + DT$, ... until $(C - E)$ changes sign.

3. The loop in (2) is repeated until $|C - E|$ is "small enough".

With this description, and some choices of initial value, we have:

procedure COMET
   input (constants)
   $DT \leftarrow 1024 : F \leftarrow -1 : T \leftarrow 0$
   repeat
      $F \leftarrow -F : DT \leftarrow -DT/2$
      //calculate $D \leftarrow (C - E)*F$ for T, $T + DT$, ... until $D \leq 0$//
   until $-D < 0.0001*E$
   print T
endproc

The role of the flag F is to keep track of (flag) the sign of $(C - E)$. It is then used to provide the absolute value of $(C - E)$ until there is a switch from *either* $+$ to $-$ or from $-$ to $+$. By filling in the details, we arrive at a more complete description of the procedure:

```
procedure COMET
  input E3, E2, E1, E0
  input C3, C2, C1, C0
  DT ← 1024 : F ← −1 : T ← 0
  repeat
    F ← −F
    DT ← DT/2
    repeat
```
$$E \leftarrow E3*T^3 + E2*T^2 + E1*T + E0$$
$$C \leftarrow C3*T^3 + C2*T^2 + C1*T + C0$$
$$D \leftarrow (C − E)*F$$
$$T \leftarrow T + DT*F$$
```
    until D ≤ 0
  until −D < 0.0001*E
  print T
endproc
```

With the limited BASIC we are using in this chapter, this becomes:

```
 10  INPUT E3, E2, D1, E0
 20  INPUT C3, C2, C1, C0
 30  LET DT = 1024
 40  LET F = −1
 50  LET T = 0
 60  LET F = −F
 70  LET DT = DT/2
 80  LET E = E3*T ↑ 3 + E2*T ↑ 2 + E1*T + E0
 90  LET C = C3*T ↑ 3 + C2*T ↑ 2 + C1*T + C0
100  LET D = (C − E)*F
110  LET T = T + DT*F
120  IF D > 0 THEN 80
130  IF −D > = 0.0001*E THEN 60
140  PRINT T
150  STOP
160  END
```

5.4.2 Statement Functions

One noticeable thing about the algorithm of the previous section is that statements [80] and [90] do essentially the same thing each time through the loop [80]-[120]. They perform a calculation according to a set formula, expressed in a single statement, which returns a *single, unique value* for any given value of T. This feature means that they perform as functions in the mathematical sense, and so they are called **statement functions**. The *form* of the expressions can be isolated in one place, as a reference or guide for the BASIC translator, and the function used in one or even several other places in the program. This isolation of a complicated expression removes some clutter from a program, which makes the program structure more apparent. As we shall see, it also carries the germ of an idea. Two statement functions can be defined by:

25 DEF FNC(X) = $C3*X \uparrow 3 + C2*X \uparrow 2 + C1*X + C0$
26 DEF FNE(X) = $E3*X \uparrow 3 + E2*X \uparrow 2 + E1*X + E0$

and then [80] and [90] may be changed to *use* these definitions by:

80 LET E = FNE(T)
90 LET C = FNC(T)

In [80], the value of FNE(T) is determined by substituting the value of T in every occurrence of X in the definition of FNE in [26]. Similarly, FNC(T) is calculated in [90] by substitution of the value of T into the expression defined in [25] at every occurrence of X. In this example, the function FNC (and FNE also) was deliberately defined with the **argument** X and used with the **variable** T to illustrate a point. What BASIC needs to know when FNC(T) is used in an expression is what to do with the value of T. The function definition determines that: do with the value of T whatever is done with the argument in the DEF statement.

A different symbol could have been used in the definition. For example:

25 DEF FNC(DT) = $C3*DT \uparrow 3 + C2*DT \uparrow 2 + C1*DT + C0$

would have given the same result. The DT in this DEF statement would not have been confused by the translator with the DT in the rest of the program. Hence, it is called a **dummy argument**—it is a place-holder for the value to be substituted for it whenever the function is used in an executable statement. (Like others which have been introduced, the DEF statement is **non-executable**—it is in the program in order to guide the translation; to give helpful information to BASIC about the program.)

The reader is cautioned that the argument of a function also has some **attributes** (properties). In Chapter 3, names like $I\%$ and $A\$$ are discussed which have certain properties because the information in the memory cells which they name are stored in a special way. With the definition in [25], to use FNC($I\%$) or FNC($A\$$) would not make sense because the definition of FNC involves a real value, indicated by the argument name X, not an integer or a character string. On the other hand, FNC($A(7)$) makes sense if a subscripted variable A appears in a DIM statement (see Chapter 4), although in that case, FNC(A) does not.

Since the functions FNC and FNE return a value, like any expression, they can be used as an expression. For example, [80], [90] and [100] all three can be replaced by one statement:

100 LET D = (FNC(T) − FNE(T))*F

Because it is only necessary to provide a value in order for the operations indicated by the function definition to be carried out, FNC(3.7) is perfectly acceptable. In many versions of BASIC, FNC(A + B*C) or even FNC(FNC(T) ↑ 2) is acceptable. For example:

10 DEF FNW(X) = 2*X − 1
.
.
.
90 LET A = 3
100 LET Y = FNW(A)
110 LET Z = FNW(FNW(A) + 1)
120 PRINT Y, Z
.
.
.

The output of this segment will be:

5   11

Statement [110] is equivalent to:

110 LET Z = FNW(Y + 1)

It is possible for a function to have more than one argument. For example:

10 DEF FND(A, B, C) = B ↑ 2 − 4.0*A*C

With multiple arguments, the fact that they are dummy arguments is very important. For example, with this definition, and with A ← 1, B ← 2, C ← 3, the expression FND(A, B, C) is equivalent to FND(1, 2, 3) and will return (4 − 4*1*3) = −8, but FND(B, A, C) is equivalent to FND(2, 1, 3) and will return (1 − 4*2*3) = −23.

These features of statement functions may be put together to simplify procedure COMET somewhat by combining FNC and FNE of that procedure into one function:

25 DEF FNP(A, B, C, D, T) = $A*T \uparrow 3 + B*T \uparrow 2 + C*T + D$
.
.
.

80 LET E = FNP($E3, E2, E1, E0, T$)
90 LET C = FNP($C3, C2, C1, C0, T$)
.
.
.

Actually, the fifth argument T is not necessary. Suppose that FNP is redefined by:

25DEF FNP(A, B, C, D) = $A*T \uparrow 3 + B*T \uparrow 2 + C*T + D$

Since T does not appear in the argument list, it is taken to be the same *variable* T which occurs elsewhere in the program. When an identifier appears *explicitly* in the argument list, it becomes a dummy argument with meaning only within the definition of the function. When an identifier appears elsewhere in the function definition, but not in the argument list, then it is taken to be a variable name.

The general form of the DEF statement is:

[N] DEF FN $\langle \alpha \rangle$ (List) = $\langle$Expression$\rangle$
where $\langle \alpha \rangle$ is any alphabetic character $A, B, \ldots, Z$ and
$\langle$List$\rangle$ is a list of dummy arguments separated by commas.

5.4.3   Library Functions

All versions of BASIC have functions which are defined within the translator itself. They may be used in expressions in any program. Some common mathematical functions normally available in BASIC are:

FUNCTION   *RETURNS*

ABS(X). . . . . the magnitude of the value of X

ATN(X)

  or

ATAN(X). . . . . the arctangent of the value of X in radians

COS(X) . . . . the cosine of the value of X, assuming it to be in radians

EXP(X) . . . . the constant $e = 2.71828...$ raised to the power (value of X)

INT(X). . . . . the largest integer less than or equal to the value of X

LOG(X) . . . . the natural logarithm of the value of X if that value is greater than or equal to zero

LOG10(X) . . . . the logarithm to the base 10 of the value of X (if X is greater than or equal to zero)

PI . . . . 3.14159...

RND(X). . . . . a pseudo-random number α, $0 \leq \alpha < 1$. If $X < 0$ it is always the same, if $X = 0$ the uses of the function in a program always results in the same sequence, and if $X > 0$ a new sequence is generated with each run of the program. In some systems, the command or statement RANDOMIZE or RANDOM plays the role of $X > 0$.

SGN(X) . . . . -1 if $X < 0$, 0 if $X = 0$, and 1 if $X > 0$.

SIN(X) . . . . the sine of X, assuming X to be in radians.

SQR(X) . . . . the square root of X

TAN(X) . . . . the tangent of a radian argument X

An example of the use of one of the library functions might occur in a program which calculates the roots of a quadratic equation:

```
           .
           .
           .
245  LET D = B ↑ 2 − 4*A*C
246  IF D < 0 THEN 280
257  LET R = (−B + SQR(D))/(2*A)
248  LET S = (−B − SQR(D))/(2*A)
           .
           .
           .
```

5.4.4   Utility Functions

There are usually some built-in functions which are interesting and useful but which vary greatly from one system to another. Built-in functions perform operations such as reading an internal clock, or re-setting it to the current date. For example, on one system PRINT *TI*$ prints the time (in "jiffies": 1/60 second) since the machine was turned on. The same system also allows the timing of routines with a clock function which returns a number (in jiffies again):

```
10 LET X = TI
20 REM ... BEGIN ROUTINE
   .
   .
   .
100 REM ... END OF THE ROUTINE
110 PRINT (TI − X)/60
```

On another machine, which stays on nearly all of the time, one may use DATE$(0%) to return the current day, month, year or use TIME$(0%) to return the time of day. (Both of the last two functions return character strings—see Chapter 3).

Another class of utility functions involves converting character strings to numbers and vice versa. Two sorts of numbers may be associated with a character. Everything that is stored in a computer must actually be stored as a number of some sort, and some numbers are used as a *code* to stand for characters (when they are recognized to be a code, and treated as such). A common code is the ASCII code in which 65 stands for an "*A*" and 100 for an "$". The other type of number which may be associated with a character is the number that a numeral stands for: the character "9" can be converted to the integer 9 (which is not its ASCII code). In one system, ASC("*X*") returns the integer code for the character "*X*", and CHR$(*N*) returns the character for which the number *N* is the ASCII code. There are other codes in use, and so you should check your system to determine which code it uses.

5.4.5   Multi-line Functions

The crucial characteristic of a function is that it returns a *single value,* unlike a GOSUB ... RETURN structure, which may do anything that can be done in a BASIC procedure (see Chapter 2). In *some* versions of BASIC, a function may be defined by more than one statement, but it is still used like a variable in any expression. Such functions are called **multi-**

line functions. An example of one which finds the absolute value of the difference of two values passed to it is:

```
100  DEF FNZ(X, Y)
110  LET FNZ = X − Y
120  IF Y < = X THEN 140
130  LET FNZ = −(X − Y)
140  FNEND
```

Of course, with the use of the library function ABS, [110]–[130] could have been replaced by:

```
120  LET FNZ = ABS(X − Y)
```

but the built-in function ABS is itself essentially the one above. The general form of a multi-line function is:

[N1] DEF *FN* $\langle \alpha \rangle$ ($\langle$Argument list$\rangle$)

         ·
         ·
         ·

[N2] LET *FN* $\langle \alpha \rangle$ = $\langle$expression$\rangle$
         ·
         ·

[N3] FNEND
where $\langle \alpha \rangle$ is *A, B, ..., Z*

The crucial feature to notice is that *FN* $\langle \alpha \rangle$ *must* appear on the left of at least one assignment statement in any path through the function definition. The assignment sets the function to its return value.

5.5 AN INTEGRATION EXAMPLE

One of the things which is extremely useful in many applications in Mathematics, Physics, psychology, etc., is to find the area which lies between two points on the x-axis and which lies between the x-axis and some curve. One of the ways to do that is to approximate the area with rectangles. The area of each rectangle can be calculated as their width times their height, and then these areas can be summed to give a total area. The slimmer the rectangles, the better the approximation.

For any point on the curve, and two points on the axis, one rectangle can be formed from the height of the curve at one axis point, and another from

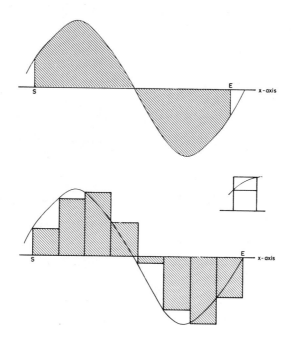

the height at the other. If the function which defines the curve is a nice enough one, then the areas determined by the left and the right axis points approach the same value. (Although there are functions for which this does not happen, they seldom occur in application areas.) We shall write a program which calculates approximate areas from both ways of forming the rectangles for a function of the form $P(X) = AX^3 + BX^2 + CX + D$, and stops when their difference is within 1% of the area of one of them. We shall use the notation $|Y|$ for ABS(Y), S for the start of the inversal of interest, and E for the right-hand end of it.

The refinements of this procedure which avoid the possible pitfalls are outside of the scope of. this book. Some of them may be discovered by experimenting with the graphs of common functions and can be incorporated into the program if desired. The simple approach involves the following:

1. Input S and E, and determine a *stepsize* (the width of the rectangles in the approximation), DX, from $E - S$.
2. Repeat a loop which, on each pass, calculates the two approximations, A_1 and A_2, of the integral of $P(X)$ between S and E, using DX. On each succeeding pass, DX is halved in order to form a better approximation.

3.   The result is printed when $|A_1 - A_2| < 0.01*A_1$.

Here is such an algorithm:

```
procedure REC
   input S, E
   DX ← (E − S)/2
   define P(X)
   repeat
      X ← S
      DX ← DX/2
      //determine A₁ and A₂, using DX//
      until |A₁ − A₂| < 0.01*A₁
   print A₁
endproc
```

The determination of A_1 and A_2 is a loop which calculates the area of each rectangle from $|P(X)|*DX$ and adds it to the appropriate sum (A_1 or A_2). Here then is the complete pseudocode and listing:

```
procedure REC
   input A, B, C, D
   input S, E
   DX ← (E − S)/2
   define P(X) = AX³ + BX² + CX + D
   repeat
      X ← S
      DX ← DX/2
      A1 ← 0 : A2 ← 0
      repeat
         A1 ← |P(X)|*DX + A1
         X ← X + DX
         A2 ← |P(X)|*DX + A2
         until X ≥ E
      D ← |A1 − A2|
      until D < .01*A1
   print A1
endproc
```

Using the stripped BASIC of this chapter, this becomes:

```
10 INPUT A, B, C, D
20 INPUT S, E
30 LET DX = (E − S)/2
40 DEF FNP(X) = A*X ↑ 3 + B*X ↑ 2 + C*X + D
50 LET X = S
60 LET DX = DX /2
70 LET A1 = 0
80 LET A2 = 0
90 LET A1 = A1 + ABS(FNP(X))*DX
100 LET X = X + DX
110 LET A2 = A2 + ABS(FNP(X))*DX
120 IF X < E THEN 90
130 LET D = ABS(A1 − A2)
140 IF D > = 0.01*A1 THEN 50
150 PRINT A1
160 STOP
170 END
```

SELF-REVIEW

1. Given $A \leftarrow 1$, $B \leftarrow 2$, and $C \leftarrow 3$, what are the values of the following expressions:

   a. $A*B − C$
   b. $A − B*C$
   c. $B \uparrow C − A$
   d. $−A − B − C$
   e. $A/B*C$

   f. $C \uparrow B \uparrow B$
   g. $3E+2$
   h. $B*B \uparrow C$
   i. $B*B/C*B \uparrow C$
   j. $(B*B)/(C*B) \uparrow C$

2. Suppose that A and C are true and B is false. What are the values of the following expressions:

   a. A AND B
   b. A OR B
   c. A AND B OR C

   d. A AND B OR B AND C
   e. NOT A OR B
   f. NOT B AND A

3. Consider the following statement function definitions:

```
10 DEF FNA(X) = X ↑ 3
20 DEF FNB(X, Y) = X*Y − 4*Y
30 DEF FNC(X) = (X + Y)/2
```

Given that $A \% \leftarrow 2$, $B \leftarrow 1/2$, $X \leftarrow 2$, and $Y \leftarrow 3$, what is the value (if any) of each of the following expressions:

a. FNA(B)   e. FNB(Y, X)   i. FNB(FNC(2))
b. FNA(B) ↑ 2   f. FNC(FNA(X))   j. FNB(FNA(2), FNC(Y))
c. FNA(B ↑ 2)   g. FNA($B*X - Y$)   k. $X + B - $ INT($X + B$)
d. FNB(Y, B)   h. FNB($A \%$, B)   l. INT(ABS(($Y - Y$ ↑ 2)/2))

PROBLEMS

P5.1 Write statement function definitions for both of the following which use a *minimum* number of parentheses:

a. $f(X, Y) = \dfrac{X - (Y/2)X^2}{Y + X}$ b. $g(X) = \sqrt{AX^2 + BX + C}$

P5.2 Define functions which calculate the area of a:

a. disk   c. parallelogram
b. triangle   d. regular polygon

P5.3 Define a function which converts a real number of the form dddd.ddddd into that required for dollars and cents displays: dddd.dd.

P5.4 Define a function which calculates the value of an investment of principle P, compounded N times per year for M years at an interest rate R.

P5.5 Write the pseudocode for a program which inputs N, then requests A_n, A_{n-1}, $\ldots$, A_1, A_0 from the user, calculates the value of the polynomial they determine, and prints that value and its magnitude. It is possible to factor $A_n X^n + A_{n-1}X^{n-1} + \cdots + A_1 X + A_0$ into the following: $A_0 + X(A_1 + X(A_2 + X(\ldots X(A_n))) \ldots)$. This is really an algorithm:

a. $k \leftarrow n$: SUM $\leftarrow A_n$
b. SUM $\leftarrow$ SUM $* X$
c. $k \leftarrow k - 1$
d. SUM $\leftarrow$ SUM $+ A_k$
e. if $k > 0$ then go back to b.

PROGRAMS

PG5.1   Write a procedure which uses the integer function INT to determine whether or not an input integer is odd.

PG5.2   Write a procedure which determines whether or not an integer is divisible by 9 by summing its digits and then determining whether or not the digit sum is divisible by 9.

PG5.3   The roots of the quadratic equation $AX^2 + BX + C = 0$ are of the form:

$$\frac{-B \pm \sqrt{B^2 - 4AC}}{2A}.$$

Write a program which finds them (after checking for $B^2 - 4AC < 0$!), for input values of A, B, and C. New values are to be repeatedly input until $A = B = C = 0$.

PG5.4   Refine the integration example so that $A1$ sums up rectangles which are entirely between the curve and the x-axis, and $A2$ sums up rectangles which all extend outside of the area between.

PG5.5   A radioactive isotope decays with time so that the amount left after Y years is $A*C^{(Y/HL)}$, where A is the amount at the beginning of the time period, HL is the *half-life*, and C is EXP(0.693). Write a program which will calculate the amount left after Y years, look up the half-life of some elements, and run it with various values of Y. You may wish to have the program loop through a number of years and print a table. Some research in newspapers and magazines will turn up half-lives of waste elements from reactors which are due to be dumped into salt mines or the ocean, and perhaps the half-lives of some of the radioactive products of nuclear testing. (For a start, HL for Strontium 90, which gets into milk, is 28 years.)

PG5.6   (Assumes Chapter 3) Construct a program which prints a plot of the values of a given function. The plct may be vertical like this:

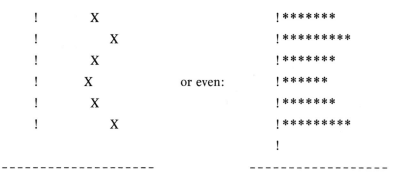

```
!       X                          ! *******
!          X                       ! *********
!       X                          ! *******
!       X            or even:      ! ******
!       X                          ! *******
!          X                       ! *********
                                   !
- - - - - - - - - - - - - - - -      - - - - - - - - - - - - - - - -
```

PG5.7   (Assumes both Chapter 3 and Chapter 4) Turn the plot of PG5.6
around and label it appropriately.

```
      SALARY         12    X        X
   (KILODOLLARS)     10  X   X   X
                      8        X
                      6
                      4
                      2
                     _____

                          2   4   6
                       EMPLOYEE  CODE
```

PROJECTS

The comments at the beginning of the project section of Chapter 3 apply
here also.

PJ5.1   One of the properties of interest of a function is the location of its
local maxima and minima. One way to look for them with rela-
tively simple calculations is as follows:

1.   Sample (calculate) the values of the function at S, $S + DX$, ...
2.   When the difference between two successive values of the
function differs in sign from the previous difference, then one
has passed over a hump or under a dip. The optimal value (for

the stepsize being used) is the one involved in the calculation of both differences.

Write a program which finds one of the optimal values of a given function on a given (input) interval with a given (input) stepsize. For more of a challenge, find *all* of the optimal values of a polynomial $P(X) = A \cdot X^3 + B \cdot X^2 + C \cdot X + D$ (A, B, C, D are to be input). For even more of a challenge, enclose your program in a loop which decreases the stepsize until the optima are located with some chosen precision. (After locating one optimum, you need to move on to the next with large stepsizes again!)

PJ5.2   Geometric series of the form: $1 + r + r^2 + r^3 + \cdots$ have a sum of the form: $1/(1 - r)$ when $|r| < 1$. Other series of the form: $s_0 + s_1 + s_2 + \cdots$ cannot be summed so neatly. One way to approximate the sum is to calculate the partial sums: s_0, $s_0 + s_1$, $s_0 + s_1 + s_2$, ... Deciding when to stop is a rich topic. Some of the problems associated with finding sums can be investigated by writing a program to sum series by the method of partial sums. Do this with a program which will decide when the successive partial sums are "close" to each other, then print both the last partial sum calculated and the number of terms involved in its calculation. The results can be compared with the correct result for various geometrical series. Many sequences may be generated from a statement function: DEF $P(R, N) = R \uparrow N$ or DEF $P(S, N) = 1/N + S$ for example. Investigate the sums of both geometric series and other types of series.

PJ5.3   The slope of a line which is tangent to the graph of a function at a point is of considerable interest to applied mathematicians of every ilk (including economists, test pilots, etc.). Given a function (perhaps defined in a BASIC statement function as $F(X)$), it is possible to find an approximation to a slope by:

1.   Calculate the value of the function at the point of interest, say P, and also at $P + DP$.
2.   Divide the difference in the two values of F by DP. This is called the slope of the secant line through $(P, F(P))$ and $(P + DP, F(P + DP))$. This slope is an estimate of the desired tangent slope.
3.   Decrease the value of DP and repeat the two steps above until "close enough".

Write programs which calculate tangent slopes of given functions. You may want to extend these programs to calculate slopes at many points on an interval and plot the results. The functions $SIN(X)$ and $COS(X)$ have particularly interesting plots of their slopes. If you have done PJ5.2, then investigate the slopes of functions near their optimum values.

PJ5.4 Generating pseudo-random numbers is a much-studied subject, but the essence of generating and printing a sequence of them is as follows:

1.   Choose X—the first of the sequence, or *seed.*
2. $P \leftarrow X*M$
3. $X \leftarrow$ (the *remainder* of P/C)
4.   **print** X, and loop to (2).

Here M, the *multiplier,* should be a power of 2 plus either 3 or 5 (4096 + 5, or 16384 + 3, etc.). The *constant* C should be approximately the square of M. The details of the best choice of M and C are highly machine dependent, but the behavior of the algorithm can be studied without optimal values. Write a program which inputs M, C, and the initial X, and prints a sequence of 20 pseudo-random numbers. The steps (2) and (3) may be done with one statement function definition and one assignment statement, using one library function (other than RND!).

Chapter 6

FILES

6.1 SAVING PROGRAMS

Anyone who has programmed on a computer system, or dealt with a large pile of paperwork, has encountered files. Files are used to store information that needs to be:

1. out of the way,
2. retrieved easily,
3. not lost, and
4. can be brought up to date, modified, expanded, and deleted.

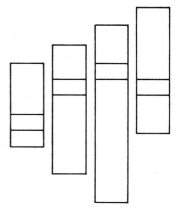

This chapter is about the where and the how of dealing with files in BASIC programs.

There is a limited amount of space available in a computer memory, and files require a great deal of storage. When control of the machine is turned over to a program, it may need to reuse the space that was previously occupied by some other program. In some systems all user programs are stored beginning at the same location, and each new program will replace an old one in memory. In all systems, programs need to be saved for reuse later. Programs need to be saved in **non-volatile** storage— storage which does not lose its contents when the user signs off. It is often necessary to have storage which is compact and portable as well as non-volatile, so that information can be stored and moved from one location to another. In some small systems, the only means provided for mass storage which is compact, portable, and non-volatile is a tape cassette, just like those on which popular music is stored. In other systems, storage is provided on magnetic disks, which look like phonograph records, but do not have grooves cut into them. The information on the disks is stored as magnetized areas, just as it is on tape. Both of these storage forms are

148

eraseable, they can be reused, and they are non-volatile, so that one must *do* something to them in order to erase whatever is on them.

No matter what storage medium is available, there must be a way to get a program onto it. Computing systems vary, but usually there is a command, SAVE, which informs BASIC that the program which is currently in memory is to be written onto the tape (or disk). The program can often be retrieved by a LOAD command. Both of these operations require, in a tape system, that the tape be in the correct starting position. The function of rewinding the tape may or may not be under program (or command) control—it may need to be done manually.

Normally, more than one program can be stored on a tape (or disk), and an identifying name is added to both tape commands, like this:

SAVE "HARDWORK"
LOAD "HARDWORK"

The retrieval of a program in some systems is done with:

OLD "HARDWORK"

rather than with the LOAD command.

Whatever form the commands may take, the response of BASIC to such a command is to store the program as a **file**. To BASIC, the program HARDWORK is a collection of data, and it is filed away on a magnetic medium under "HARDWORK". What is stored in the file is a collection of **records**, which play the same role as the pieces of paper in a file folder stored in a cabinet. The records for this kind of file are BASIC statements. They are likely to be ordered by statement numbers, since that is the way in which BASIC arranges them while a program is being developed by the user.

6.2 PROGRAM FILES

Consider some of the things which the BASIC translator, acting as an editor, must do as a program is being written:

1. BASIC must **create** a file in which to put the program. The BASIC translator is alerted to the fact that a program is being written when it encounters input which resembles a valid BASIC statement. If there is already a program in the part of memory assigned to the user, then BASIC needs to be told to start a new program file. In some systems the command to form a new program file is simply NEW®.

2. BASIC must be told whether or not an incoming statement is a *new*

record to be added to the list of records in the file, or if it is a *replacement* for an old one. One purpose of statement numbers is to provide a **key** by which statements are recognized, even if they are changed drastically. The key (statement number) also determines the final order of the statements, but not their **entry sequence**: statements can be input in any order. The key also does not determine the order of execution—there are branch statements in the language. We shall call the order determined by the key the **list order** of the statements, and the order of execution their **logical order**. It is the list order which is used for sorting a file, or searching for a record in it. Consider these statements:

    20 PRINT *A*
    10 INPUT *A*
    30 GO TO 10

The entry sequence of the statements above is [20], [10], [30]. Their list order is [10], [20], [30]. Their logical order is an infinite loop: [10], [20], [30], [10], [20], ...

3. If the incoming record has a key (statement number) which differs from any in the current list, then the record (statement) is added to the list. If it has a key which matches the key of a record already in the list, then the record with the matching key is removed, and the new record replaces it in the list. The replacement process is called **updating** a record of the file. If the input is a number followed by ®, then even the key of the record is removed, and the record with that key is said to be **deleted** from the file. Deletion is to be distinguished from updating. For example, if the statement file holds:

    10 INPUT *A*
    20 PRINT *A* + 7
    30 STOP
    40 END

then there are four records in the file. If

    10®

is entered, then there will only be three records, whereas

    10 INPUT *A, B*

will cause an update of the record with key [10] but it will cause no deletions. To summarize:

The operations of creating, adding, and deleting records all come under the heading of **file maintenance**. They affect the structure of the file. The operation of updating does not affect the file structure, it affects only the contents of a record.

---

4. BASIC must either keep the statements in list order or sort them every time it receives the command LIST. It does the former of these two things, and the techniques most commonly applied to this task are discussed in Chapter 7.

   The file handling done by BASIC is not under the control of a user's program. The files which *do* come under program control are *data files* of three control types: **transparent**, **explicit**, and **mixed**. We shall deal with all three to a limited extent.

6.3   AN EXPLICIT FILE EXAMPLE

Some versions of BASIC offer a great deal of support for file handling, but quite often a file must be designed and then explicitly maintained and updated with detailed programming. The operations involved are done in memory, no matter what sort of permanent storage is used for the file, and they naturally require some procedures and techniques designed specifically for files. We will illustrate file-handling for an explicit file through an example: a class file with last names only, and a single test score for each student name. The following things need to be done to it:

1. Input the tentative roll (create the file).

2. Sort the file in the alphabetical order of the student names.

3. Add records (there may be late enrollees).

4. Enter scores (update the records).

5. Correct a record (misspelled names, incorrect scores, etc.).

6. Sort the file by scores while *retaining* the order of the records in it in the alphabetical order of the student names. This requires that the records can be accessed in score-order while still physically stored in name-order.

7. Delete the records of students who drop the course or who do not take the exams.

All of these can be managed if a file is created in which the records contain three entries: a name, a score, and a student number. We shall create such a file and call it CLASS.

The name and the student number in a record of CLASS are character data, whereas the score is a number. (A "student number" is actually used as an identifier, just like a name, and no arithmetic is done with it.) This is typical of file structures, in which each record is often quite complex, and may be made up of more than one data type. The individual items into which a record is divided are called the **fields** of the record. Each record of the file CLASS has three fields, and each field has its own data type. In our case a record may be diagrammed like this:

field 1	field 2	field 3
NAME (character)	NUMBER (character)	SCORE (numeric)

In a more complete record, there might be fields for addresses, class level, etc. Some of the fields might themselves be divided into subfields. For example, an outline of a record in a different file might appear as:

1. NAME
  1.1 LAST
  1.2 FIRST
2. NUMBER
3. SCORES
  3.1 TEST 1
  3.2 TEST 2
    3.2.1 PART 1
    3.2.2 PART 2
  3.3 TEST 3

Files are such a common way of thinking of data that some languages are designed around the ideas involved in managing files. BASIC is not, and so files usually must be created as logical structures which are physically stored within arrays. The structures which result are files because of the way the program logic treats them, rather than because of their naming scheme. In either case, they form a data structure which is logically distinct from a subscripted variable or a READ ... DATA structure.

6.3.1 Creating a File

The classroom example of the previous section may be developed as follows: If it is assumed that the classroom holds a maximum of 40 students, then a file with 40 records is required. The file can then be supported in arrays with dimension 40. Since some of the information is string data and some of it is numeric data, at least two arrays are required. Although a different array could be used for each item, we shall use only two, STU$ and SCORE:

STU$($I$, 1) for the Ith student name
STU$($I$, 2) for the Ith student number
SCORE(I) for the Ith score

With the structure indicated by the items above, the index I points to a record (using both arrays). For example, $I = 17$ indicates the 17th record:

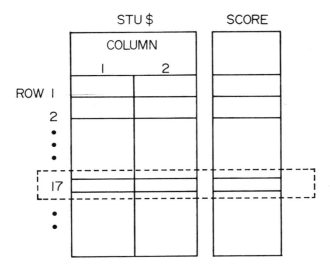

Inside of the dashed line is the 17th record in the file, which we shall refer to as CLASS[17]. In general, the Ith record will be referred to as CLASS[I], which is not an array cell, but indicates the entire collection

$$\{ \text{STU\$}(I, 1), \text{STU\$}(I, 2), \text{SCORE}(I) \}.$$

Field 1 of CLASS I is then STU$($I$, 1), field 2 is STU$(I, 2), and field 3 is SCORE(I).

The storage for the 40 records of the file can be allocated by:

DIM STU$(40, 2), SCORE(40)

Scores and numbers can be entered into the file just by assignment to the arrays STU$ and SCORE.

An instructor using the CLASS file would first create it by using an input routine which accepts the initial class roll of names and numbers. The other file operations can then be applied to add test scores, to add and delete student records, and to correct errors.

At the time when the initial roll is available, test scores normally are not available, and so they are initialized to an arbitrary value of -1. The choice of -1 is made here because if differs from any actual test score, and so after test scores are added, a record which contains a -1 in field 3 must represent a student who failed to take the exam. It is then possible to locate such records and deal with them as desired.

Some way must be provided to enter less than 40 names, and so the entry of "*" as a name can be used to signal the completion of valid input. The number of valid input records is preserved in a variable, N, which can be used to control loops for the other operations. With these considerations, an outline of the logic of the input procedure is:

```
procedure IN
   I ← 1
   N ← 40
   while I ≤ 40 do
      //initialize CLASS[I]//
      if field 1 = "*"
        then N ← I − 1
             exit
        endif
      I ← I + 1
   endwhile
endproc
```

In this particular example, "initialize CLASS[I]" translates into:

```
input STU$(I, 1), STU$(I, 2)
SCORE(I) ← −1
```

This routine could be used for the creation of a file with different fields by changing the initialization details. The "field 1" of the record is, in our example, STU$(I, 1).

6.3.2   Sorting a File

It is convenient to store the records in a file in some particular order, and doing so frequently makes it easier to use the file and makes it possible to speed up retrieval of records from the file. We need to be able to list the records of CLASS in alphabetical order—that is, with the *names* of the class members in alphabetic order. The field for the names STU$(I, 1) is a **key** which is to be used to sort the records. We also will use a second key, the field which contains SCORE(I), and will want to sort the records according to scores. We shall keep the records in memory sorted according to the *name key*, and sort the records according to the *score key* by a different method.

There is a **collating sequence** for the character set which a version of BASIC is designed to use. There may be variations for special characters, but essentially the collating sequence determines that

$$\text{``}A\text{''} < \text{``}B\text{''} < \text{``}C\text{''} < \ldots < \text{``}Z\text{''}$$

when they appear in a condition. With that, the names in the file may be sorted alphabetically. (Beware that "101" < "20", simply because "1" < "2"!) The remaining question is: How does one do a sort at all? The answer is that there are many ways to sort, and the study of sorting algorithms is an area of research in Computer Science. (See PG4.8, PJ4.3, and PJ4.4.) The sort procedure given below is a simple way—with a switching loop. It is *not* often used by experienced programmers because there are several procedures which are more efficient, but it must be understood if the more elegant procedures are to be appreciated.

Sorting by repeated switches of adjacent elements in a file is called a *bubble sort* or a *sinking sort*. To see how it works in practice, consider the sequence of numbers: 10, 26, 17, 54, 13, 9. Examine the first pair, 10 and 26. They are not out of order in relation to each other, so they are not switched. Now examine the second pair, 26 and 17. They *are* out of order, so they are switched. Then the third pair are examined and the process is repeated. Snapshots of the process as it rearranges the numbers look like this:

10⌉	10	10	10	10	10
26⌋	26⌉ switch	17	17	17	17
17	17⌋	26⌉	26	26	26
54	54	54⌋	54⌉ switch	13	13
13	13	13	13⌋	54⌉ switch	9
9	9	9	9	9⌋	54

That is one *pass*. The effect will be to move the largest item to the last position, since it will be switched with every item which followed it before the pass began.

An identical second pass will move the next-to-largest item down to the next-to-last position:

10⌉	10	10	10	10	10
17⌋	17⌉ switch	17	17	17	17
26	26⌋	26⌉	13	13	13
13	13	13⌋	26⌉ switch	9	9
9	9	9	9⌋	26⌉	26
54	54	54	54	54⌋	54

Note that the last pair does not even need to be examined: the largest item is already in last position, and so no switch will occur. The third pass will need to examine one less pair than the second pass, and will leave the largest *three* items in their correct position. In general, the pass only needs to involve N items, the second $N - 1$ items, the third $N - 2$ items, etc. The final pass only involves comparing the first two items (if the second through the Nth items are in place, the first one must be also.) The general procedure is thus:

procedure SINKING SORT
   $J \leftarrow N$ //J is the index of the last item to be compared//
          //during a pass.//
   while $J \geq 2$ **do** //control of the number of passes//
      //make a pass: compare and if necessary, switch the//
      //items in successive pairs, using items 1, 2, ..., J//
      $J \leftarrow J - 1$
   endwhile
endproc

A single pass itself consists of a loop, the crux of which is:

   //if the Ith item is larger than the $(I + 1)$st item,//
   //then switch them//

With the details of a pass tailored to the CLASS file, we have:

procedure SINKING SORT
   $J \leftarrow N$ //J is the index of the last item to be compared//
          //during a pass.//
   while $J \geq 2$ **do** //control of the number of passes//
      $I \leftarrow 1$
      while $I \leq J - 1$ **do** //loop for a single pass//
         if STU\$$(I, 1) >$ STU\$$(I + 1, 1)$
            then switch CLASS[I] and CLASS[$I + 1$]
            endif
         $I \leftarrow I + 1$
      endwhile
      $J \leftarrow J - 1$
   endwhile
endproc

In order to switch all three fields of the records of CLASS, the following procedure is required:

procedure SWITCH
  TEMP$ ← STU$($I$, 1)
  STU$($I$, 1) ← STU$(I + 1, 1)
  STU$($I$ + 1, 1) ← TEMP$
  TEMP$ ← STU$($I$, 2)
  STU$($I$, 2) ← STU$(I + 1, 2)
  STU$($I$ + 1, 2) ← TEMP$
  TEMP ← SCORE(I)
  SCORE(I) ← SCORE(I + 1)
  SCORE(I + 1) ← TEMP
endproc

As an example of how a collection of names in STU$(*, 1) is sorted by procedure SINKING SORT, consider the following set:

  JONES, SMITH, XEBLE, HAAKEN, ALOURS, NEVERS

The effect of the algorithm upon this list is as follows:

$$J = 6$$

	$I = 1$	$I = 2$	$I = 3$	$I = 4$	$I = 5$
JONES	JONES	JONES	JONES	JONES	JONES
SMITH	SMITH	SMITH	SMITH	SMITH	SMITH
XEBLE	XEBLE	XEBLE	HAAKEN	HAAKEN	HAAKEN
HAAKEN	HAAKEN	HAAKEN	XEBLE	NEVERS	NEVERS
NEVERS	NEVERS	NEVERS	NEVERS	XEBLE	ALOURS
ALOURS	ALOURS	ALOURS	ALOURS	ALOURS	XEBLE

Here are the results of the other passes for this set of names, with an asterisk placed in front of a name that is guaranteed to be in place by the execution of the pass:

$J = 5$	$J = 4$	$J = 3$	$J = 2$
JONES	HAAKEN	HAAKEN	*ALOURS
HAAKEN	JONES	ALOURS	*HAAKEN
NEVERS	ALOURS	*JONES	JONES
ALOURS	*NEVERS	NEVERS	NEVERS
*SMITH	SMITH	SMITH	SMITH
XEBLE	XEBLE	XEBLE	XEBLE

6.3.3   Adding Records to a File

Adding a record to a file after the file has been sorted creates a problem. The new record could simply be added as the $(N + 1)$st one, and the file sorted again, but this tends to be inefficient because sorting takes a lot of time, especially for large files. Another way to deal with a new record is to insert it directly into its correct position. Insertion requires making room for the new record by moving the items which should be below it down one place in the file. The first requirement for insertion is searching for the position in which the record belongs. Here is a search procedure which determines the index P of the record to be replaced by the new record, which is input as $A\$, B\$, S$—name, number, score.

1. Check to make sure that there is room for another record in the file. In order to simplify the process of place-finding, we shall leave this task to the overall file managing routine, and assume that the place-finding procedure will only be called when there is room in the file for another record.

2. Clearly CLASS$[N + 1]$ is where the input record should be placed if it has the "largest" key of any record in the file, and so if the search for a place fails, P should have the value $N + 1$ at the end of the search. This can be done by initializing P to $N + 1$ when a record is input.

3. Form a loop which compares the name, $A\$$, in the new record to STU$\$(I, 1)$ for $I = 1, 2, \ldots, N$. The first value STU$\$(I, 1)$ greater

than $A\$$ determines $P = I$, since the new record then belongs between the current CLASS[$I - 1$] and CLASS [I].

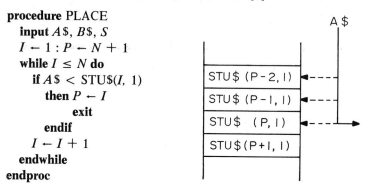

procedure PLACE
  input $A\$$, $B\$$, S
  $I \leftarrow 1 : P \leftarrow N + 1$
  while $I \leq N$ **do**
    if $A\$ < $ STU$\$(I, 1)$
      then $P \leftarrow I$
         exit
    endif
    $I \leftarrow I + 1$
  endwhile
endproc

Once P has been determined, records may be copied into their new positions by:

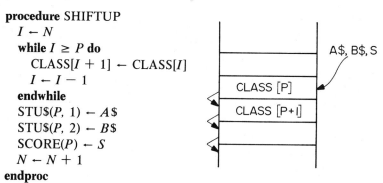

procedure SHIFTUP
  $I \leftarrow N$
  while $I \geq P$ **do**
    CLASS[$I + 1$] $\leftarrow$ CLASS[I]
    $I \leftarrow I - 1$
  endwhile
  STU$\$(P, 1) \leftarrow A\$$
  STU$\$(P, 2) \leftarrow B\$$
  SCORE(P) $\leftarrow S$
  $N \leftarrow N + 1$
endproc

In our particular example, CLASS[$I + 1$] $\leftarrow$ CLASS[I] becomes:

    STU$\$(I + 1, 1) \leftarrow$ STU$\$(I, 1)$
    STU$\$(I + 1, 2) \leftarrow$ STU$\$(I, 2)$
    SCORE($I + 1$) $\leftarrow$ SCORE(I)

6.3.4   Entering Scores Into CLASS

In order to enter scores into the file, they must be matched with the person to whom they belong. Fingers and keyboards being what they are, typing a name like BIRKHEIMEISTER is frought with danger. It may not match the original version! In that case, searching through the file for a match for the input would be fruitless. One way around this is to list the names (and numbers) in the file along with their index, and input scores in the form P, SCORE(P). Since the scores have been initialized to -1 in procedure IN, those which still contain -1 after all scores have been entered indicate records to be deleted from the file. The listing and the input procedures we leave to the reader, but the deletions will be discussed.

There are basically two different ways to handle deletions:

1. Mark the records which are not to be used, but leave them in place.

2. Shift undeleted records into storage vacated by deleted records.

Technique 1 is an easy way to delete records, and scores of -1 serve as a suitable mark (deletions could also be handled simply by inserting "*" into the name slot, etc.). Since procedures PLACE and SHIFTUP are to be used *after* deletions may have occurred, they need to deal with cells in the array which contain records no longer in the file. They have been written so that they simply shift all records, deleted or not. This technique also wastes some storage space. The extra space is already allocated by the DIM statement, but suppose that 39 people sign up for the class, four drop (or do not take the exam) and three more wish to sign up late. There is still room in the class, but not in the memory cells in which the file must reside. In a sense, the file is not full either, since it does not contain 40 *active* records. To distinguish between the Ith element of CLASS and the Ith element of the two arrays in which it is stored is more easily done with data structures developed in Chapter 7. In this instance, then, we opt for technique 2, although technique 1 has its uses in other situations. This technique is called **garbage collection**, since it brings together unused storage. The required procedure is similar to SHIFTUP except that as it works through the file, it must keep track of the number of deletions, stored in the variable DI. Here is what must be done:

1. The procedure must keep track of the number of *active* records, I, which is encountered as it moves through the file, and also the number of *inactive* records, DI. At a given point in the file, DI is the number of places that the next active record is to be shifted in the underlying array structure. Hence $I \leftarrow 0$, $DI \leftarrow 0$ is the initialization.

2. Loop through CLASS: when an active record is encountered, increment I, and when an inactive record is encountered, increment DI.

The index of the record being examined is $I + DI$, hence an active record is moved by: CLASS[I] ← CLASS[$I + DI$]. The termination of the loop occurs when $I + DI = N$.

Here is the scheme in pseudocode:

```
procedure COMPACT
  I ← 0 : DI ← 0
  while I + DI < N do
    if SCORE(I + DI + 1) ≥ 0
      then I ← I + 1
           CLASS[I] ← CLASS[I + DI]
      else DI ← DI + 1
    endif
  endwhile
  N ← I
endproc
```

DI = 0
DI = 1
DI = 3
DI = 3

6.3.5   Sorting Indirectly

If the records were now physically resorted according to the scores, they would no longer be sorted alphabetically. The awkwardness inherent in this situation is one of the several reasons for the list structures discussed in the next chapter. However, the records of CLASS can be sorted *logically* by order of score without physically moving them. Such a sort is said to be *indirect*. We shall create an **index map**, an array of indices which are sorted by the scores they point to, rather than by their own values. The index in the first position of the array is the index of the record with the highest score. The second position points to the next highest score, etc. Except for its indirectness and the need to float high scores to the top, rather than sink them to the bottom, the procedure which creates the index map is much like procedure SINKING SORT. Before tailoring these ideas to the CLASS file, we will develop them for the simpler case of an array X, containing N numbers, and observe how they perform on X:

Let X have the values of the numbers in 6.3.2:

$X(1) = 10$
$X(2) = 26$
$X(3) = 17$
$X(4) = 54$
$X(5) = 13$
$X(6) = 9$

Suppose that for $I = 1, 2, 3, \ldots, N$, MAP$(I) = I$. Then the output of the following print loop:

$I \leftarrow 1$
while $I \leq 6$ do
  print $X(\text{MAP}(I))$;
  $I \leftarrow I + 1$
endwhile

is simply the values of X in their original order:

    10 26 17 54 13 9

Now suppose that a sorting pass compares values of X, but switches values of MAP:

$I \leftarrow 1$
while $I \leq J - 1$ do
  if $X(\text{MAP}(I)) > X(\text{MAP}(I + 1))$
    then switch MAP(I) with MAP$(I + 1)$
    endif
  $I \leftarrow I + 1$
endwhile

The comparisons and switches for a pass will proceed much like the example of 6.3.2:

The result of executing the print loop will now be:

10   17   26   13   9   54

which is the *same* result that would have occurred if the values of *X itself* had been switched and the print loop had used simply **print** $X(I)$. We have exchanged *information* about where the values are located instead of the values themselves. The result of succeeding passes will be:

pass 2			pass 3			pass 4		
I	X(I)	MAP(I)	I	X(I)	MAP(I)	I	X(I)	MAP(I)
1	10 ← 1		1	10 ← 1		1	10 ← 1	
2	26	3	2	26	5	2	26	6
3	17	5	3	17	6	3	17	5
4	54	6	4	54	3	4	54	3
5	13	2	5	13	2	5	13	2
6	9	4	6	9	4	6	9	4

pass 5		
1	10	6
2	26	1
3	17	5
4	54	3
5	13	2
6	9	4

Execution of the print loop after pass 5 will produce:

9   10   13   17   26   54

With this general scheme tailored to CLASS, the detailed pseudocode is:

```
procedure SCORDEX
    I ← 1
    while I ≤ N do //initialize MAP//
        MAP(I) ← I
        I ← I + 1
    endwhile
    J ← N //J is the index of the last item to be compared//
    while J ≥ 2 do //control of the number of passes//
        I ← 1
        while I ≤ J − 1 do //loop J − 1 times for a single pass//
            if SCORE(MAP(I)) < SCORE(MAP(I + 1))
                then
                    TEMP ← MAP(I)
                    MAP(I) ← MAP(I + 1)
                    MAP(I + 1) ← TEMP
                endif
            I ← I + 1
        endwhile
        J ← J − 1
    endwhile
endproc
```

The records may then be printed in the order of their MAP.

6.3.6 The Management of the CLASS File

The procedures devised in the previous sections could be written as either separate programs or with the GOSUB ... RETURN structure in one large program. A main program might be written to print instructions and indicate the options available, prompt input, and branch to the subroutines required by the user for a specified task (update, delete, print scores, etc.). A programmer who attempted to simply write this package as one procedure would be asking for mass confusion. Debugging of such a procedure would be troublesome. The fact is, that it is *much* better in the long run to break the problem into tasks as we have done, and *much* more likely to work properly. It is effective, and it is one of the standard professional approaches to develop the general plan of attack on a problem—normally by dividing it into subproblems—before any details of the solution are developed. However, this is not honestly reasonable until it is known what sort of procedures *can* be done and *should* be developed to solve subproblems. When a problem is of a type which is unfamiliar to the programmer or is being approached with an unfamiliar general plan, it may be helpful to explore the details of subproblems before meshing them together in an overall solution. That is the approach to file-handling which has been taken in this chapter. Once the problem is well understood, however, the solution should be one which *can* be presented in a stepwise fashion for the sake of clarity. Some stepwise refinement is essential for readability in the display of the logic of a substantial program.

Now that some of the common file-handling procedures have been explored, the management of a file should be approached by first blocking out the subtasks to be done.

With the procedures which have been developed in the preceding sections available, a general plan for managing the CLASS file is to give the user the *option* of which of these procedures to apply to CLASS. Instructions are needed to help the user make a choice between options, and output is needed to feed information about the effect of the user's actions on CLASS back to the user. A list of options to be available to the user might be:

1. Input a new roll. Procedure IN will do this. If the records are sorted immediately after IN is finished, then PLACE and SHIFTUP will keep CLASS in alphabetic order, hence procedure SORT may be called automatically by this option. This option initializes the number of records, N, and the scores.

2. Make additions to the roll. This may involve trying to overfill the file, or getting rid of deletions in order to make room in the file. One approach is to call COMPACT if $N \geq 40$. If $N \geq 40$ *after* COMPACT executes, then the file is full and a message to the user must be generated, after which the user should be given the choice of what to do next. The user must be given a way to stop making additions, with the entry of "*" for a name. If all of these tests have been made, there is an addition request, and if there is room for it in CLASS, then procedures PLACE and SHIFTUP will effect the entry, while preserving alphabetic order in the file.

3. The user may want to see the records in the file, and for that a procedure (and option) must be provided which displays an alphabetic listing of the current file. By including the *index* of each record in this display, we make it possible to add scores and update records by specifying the index of a particular record to be changed.

4. Add scores to the records. This option can also be used for the deletion of a record by simply the input of -1 for its score. After the scores are added, the records may be sorted indirectly by building an index map.

5. An option should be provided to display the records arranged by their SCORE value.

6. An option is needed to update any record in the file, to change entries invalid for any reason.

When displayed as pseudocode this scheme is:

procedure MAIN
  print (instructions and options available)
  repeat
    case of options
      : new roll : **proc** IN   //input names as STU$($I$, 1) and//
                                     //numbers as STU$($I$, 2), and//
                                     //initialize scores to -1//
                    proc SORT //sort records by name//
      : additions : **repeat**
                if $N \geq 40$ **then procedure** COMPACT **endif**
                if $N < 40$ **then input** $A\$, B\$, S$
                          else (print file full message)
                                exit
                              endif
                if $A\$ = $ "*" **then exit endif**
                proc PLACE   //determine the order of an//
                                  //input record as index P//
                proc SHIFTUP //shift following records//
                                  //one index and insert the//
                                //input record at index P//
           forever
      : alpha-list : **proc** LIST //listing of the records by//
                            //alphabetic order//

```
          : scores in :  input P, SCORE(P) //for all desired values of P//
                                            //that are valid.//
                         //Note that SCORE(P) ← − 1 is a deletion//
                         proc SCORDEX //build an index map in//
                                      //array MAP of scores in//
                                      //largest-first order.//
          : score-list : proc OUT //list records by scores, using MAP//
          : update :  repeat
                         input P
                         if P < 0 then exit endif
                         if P > N then print (warning message)
                                  else input STU$(P, 1), STU$(P, 2), and
                                                  SCORE(P)
                                  endif
                      forever
        endcase
        if (the user is through) then exit
      forever
endproc
```

NOTE

Some of the specific features which are discussed in the sections which follow are not available on all systems. In particular, the virtual array capability discussed in the next section is modeled on that feature as it is implemented in the PDP11/70 computer. Some statement syntax in this chapter is more closely modeled on the Commodore PET system. The general file-handling features which are developed in the following sections are common enough to many systems and can be transferred readily—all that is required is a manual (and understanding). Implementations of file-handling differ quite a bit in their details, however. The understanding of file management is of fundamental importance for most commercial applications.

6.4   VIRTUAL STORAGE

In many computing systems, BASIC is only one of the programming languages available for the machine, and the user can specify which one of them is to be used through commands. In such a system, the BASIC translator is a subsystem within a larger **operating system**. An operating system does many more things than can be discussed here, but one thing that is of particular interest is the management of **virtual memory**. The idea of virtual memory is that the memory available for a program is not just the main memory, but also includes the peripheral storage, usually magnetic disks. This extra memory is deliberately **transparent**—the management of it is not visible to the user. In a system which has peripheral storage, a program can include a request for virtual memory, and then be written as it would be if the main memory were simply larger than it actually is. The input and output from and to disk storage is handled by the operating system as it is needed.

The reasonable use of the procedures which have been devised for CLASS calls for non-volatile storage. Consequently the three arrays STU$, SCORE, and MAP would reasonably reside as virtual arrays on disk storage. If that were not available, they would reside on magnetic tape and be swapped into and out of main memory as needed.

The power of virtual memory lies in its size as well as its permanence. A byte of information is enough to store one character. A typewritten page (double-spaced) would require perhaps 1250 bytes of storage in a computer memory (25 lines of 50 characters each). Normally, a kilobyte is considered to be 1024 bytes, or 1K, and the square of that number is a megabyte, or 1M. A typical personal computer has a main memory of anywhere from 4K to 32K equivalent to about 4 to 40 typewritten pages. A storage area iK holds about fifty lines of a BASIC program that contains no arrays.

The BASIC translator itself takes up room in main memory. A typical disk storage unit for such a system might have 500K of disk storage available at a time. A typical time-sharing minicomputer in a school might have a 256K main storage, and a 200M disk storage. The price paid for the use of this extra storage is the time spent to copy records in and out of the disk system during the management of virtual storage (or during other use of the disk system). Many compromises are called for in a system with disk storage, and that is a topic which lies outside the scope of this book.

6.5 OPEN AND CLOSE

Files which are on disks or tapes are permanent until erased, but they *can* be erased or written over. Hence, file management involves protecting the area in which the file is stored from accidental use. Statements which affect files must specify the peripheral device involved, since many systems have tapes, disk packs, terminals, printers, etc., all available. File handling statements also need to specify a file name, since more than one file can be stored on a device. Finally, files can be protected more carefully if the option is given to the programmer to decide if the file is to be written on or merely read from, or both. The standard way to place some file protection under program control is to insist that files be **opened** before they are used, and **closed** when they are no longer needed by a program.

Since the statements for opening and closing files vary greatly from one system to another, the ones given here are intended to be merely typical examples. A typical OPEN statement looks like this:

10 OPEN "STASH" FOR OUTPUT AS FILE 1

This statement allows the program in which it appears to store information onto device number 1 in a file named "STASH". In order to check the information in non-volatile memory for accuracy or to list it, for example, it is necessary to read information from the file into main memory. Hence, the file must be opened for *input* also:

20 OPEN "STASH" FOR INPUT AS FILE 1

The two statements above can be replaced by a single statement:

15 OPEN "STASH" AS FILE 1

When a program has finished using a file, it should close the file:

1040 CLOSE 1

> Various unhappy things occur, depending upon the circumstances and the system, if a file is left unclosed.

6.6 VIRTUAL ARRAYS

One of the common things that is done with virtual storage is to use it for storage of arrays:

> There are three kinds of arrays for which virtual storage is particularly useful:
>
> 1. those arrays which are too large to keep in main memory,
>
> 2. those arrays which store information to be used by more than one program, and
>
> 3. those arrays which will be needed by more than one run of a program.

Item 1 expands the range of program size available with a given memory. Item 2 is related to the process of breaking up large problems into smaller ones, and provides a communication link between the pieces; a link through shared data. Item 3 is relevant to files which must be maintained or updated.

Virtual arrays are distinguished from those in main memory by their location, hence there must be a way to inform the BASIC translator which is which. This is done with dimension statements, which typically look like this:

    30 DIM #1, $A(1000)$, $C(1)$
    40 DIM $B(5, 7)$

Here [30] places the arrays A and C in virtual storage, while [40] places B in main memory. The "#" must match with the device number of an OPEN and a CLOSE statement.

With the special statements discussed in this section, storage into a virtual array is simply done by having a cell of it appear on the left of an assignment. Except for the statements mentioned above, there is no difference in the way virtual arrays and main memory arrays are used in a program. For example:

    184 LET $A(73) = B(4, 2) + 107.3$

gives no indication whether $A(73)$ or $B(4, 2)$ are in main memory or are in virtual storage. Retrieval from a virtual array is done by its appearance in an expression. The array A in the following statement will be in virtual storage or will not be, depending only upon the dimension statement in which it is declared:

    200 LET $Z = A(10)*A(25)$

6.6.1 Example STASH

What follows is a pair of programs; one of them creates a file as a virtual array, the other lists what is in the file and adds records to it. They are deliberately left to be studied by *reading* them. Reading algorithms is one of the essential skills of a programmer. In fact, reading algorithms for what they say, rather than what they *should* say, is part of the art of debugging—at the stage of program development in which the debugging of algorithms belongs. (This pair, however, will not require debugging, merely understanding.)

procedure STASH
  open "STASH" **for output on** 1
  $A(0) \leftarrow 1000$
  $I \leftarrow 1$
  while $I \leq 1000$ **do**
    input $A(I)$ //input into program, and output onto file//
    if $A(I) < 0$ **then**
            $A(0) \leftarrow I - 1$
            exit
            endif
    $I \leftarrow I + 1$
  endwhile
  close 1
endproc

procedure APPEND
  open "STASH" **on** 1
  $I \leftarrow 0$
  while $I < A(0)$ **do**
    $I \leftarrow I + 1$
    print $A(I)$ //input from file and output from program//
  endwhile
  while $I < 1000$ **do**
    $I \leftarrow I + 1$
    input $A(I)$ //input into program and output onto file//
    if $A(I) < 0$ **then exit**
  endwhile
  $A(0) \leftarrow I - 1$
  close 1
endproc

6.7   SEQUENTIAL FILES

Virtual arrays are stored on magnetic disks, which are **random access** devices, that is, one may address any part of them directly, ignoring all of the rest. Whenever $A(17)$ is stored in a virtual array A, assignment can be made to it without need to involve $A(1)$, $A(2)$, ..., $A(16)$. The operating system may do quite a bit of calculating to find the address of $A(17)$, and will need to position a read-head in the correct track (which is somewhat like a groove on a phonograph record), and may have to wait for the right sector of the track to spin under the head, but it deals with $A(17)$ directly, not with an entire file.

At one time, the mass-storage devices in common use were magnetic tapes, and they are still widely used, even though there are other options available for mass-storage. They have the property that to use them, one must follow Lewis Carroll's advice about telling a story:

> Begin at the Beginning, and stop when you come to the End.

The data stored on tape is a file which is arranged as a sequence of records, a **sequential file**. Lines of output of a program may also be thought of as a sequence of records, with one line per record. The essential difference, of course, is that one may input from a file on tape, but not from a printer—or display screen.

Sequential files are of *mixed* control type, since they can be maintained, and the records in them updated, only in ways that are rather limited and sometimes awkward. They also have advantages: because the records of a sequential file are stored one after the other, when the file is to be read (or written) as a whole, it can be done as rapidly as the tape flows by (or the disk spins around). Sequential files are a very natural form in which to store one-dimensional arrays and sequences of data points which are available for storage one at a time, in order, and are to be accessed the same way.

The statements which deal with sequential files require a device number, and they vary in the details of their syntax from one version of BASIC to another, but are otherwise similar to statements previously discussed. Here is a pseudocode segment which inputs a sequence of data points and outputs them into a sequential file:

open "SEQ" **for output on** 5
rewind 5
repeat
  input $X, A\$$
  if $A\$ =$ "*" **then exit**
  print on 5, X
forever
close 5

It must be noted that the **rewind** command does not exist in all versions of

BASIC. Some small systems require rewinding with hand controls, such as the buttons on a tape deck.

The input statement in the above procedure may be responded to by:

−187.35, ®
93.7, ®
    .
    .
    .

until all of the data is in, and then 0,* will cause exit from the loop. It is not necessary for the program to count the records written on a tape unless there is concern about running out of tape.

We shall assume that the **close** statement writes a special record on the tape, called the **end of file**, or EOF. It is the EOF which is used to decide when to stop reading as the data on the file is being retrieved. The way in which data is retrieved depends upon the system. What we shall do is assume a system which has the commands which make it convenient to use. Here they are:

1. There should be a way to recognize the EOF when reading. We shall invent the pseudocode:

    input #⟨D⟩ (**exit on** EOF), ⟨list⟩

    which is meant to imply that when the EOF is detected, the result is an exit from the loop which contains the **input** statement.

2. There should be a way to backspace one record. This means to rewind the tape a small amount, enough to get back past the record just read, and reposition ready to read it again. This is asking quite a bit from a tape drive, but it may be available. In pseudocode: **backspace** ⟨n⟩.

With these statements, the file written above may be updated and appended, but deleting a record can only be done by updating it to a recognizably nonsense value (such as "*" for a name), or writing out the rest of the data onto a second file, omitting the record(s) to be deleted. Here is our procedure, which rewrites every record X that has a value greater than 100 so that it has the value 100:

```
procedure ADDON
  open "SEQ" on 5
  rewind 5
  repeat
    input #5 (exit on EOF), X
    if X > 100
      then
        backspace 5
        print on 5, 100
      endif
  forever
  backspace 5
  repeat
    input X, A$
    if A$ = "*" then exit
    print on 5, X
  forever
  close 5
endproc
```

SELF-REVIEW

1.   Suppose that a programmer inputs:

        NEW
        20 PRINT A, B
        10 INPUT A
        30 GO TO 10
        10 INPUT A, B
        25 STOP
        40 END
        25®

     What is:

     a.   The entry sequence,
     b.   the list sequence, and
     c.   the logical order

     of the statements above?

2. Classify the statements in item 1 as:

    a. creating,
    b. updating,
    c. adding to, or
    d. deleting from

    a file. Skip the statements which do none of the above.

3. What is the difference between a record and an array?

4. In procedure SINKING SORT, why is the condition of the outer loop $J \geq 2$ instead of $J \geq 1$? Why is the condition of the inner loop $I \leq J - 1$ instead of $I < N$?

5. In procedure PLACE, is it necessary to initialize P before the loop? Why $P \leftarrow N + 1$ instead of $P \leftarrow 1$ or $P \leftarrow N$?

6. In procedure COMPACT, what will happen to other procedures called by MAIN if all of the records have been marked for deletion, and $N \leftarrow 0$ just before exit? Is it possible to initialize COMPACT with $I \leftarrow 1$ and use the branch

    if SCORE($I + DI$) ≥ 0

    within the loop?

7. In procedure SCORDEX, what would happen if the initialization of MAP were done using MAP(I) $\leftarrow N - I + 1$ or using MAP(I) $\leftarrow 1$?

8. If procedure SCORDEX were applied to the following four scores, what would be in MAP after each pass?

I	SCORE(I)
1	67
2	92
3	76
4	81

9. What is the role of $A(0)$ in procedure STASH? in APPEND?

10. What statements in STASH and in APPEND actually move data to and from the disk storage?

11. What would happen if $I \leftarrow I + 1$ and **input** $A(I)$ were switched in APPEND?

PROBLEMS

P6.1 Locate the two logical errors in the following program:

```
10 OPEN "GOLD" FOR INPUT AS FILE 3
20 DIM #5, A(100)
30 FOR I = 1 TO 10
40   A(I) = A(I + 10) + A(I)
50 NEXT I
60 CLOSE 5
70 STOP
80 END
```

P6.2 Rewrite both IN and SINKING SORT in pseudocode, assuming that both first and last names are to be used, but assuming that both are stored in a record in separate fields.

P6.3 Write a procedure in pseudocode which searches the student file of MAIN for all scores less than or equal to 50 and prints the corresponding record (all of it).

P6.4 Rewrite PLACE and SHIFTUP, assuming that no records are moved with deletion, but that the name STU$(I, 1) is changed to "*".

P6.5 Write a procedure in pseudocode to list the student records of this chapter, in alphabetical order, and another to input the scores.

P6.6 Create the pseudocode which will count and print the number of students in CLASS in each of the following categories:

A	88–100
B	76–87
C	63–75
D	50–62
F	below 50

P6.7 Create the pseudocode to look up a student in CLASS by the use of his/her student number only.

P6.8 Create all the routines required to use the student number as a key in dealing with CLASS, as well as the scores and names. An index map must be built by one routine, and a routine must be written to list records by student number.

PROGRAMS

PG6.1   Do the update problem of Chapter 4, PG4.3.

PG6.2   Write a program which will input an 8 by 5 table of values and sort each row so that entries increase with column numbers, and then sort the rows so that they are in decreasing order in the *second* column. Example:

INPUT						OUTPUT				
17	13	12	0	18		4	47	48	56	65
80	81	90	12	40		12	40	80	81	90
65	47	48	56	4		0	12	13	17	18
11	13	12	10	17		10	11	12	13	17
.						.				
.						.				
.						.				

PG6.3   Write a subprogram which will list the rows of the table in PG6.2 in the order of the items in *column* 5, without physically resorting the table.

PG6.4   Create a subprogram which will input row deletion information for the table in PG6.2, and mark the rows accordingly, then list the active rows.

PG6.5   Write a program which will search the table of PG6.2 for *all* entries greater than an input value. Assume that this little table is a model for a large system, and use the ordering of the second column efficiently. Search down to the rows of interest, and then search both (if necessary) directions for values of interest.

PG6.7   Write a sorting procedure which starts with a single pair of records, puts them in order, and inserts the other records, one at a time, in their proper place. (See PJ4.3.)

PG6.8   Files must frequently be searched for the value of a key, whether to prepare for deletion, or to retrieve the entire record which accompanies a key. A straightforward method is simply to run through the keys in sequential order until the desired one is located. Write a program which inputs 20 numbers, sorts them, inputs a value, and prints its *position* in the column. If the input number is not one of the 20, then print an error message.

PG6.9 The linear search of PG6.8 is not optimal in many situations. One common approach for finding X in a sorted key array can be described by:

1. For N items, initialize the left end of a search interval by $I \leftarrow 1$ and the right end by $J \leftarrow N$.

2. Repeatedly determine $K \leftarrow INT((I + J)/2)$ and if $X > A(K)$, then $I \leftarrow (K + 1)$, otherwise $J \leftarrow (K - 1)$. When $A(K) = X$ or $I > J$, the search is over.

This is called a **bisection search** or **binary search**. Before you program this, try your pseudocode with five or six numbers on paper. For example, look for 17, for 1, for 20, and for 18 among: 2, 3, 9, 16, 17, 17, 19.

PG6.10 The exchange sort, such as that of procedure SINKING SORT, may be improved by noting that everything below the last exchange actually made on a pass is already in order. It is not necessary to look beyond the index of that exchange on the next pass. Program this improvement and try it on 20 input items.

PG6.11 Files often need to be **merged**. For example, a class file from a university extension course may come in late, and need to be added to a current-session file which is already sorted. If the class file is already sorted, one merges them by:

1. Compare the "smallest" items, $F1(1)$ of File 1 and $F2(1)$ of File 2. Suppose that $F1(1) < F2(1)$.

2. Move the items of File 1 into the merge file M, up to, but not including, the first File 1 item, say $F1(N)$, which is larger than $F2(1)$.

3. Move the items of File 2 into M, beginning with $F2(1)$, up to, but not including, the first File 2 item which is larger than $F1(N)$.

4. Repeat this process, switching back and forth between the files.

After exploring this idea with two sets of 10 or so numbers on paper, write a program which picks up one column of 15 numbers from DATA statements, and one from input data, merges them, and prints the resulting merge file.

PG6.12   If your system will support virtual arrays, then translate STASH
and APPEND into BASIC, using the syntax of your version, and
run them.

PROJECTS

The comments at the beginning of the projects in Chapter 3 also apply to
the following:

PJ6.1   Translate into BASIC the procedures which were developed in this
chapter to manage the file CLASS and run them.

PJ6.2   The algorithm of PG6.10 may be further improved by noting that
during a pass, "light" items move no more than one position,
whereas "heavy" items may be carried down several positions.
Reversing directions after each pass will even the moves out a bit.
Every other pass proceeds from bottom-to-top, and exchanges so
that the light items are moved up. Write and run a program which
incorporates this improvement.

PJ6.3   In the straight insertion sort of PJ4.3, it is necessary to search
through the previously sorted items in order to find out where the
next one goes. The algorithm indicated in PJ4.3 included a linear
search to find the position. Combine the binary search technique of
PG6.9 with insertion to create a binary insertion sort and try it on
a column of 20 numbers.

PJ6.4   Write a program which catalogs an LP record library. A record (of
the file) may contain such items as the album label, title, date of
publication, lead instrumentalists, orchestra, conductor, singer(s),
and possibly information about songs on individual bands of the
(phonograph) record. Provision must be made for maintaining the
file and updating records, and for searching the file for items of
interest. A complete system would require several keys, and would
be a major project. Start small and modularize.

PJ6.5   Write a program which manages a file of stockmarket transactions,
allowing maintenance of the file and updating of records. The
records should include date of purchase, number of shares, date(s)
of sale of blocks of stock, additional blocks of a current stock pur-
chased (with the date), purchase prices, sale prices, transaction
costs. Records for which all shares have been sold should be marked,
but not deleted until after tax liability is invalid.

PJ6.6 Write a program to manage a collection of files of household records for Income Tax reporting. Possible files include charitable contributions, medical expenses, interest payments, work-related travel, books and supplies, miscellaneous expenses, and energy-saving home modifications.

PJ6.7 Write a program to manage a household budget. The entry of an expense which causes an account to exceed its budgeted limit in a given month should generate a warning message. Deficits should be carried over into the next month. A variety of categories are possible, and probably include rent or mortgage payments, utilities, food, clothing, vacation expenses, car payments, savings, medical expenses, insurance costs, and perhaps a small amount for gracious living.

PJ6.8 Write a main program which generates data and then runs two or more sorting procedures for the same data, comparing their performance. The procedure SINKING SORT could be compared with those described in PJ4.3, PJ4.4, PG6.9, PG6.10, PJ6.2, PJ6.3, and to the following two sorting procedures:

```
procedure DELAYED-REPLACEMENT SORT
  K ← 1
  while K < N do
    I ← K
    J ← K + 1
    repeat
      if D(J) > D(I) then I ← J
      J ← J + 1
    until J > N
    if I > K then
            T ← D(I)
            D(I) ← D(K)
            D(K) ← T
        endif
    K ← K + 1
  endwhile
endproc
```

```
procedure SHELL-METZNER SORT
  M ← INT(N/2)
  while M ≥ 1 do
    K ← N − M
    J ← 1
    while J ≤ K do
      I ← J
      repeat
        L ← I + M
        if D(I) > D(L) then
                              T ← D(I)
                              D(I) ← D(L)
                              D(L) ← T
                              I ← I − M
      until I < 1          endif
      J ← J + 1
    endwhile
    M ← INT(M/2)
  endwhile
endproc
```

Chapter 7

STRINGS AND LINKED LISTS

7.1 TEXT EDITING

When a letter, a report, a legal document, or similar prose is being prepared at a keyboard from a rough draft, there are three distinct aspects of the process involved. One aspect is thinking of what is to be typed or corrected, a second aspect is actually pushing the correct keys, and the third aspect is making it possible for the input characters to be placed correctly. The third aspect, if done on a standard typewriter, may require erasing by some means, moving paper and carriage into the correct position, or perhaps even retyping most of a page of material which itself does not need correction. This final aspect is the most troublesome, and the slowest. It can be  eliminated almost entirely if the keyboard is part of an interactive computing system, and the shifting of characters, words, and paragraphs into their desired position is done by a program. A program which provides for text to be rearranged one line (one record) at a time within a text file, and which allows individual lines to be altered (updated) character by character, is called a **text editor**. Many small computing systems are currently marketed for the specific purpose of text editing, and editing is one of the common uses of multi-purpose interactive systems. In order to do text editing, it is necessary to manipulate strings of characters—take them apart and put them back together with insertions and deletions. This is called **string processing**, and it is one basis for more general manipulations involved in text editing. Text editing itself can be extended to include the management of text treated as *natural language*, in terms of sentences, paragraphs, addresses, and so on. This is called **word processing**, which is playing an increasing role in Law, Government, Newspaper Edit-

183

ing, etc. Although word processing as a whole is a complex task, it involves many subtasks, some of which are not complicated. For example, one operation that is involved in word processing is the searching of a file for a key word.

7.2 KEYWORD SEARCHING

Searching a text for **keywords** is a common but tedious job. For example, newspaper files or law cases may be searched for information relating to particular subjects. Usually the subject of the search is associated with particular words which are likely to show up in any discussion of it, and which usually indicate that it is being dealt with. If a file of this type is stored in a computing system, then the file probably resides on tape or disk storage as a sequence of records. For the sake of a simple example, assume that a file is to be typed from a keyboard, one string (or input line) at a time, and searched for any one of a collection of keywords, stored in array KEY$. For simplicity, again, assume that input strings do not split words. By that we mean that a word will not begin at the end of one input string, and be completed at the beginning of the next input string. If words can be split between input strings, then the keyword search algorithm must be designed to deal with this special case. The simpler case in which there are no split words will be solved in this section.

The general procedure, then, will be to repeatedly input strings, one at a time, until a nonsense string, say "*", is encountered. As each string A is entered, it is searched for N keys stored in array KEY$, one at a time. At this point we have:

procedure KEY
  repeat
    input A
    if A = "*" **then exit**
    //search A for KEY$(1), KEY$(2), ..., KEY$(N)//
  forever
end KEY

The keys in KEY$ can be accessed one at a time with a straightforward **while** ... **do** loop, and copied into B. The heart of the algorithm is a procedure, which we shall call MATCH, which searches in A for a copy of B. For example, "UNTHINKINGLY" contains a copy of "THIN" beginning at the 3rd character position, and a copy of "KING" beginning at the 7th. A fairly generalized matching procedure would return the *position* of the copy of B found in A as the value of a variable, say S. Then if S is returned as 0 by procedure MATCH, it will serve as a flag to indicate that *no* copy of *B$* was located in *A$*. The details of MATCH must be postponed until some string-handling capabilities are discussed, but the use of it in procedure KEY is straightforward:

```
procedure KEY
  repeat
    input A$
    if A$ = "*" then exit
    I ← 1
    while I ≤ N do
      B$ ← KEY$(I)
      procedure MATCH(A$, B$, S)
      if S ≠ 0 then
                  print ("found" message and KEY$(I))
                  exit
                endif
      I ← I + 1
    endwhile
  forever
end KEY
```

7.3 STRINGS

When string variables were introduced in Chapter 3 it became possible to deal with data which is in the form of a string of characters. The maximum length of these strings varies from one BASIC to another, but in any version, when they are stored in a variable such as *A$*, they form a unit. Access to an entire string is quite sufficient for many applications, but for some it is not. As a familiar example, consider people's names. They appear quite often in two forms: "Quigley, Stanley J." and "Stanley J. Quigley". As the reader may have discovered, if one attempts to input the first form with INPUT *A$*, then *A$* ← "Quigley". It is possible to input the entire name with INPUT LAST$, FIRST$ which then has the effect LAST$ ← "Quigley" and FIRST$ ← "Stanley J.". The pieces can be put back together with FULL$ ← FIRST$ + LAST$, which then catenates them as "Stanley J.Quigley". The missing space is rather annoying. It can be inserted with:

FULL$ ← FIRST$ + " " + LAST$

This sort of manipulation is all that is available with some versions of BASIC. Other versions allow programs to take strings apart and put them back together in new forms.

7.4 SUBSTRINGS

In many interactive programs, it is common for a program to prompt the user to make a decision with something like this:

```
1190 PRINT "ANSWER 1 FOR YES AND 2 FOR NO:"
1200 INPUT "DO YOU WISH TO PLAY AGAIN"; ANS
1210 IF ANS = 1 THEN 40
```

This can be improved with:

```
1200 INPUT "DO YOU WISH TO PLAY AGAIN"; ANS$
1210 IF ANS$ = "YES" THEN 40
```

There are many mishaps which can occur here. The user may intend to answer YES® but actually enter YE®, YESS®, YE S®, etc. An additional improvement can be made by checking for the "Y", which is only part of the string in ANS$. The separation of parts of strings from the entire string is one of the operations needed in word processing of all kinds.

In order to deal with portions of a string, the string is treated as a sequence of characters. In "YES", "Y" is the first letter, "E" is the second, and "S" the last one. Often, the number of characters in the string is not known, and that is not always crucial, as we shall see. What is of particular interest is **substrings**—strings which are part of other strings. For example, "DAY" is a substring of both "DAYLONG" and "YESTERDAY". We would like to be able to determine that "DAY" is a substring of the given strings, locate it within the two strings, extract it from one of them, or substitute a different substring for it, etc. All of these operations are possible if string operations are built into the language.

7.5 STRING OPERATIONS

We shall work from a minimal set of string operations, and derive others from them:

A minimal set of string operations is:

1. Determine the length of a string.

2. Determine the first N characters of a string.

3. Determine the characters of a string, beginning at the Nth one.

The procedures which do these things are **functions**—that is, given a particular argument (a string), they return a single, unique value (a substring or a number). (Other functions are discussed in Chapter 5.) The syntax for such procedures varies, and so we will define our own, which look much like the common versions:

LEN(⟨string⟩) returns the length of ⟨string⟩.

LEFT$(⟨string⟩, N) returns the leftmost N characters of ⟨string⟩.

RIGHT$(⟨string⟩, N) returns the rightmost characters of ⟨string⟩, beginning at the Nth character.

With the function LEFT$, the example of the previous section can be improved:

```
1200 INPUT "DO YOU WISH TO PLAY AGAIN"; ANS$
1210 IF LEFT$(ANS$, 1) = "Y" THEN 40
```

Note that N in LEFT$ is the *length* of the **head** of a string, and that N in RIGHT$ is the *starting position* of the **tail** of a string.

If A$ ← "UNTHINKINGLY", then LEN(A$) has the value 12, LEFT$(A$, 6) has the value "UNTHIN", and RIGHT$(A$, 7) has the value "KINGLY".

The definitions as well as the syntax of essential string functions vary. For example, in some versions the roles of LEFT$ and RIGHT$ may be replaced by MID$(A$, M, N), which returns N characters, beginning with the Mth. Another scheme is to define A$(M:N) to return characters M through N of A$.

7.6   EXTENSIONS

Perhaps the best way to see what can be done with the minimal functions listed above is to build useful procedures with them. For example, a string B$ may be inserted into a string A$, beginning at some location N in A$. Suppose that B$ ← "FOR" is inserted into A$ ← "TITTAT" in the fourth position. The result is "TITFORTAT". The variables A$, B$, and N are **arguments** of the insertion procedure, and the result of executing the procedure is one of the arguments; with the given A$, B$, and N it is "TITFORTAT". The same procedure will work, of course, no matter what the values of A$, B$, and N are. Arguments are included in the pseudocode so that it will be clear what information is needed by the procedure, or is produced by it. Here is an insertion procedure:

procedure INSERT($A\$$, $B\$$, N)
    $A\$ \leftarrow$ LEFT\$($A\$$, $N - 1$) + $B\$$ + RIGHT\$($A\$$, N)

end INSERT

Note that the result is an alteration of $A\$$. The procedure could have been written to leave $A\$$ unchanged and put the catenated string in still a third location, but the given version is the one normally required. Procedure INSERT is said to **edit** the string $A\$$ with an insertion.

Another useful procedure is one which extracts (copies) the characters M through N of a string:

procedure EXTRACT($A\$$, $B\$$, M, N)
    TEMP\$ $\leftarrow$ LEFT\$($A\$$, N)
    $B\$ \leftarrow$ RIGHT\$(TEMP\$, M)
end EXTRACT

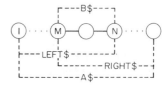

A more concentrated form of the same procedure is:

procedure EXTRACT($A\$$, $B\$$, M, N)
    $B\$ \leftarrow$ RIGHT\$(LEFT\$($A\$$, N), M)
end EXTRACT

Note that $B\$$ is included in the argument list through which the procedure communicates with the outside world. $B\$$ is included because the result of EXTRACT is stored in it—$B\$$ is changed by the procedure. If $A\$ \leftarrow$ "WEEK-DAY-NIGHT", then EXTRACT($A\$$, $B\$$, 6, 8) will change $B\$$ from whatever it was to "DAY". This procedure differs from the functions which were discussed in Chapter 5 and from LEFT\$ and RIGHT\$ in a technical sense—those functions *return a value,* and may be used in expressions, as LEFT\$($A\$$, N) is above.

Another useful procedure is one which finds the location of a given string, say $B\$$, within another string, say $A\$$. If $B\$$ is not present as a substring of $A\$$, then the procedure should indicate that this is so. That procedure will serve as the procedure MATCH required by procedure KEY in 7.2, and so it should return $S = 0$ if no match is found, and set S to the starting position of the copy of $B\$$ in $A\$$ if there is one in $A\$$. One way to approach the problem is to extract a substring of $A\$$ which is equal in length to $B\$$, and compare them. If they are not the same, another substring is extracted and compared. This continues until $A\$$ is exhausted. If the position of the beginning of the extracted substring of $A\$$ is L, and the position of its rightmost character is R, then initially L is 1 and R is LEN($B\$$). Each time both L and R are incremented, the substring moves to the right one position. The process stops when R is the length of $A\$$ (the position of its rightmost character) or when a match is found:

procedure MATCH($A\$$, $B\$$, S)
   $N \leftarrow$ LEN($A\$$)
   $R \leftarrow$ LEN($B\$$)
   $L \leftarrow 1 : S \leftarrow 0$
   while $R \leq N$ **do**
      //compare $B\$$ to the substring which is the Lth through//
      //the Rth characters of $A\$$ and exit if a match is found//
      $R \leftarrow R + 1$
      $L \leftarrow L + 1$
   endwhile
end MATCH

The comparison can be made between $B\$$ and the extracted substring of $A\$$, say TEMP$. (The compact form of EXTRACT in 7.6 can be directly incorporated into MATCH as a single statement.) To see how this procedure behaves, suppose that $A\$ \leftarrow$ "UNTHINKINGLY", and $B\$ \leftarrow$ "INKING". Then N is 12, R is initialized to 6, and the successive values of L, R, and TEMP$ will be:

L	R	TEMP$
1	6	"UNTHIN"
2	7	"NTHINK"
3	8	"THINKI"
4	9	"HINKIN"
5	10	"INKING" ... a match

In more detail, the algorithm is:

procedure MATCH($A\$$, $B\$$, S)
  $N \leftarrow$ LEN($A\$$)
  $R \leftarrow$ LEN($B\$$)
  $L \leftarrow 1 : S \leftarrow 0$
  while $R \leq N$ **do**
    TEMP$\$ \leftarrow$ RIGHT$\$$(LEFT$\$$($A\$$, R), L)
    if TEMP$\$ = B\$$
      then $S \leftarrow L$
        exit
    endif
    $R \leftarrow R + 1$
    $L \leftarrow L + 1$
  endwhile
end MATCH

Note that $S \leftarrow 0$ if no match is found, and that the position of the *leftmost* occurrence is the one located by the procedure. If $A\$ \leftarrow$ "RATTATTAT" and $B\$ \leftarrow$ "TAT", then MATCH will set S to 4. If $B\$ \leftarrow$ "RATA", then S will remain 0, and so S becomes a **flag** which indicates that no occurrence of $B\$$ was located by MATCH.

If a substring can be located, then it can be deleted. This can be done with the procedure EXTRACT, but it requires the first and last positions of a substring to be known. A more general extraction procedure can be formed which uses MATCH to locate the first occurrence of a substring and then extract it. Here is one:

procedure DEL($A\$$, $B\$$, S)
  procedure MATCH($A\$$, $B\$$, S)
  if $S = 0$ **then exit**
  $A\$ \leftarrow$ LEFT$\$$($A\$$, $S - 1$) + RIGHT$\$$($A\$$, $S +$ LEN($B\$$))
end DEL

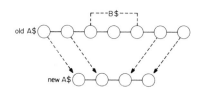

Finally, a substring $B\$$ of $A\$$ may be replaced with a different string $C\$$. For example, if $A\$ \leftarrow$ "CONCENTNATION", $B\$ \leftarrow$ "CENT" and $C\$ \leftarrow$ "DEM", then the resulting $A\$$ should be "CONDEMNATION".

procedure SUB($A\$$, $B\$$, $C\$$, S)
  procedure MATCH($A\$$, $B\$$, S)
  if $S = 0$ **then print** (an error message)
          exit
        endif
  $A\$ \leftarrow$ LEFT\$($A\$$, $S - 1$) + $C\$$ + RIGHT\$($A\$$, S + LEN($B\$$))
end SUB

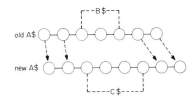

7.7 PACKED BASIC

Consider the characters which are encountered by BASIC as it scans a statement from left to right.

Statements always begin with a number—a sequence of digits. This sequence is often followed by one or more blanks. The next sequence of related characters to be encountered (often called a **token**) is an identifier, a keyword, and in some format schemes, a colon. For an assignment statement, the initial token is a variable name, and for statements like the IF, END, GO TO, etc. it is a keyword. In each case, the second token is some specific type of character sequence, else the statement is invalid. For a GO TO statement it is a statement number. For an assignment statement, it is an "=". An IF statement is more complex to decipher, but it can be dissected in the same manner.

All of the valid statements can be traced, token by token, until they reach the ®. In no case are blanks absolutely necessary in order to determine the information content of a statement of known type, although requiring them to be present may make it easier to program the BASIC translator. Consequently, in many versions of BASIC, blanks may be left out of statements. Not only may they be left out, but if the blanks are *removed* as each statement is filed away, the statement can still be reconstructed, with or without blanks, when the LIST command is entered. Some systems, particularly the small ones, *pack* statements by removing blanks before filing, which saves storage space. If ® is always the last "character" in a statement, A\$, then the blanks can be removed to produce a **packed statement** P\$ by:

```
procedure PACK(A$, P$)
   P$ ← A$
   repeat
      procedure MATCH(P$, "   ", S)
      if S = 0 then exit
      P$ ← LEFT(P$, S − 1) + RIGHT$(P$, S + 1)
   forever
end PACK
```

7.8   LISTS

The procedures discussed in the previous sections can be put together to do quite a bit of text editing, but in most systems there is a limit to how many characters can be stored in a single string variable. Even without a system limit to the number of characters, too many of them in one string is inefficient and unwieldy to manage. It is far more convenient to tie together a collection of strings than to put all characters of interest into one string. Individual strings in the collection may be added or deleted, or they may be updated (altered) with procedures like those which have been discussed. The techniques of Chapter 6 may be applied to this problem, but they tend to be unsatisfactory because word processing uses such large amounts of memory unless it is managed well (and even then!). A technique for dealing with the storage-management problem for text is **list processing**. Lists are valuable data structures for a variety of applications, but we will develop them around the subject of text editing, and by doing so, illustrate some of the list managing techniques which form the core of list processing.

7.9   LINKS

Suppose that a program is to be written which is to input pieces of text, one at a time, edit them, and then print the edited text. Suppose further, that this is to be done within a limited memory (perhaps on a personal microcomputer). The pieces of text, which we shall call *lines*, can be stored in an array, $L\$$, with maximum index 100. The lines $L\$(I)$ form a file and each one is a record, in accordance with the terminology of Chapter 6. The editing process in-volves getting started (creating the file), deleting 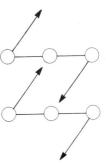 records, adding records, and updating a record. The updating can be done with the string processing procedures developed above, and will not be pursued farther. For example, suppose the following were entered:

$L\$(1)$ "NOW"
$L\$(2)$ "IS THE"
$L\$(3)$ " PLACE FOR"
$L\$(4)$ " ALL GO"
$L\$(5)$ "OD MEN TO COME"

The editing tasks which might be desired are to delete $L\$(3)$, to add "TO THE AID OF THE PARTY.", to update either $L\$(1)$ or $L\$(2)$ in order to insert a blank between W and IS, and to insert the record " TIME FOR" in the appropriate place. These changes should produce "NOW IS THE TIME FOR ALL GOOD MEN TO COME TO THE AID OF THE PARTY.".

As in Chapter 6, it is necessary to avoid using too much of the available memory for a small file simply because deletions and insertions are made in it. The purpose of a text editor is to *support* whatever file maintenance and updating are required by the task at hand. The technique which has been invented for this is conceptually simple, if one separates the physical order of the entries in $L\$$ from their logical order. Suppose that when $L\$(3)$ is deleted, it is done merely by *marking* the physical space that it occupies as being available for further use. Then when the concluding record is added, it could be stored into that space. Even if it is stored in $L\$(3)$, it may not be the third logical record. This operation is not an up-date, precisely because the concluding record is the *last* record in the logical order, not the third. Now when " TIME FOR" is inserted, it can go into $L\$(6)$, but it is still to be the third record in the logical sense. The arrows in the following diagram indicate which line follows a given one in the logical order:

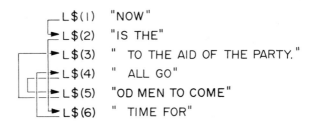

L $(1)   "NOW"
L $(2)   "IS THE"
L $(3)   " TO THE AID OF THE PARTY."
L $(4)   " ALL GO"
L $(5)   "OD MEN TO COME"
L $(6)   " TIME FOR"

In order to unscramble the physical order into the correct logical order, a way is needed to *link* the records in their correct logical order. The **link** of the (logical) first record should point to the physical location of the (logical) second record, etc. It is convenient, especially for deletions, to have backward links to the previous record, as well as forward links to the next one. Linking can be accomplished by adding the following to the structure used to manage the data:

AVAIL(100) for flags which indicate available storage.
FLINK(100) for forward links.
BLINK(100) for backward links.

These three arrays will contain integers—flags in AVAIL and indices to locations in *L*$ in the other two. The link and flag arrays generally take up much less memory than *L*$, because of the difference in the ways that string data and integer data is stored. The *I*th cell in these arrays can be thought of as part of the *I*th record in the file like this:

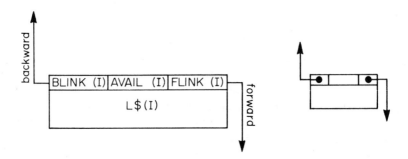

With this data structure in hand, the management of the file can be approached. (We will delay illustrating the use of links until some management procedures have been developed.)

7.10   CREATING A LINKED LIST

The first task in file management is to create the file—to get the first record into the file and start the linking process. After some editing has been done, $L\$(1)$ may not contain the first item in the list. Hence if the list is to be searched for some substring (the links make it possible to treat $L\$$ as one large string), or if the final result is to be printed, then the starting point must be known. Because arrays in BASIC provide a 0th position, FLINK(0) may be used as the **head** of the list. Initially, it is set to 0, indicating that the list is **null**: it contains no records. Whenever the list is not null, FLINK(0) will point to the (logical) first record, and hence it will *not* be 0. It must be possible to detect the last record as the list is searched. In order to do that, FLINK of the last record can also be set to 0, since $L\$(0)$ is explicitly not for records and cannot be the next one. When the file is created, all of $L\$$ is to be available, so the initialization procedure looks like this:

```
procedure CREATE
   FLINK(0) ← 0
   I ← 1
   while I ≤ 100 do
      AVAIL(I) ← 0
      I ← I + 1
   endwhile
end CREATE
```

7.11   ADDING TO A LINKED LIST

The first record can be added to the **null list** (no records) just as any other record can be added, hence the general problem can be attacked at once. In order to add a record, AVAIL must be searched for the first available space in $L\$$, loaded with the entry record, say $A\$$, and linked to the rest of the list. This process may be broken into two parts, the first of which finds available space, puts $A\$$ into it, and removes that space from the available list:

procedure SPACE($A\$$, J)
  $J \leftarrow 0 : I \leftarrow 1$
  while $I \leq 100$ **do**
    if AVAIL(I) $= 0$
      then $J \leftarrow I$
         exit
    endif
    $I \leftarrow I + 1$
  endwhile
  if $J = 0$
    then print (no available space message)
    else $L\$(J) \leftarrow A\$$
       AVAIL(J) $\leftarrow 1$
  endif
end SPACE

The index J is put in the argument list of SPACE because it is useful information for both procedure TAIL below, and procedure INSERT to be discussed later. In general, SPACE would call an error handling routine, rather than just printing a message when no space was available. When space is available, a procedure is needed to run down the list in order to find the last record. The new record must then be linked to it. Procedure TAIL also updates the number of active records, N.

procedure TAIL(J, N)
  $K \leftarrow$ FLINK(0)
  while FLINK(K) > 0 **do**
    $K \leftarrow$ FLINK(K)
  endwhile
  FLINK(K) $\leftarrow J$
  BLINK(J) $\leftarrow K$
  FLINK(J) $\leftarrow 0$
  $N \leftarrow N + 1$
end TAIL

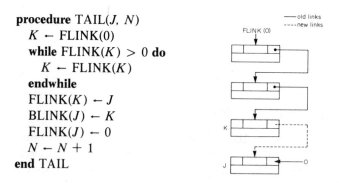

7.12 OUTPUT OF A LINKED LIST

The user of a word processor needs to have a listing of the contents of the file before deleting and inserting, so that s/he can specify *where* in the list these operations are to take place. In order to make this possible a line number will be printed with each active entry in $L\$$ as the list is printed:

procedure LIST
    $I \leftarrow$ FLINK(0)
    $L \leftarrow 0$
    while FLINK(I) > 0 **do**
        $L \leftarrow L + 1$
        print L, $L\$(I)$
        $I \leftarrow$ FLINK(I)
    endwhile
end LIST

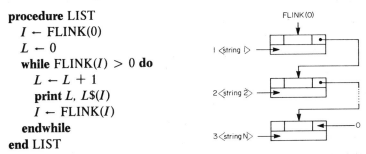

The listing for our example, before deletions, additions, and insertions, might look like this:

    1 NOW
    2 IS THE
    3   PLACE FOR
    4   ALL GO
    5 OD MEN TO COME

The underlying data structure at this point can be tabulated as follows:

I	L	BLINK(I)	$L\$(I)$	FLINK(I)
1	1	0	"NOW"	2
2	2	1	"IS THE"	3
3	3	2	" PLACE FOR"	4
4	4	3	" ALL GO"	5
5	5	4	"OD MEN TO COME"	0

Note that if the listing includes the index I of each record, *updating* becomes simply:

   Input $L\$(I)$

Without this information, it is necessary to follow the links down the list to the Lth record. It is more common to omit the index in the listing, so that the data structure is completely transparent to the user. You are asked to do it the hard way in P7.9.

7.13 DELETION FROM A LINKED LIST

We may assume that the user has a listing like the one shown above which has accompanying line numbers L, and that the user wishes to delete a line. The input will consist of the line number L and some means of giving the command to delete it. The deletion operation involves relinking the list, and that requires:

P, the index of the predecessor of line L in $L\$$
D, the index of line L in $L\$$
S, the index of the successor of line L in $L\$$

procedure DELETE(L)
  $S \leftarrow$ FLINK(0)
  $J \leftarrow 1$
  while $J \leq L$ **do**
    $P \leftarrow$ BLINK(S)
    $S \leftarrow$ FLINK(S)
    $J \leftarrow J + 1$
  endwhile
  $D \leftarrow$ BLINK(S)
  FLINK(P) $\leftarrow$ FLINK(D)
  BLINK(S) $\leftarrow$ BLINK(D)
  AVAIL(D) $\leftarrow 0$
end DELETE

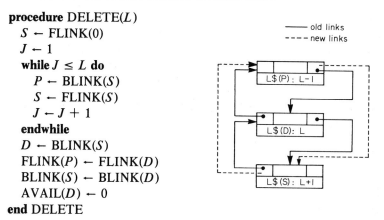

A snapshot of the example data structure immediately after the deletion of line 3, and after "NOW" is updated to "NOW ", is:

I	L	BLINK(I)	L$(I)	FLINK(I)
1	1	0	"NOW "	2
2	2	1	"IS THE"	4
3	—	—	—	—
4	3	2	" ALL GO"	5
5	4	4	"OD MEN TO COME"	0

After the addition of " TO THE AID OF THE PARTY", the data structure will be:

I	L	BLINK(I)	L$(I)	FLINK(I)
1	1	0	"NOW "	2
2	2	1	"IS THE"	4
3	5	5	" TO THE AID OF THE PARTY"	0
4	3	2	" ALL GO"	5
5	4	4	"OD MEN TO COME"	3

7.14   INSERTION INTO A LINKED LIST

The insertion of a record is similar as a process to the deletion of one, except that L is the statement number *after* which a new statement is to be inserted:

procedure INSERT($A\$$, L)
  procedure SPACE($A\$$, J)
  $S \leftarrow$ FLINK(0) : $K \leftarrow 1$
  while $K \le L$ **do**
    $S \leftarrow$ FLINK(S)
    $P \leftarrow$ BLINK(S)
    $K \leftarrow K + 1$
  endwhile
  FLINK(P) $\leftarrow J$
  BLINK(S) $\leftarrow J$
  FLINK(J) $\leftarrow S$
  BLINK(J) $\leftarrow P$
end INSERT

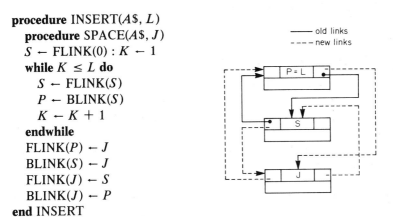

Note the switch in the order in which S and P are assigned in the inner loop, and also that the line numbers for statements which come after the insertion will automatically be incremented in the listing process:

I	L	BLINK(I)	$L\$(I)$	FLINK(I)
1	1	0	"NOW "	2
2	2	1	"IS THE"	6
3	6	4	" TO THE AID OF THE PARTY."	0
4	4	6	" ALL GO"	5
5	5	4	"OD MEN TO COME"	3
6	3	2	" TIME FOR"	4

The statement numbers indicate the logical order of these records, although the data processing of the list is *actually* done with the links. (This distinction frees the statement numbers to be 10, 20, 40, 90, 100, 101 for example, instead of 1, 2, 3, 4, 5, 6.) The listing produced for our example will be:

1 NOW
2 IS THE
3   TIME FOR
4   ALL GO
5 OD MEN TO COME
6   TO THE AID OF THE PARTY.

7.15   TEXT EDITING COMMANDS

The existence of the list-processing routines which are treated in this chapter makes it possible to construct a text editor, one of the things necessary as support for an interactive language like BASIC, which must have editing capabilities. By themselves, however, list-processing routines do not give the user of a program which incorporates them the interactive facility that is needed to use them. Such routines must be combined with **commands** which allow the user to call upon them.

Possible commands are *I* (insert), *D* (delete), *L* (list), *A* (add), etc. A set of them naturally includes string processing commands for updating records in the list. For example:

S[12]/DEM/CATE/

might indicate that in line 12 the first occurrence of "DEM" is to be replaced by "CATE". Commands must also be combined with a means to inform the processing program that a command, rather than a list item, is being input, and which data object it is to be applied to. One way to do this is to have the processor print a signal, like "*" and wait for an input command. The input which follows the command is taken as data upon which the command operates. The user's response might then be a command followed by a line number or some text. The resulting display while using an editor could look like this:

*D[3]®   *D/3/®
                          or
*I[2] TIME FOR®   *I/2/®
*   perhaps: TIME FOR®
                                          *

Clearly, a great deal of power is to be gained (and may be needed) in text editing by combining the procedures of this chapter with the mass-storage techniques of Chapter 6.

It is the collection of available commands which makes much of the difference in quality between text editors, but we shall have to leave it at that.

SELF-REVIEW

1. How many procedure KEY (page 185) be changed so that it prints *all* of the keys in KEY$ which are found in the textural material being searched?

2. In what way would the partitioning of strings into words and punctuation marks be involved in newspaper typesetting?

3. How might a law office use a word-processing program which locates keywords?

4. What kinds of word-processing would be of use in a public library?

5. How can word-processing be used to create form letters?

6. Suppose that RIGHT$($\langle$string$\rangle$, N) returned the *last* N characters in $\langle$string$\rangle$. How would the following procedures be changed?

    a. INSERT (page 188)
    b. EXTRACT (page 188)
    c. MATCH (page 189)

7. What are the tokens in the following statements?

    a. 100 STOP
    b. 90 GO TO 145
    c. 20 IF $A < B$ THEN 40

8. Suppose that 20 triplets of numbers (A, B, C), together with all of the links that are required to list them in order by the values of A or B or C, are to be supported in a single table. How many columns will it need to have?

9. What happens when the assignments

    $P \leftarrow$ BLINK(S)
    $S \leftarrow$ FLINK(S)

    are switched in procedure DELETE? (page 198) in procedure INSERT? (page 199)

10. Consider the linked list at right: What is the linkage resulting from the operations which follow, done in sequence?

cell	BLINK	item	FLINK
0			3
1	3		5
2	5		4
3	0		1
4	2		0
5	1		2

a. Delete the second item in the list.
b. Exchange the third and fourth items.
c. Add another item, which comes last in the list.
d. Add another item, which comes second in the list.

PROBLEMS

Write the following in pseudocode.

P7.1 Write a procedure which, given a string $A\$$, will alter it by removing a given string $B\$$ from $A\$$ if it is there. The procedure should print an error message otherwise.

P7.2 Write a procedure which will remove *all* of the multiple blanks (spaces) from a given string and print the result.

P7.3 Write a procedure which will delete *every* occurrence of a substring $B\$$ from a string $A\$$, and leave the result in $A\$$.

P7.4 Rewrite procedure INSERT, assuming that L is the statement *before* which the new statement is to be inserted. (One should be able to insert the very first record, as well as add it.)

P7.5 Write a procedure which will search a linked list for a given record.

P7.6 Write a procedure which will search a linked list for a given string. (It may even overlap records!)

P7.7 Develop a procedure which will sort a linked list. (You may assume numerical records.)

P7.8 Develop a procedure which searches a linked list of strings to determine *letter frequencies*—the number of occurrences of the letters A, B, ..., Z in the list.

P7.9 Develop a procedure for updating a linked list.

PROGRAMS

In a biological cell, proteins are synthesized from a pattern of triplets of bases in messenger RNA (mRNA). The four bases have codes *A, C, G,* and *U* for Adenine, Cytosine, Guanine, and Uracil, respectively. The triplets may be in any combination from *AAA* to *UUU,* except that the triplets *UGA, UAA,* and *UAG* must appear at each end, and *only* at the end of a synthesis string. Their occurrence determines the *active sections* of an mRNA molecule. We shall call these the *end-codons,* and the other triplets just *codons.*

PG7.1   Write a procedure which inputs an mRNA string, searches it for end-codons, and prints out the list of active sections. If the ends of the mRNA string itself are not end-codons, an error message is to be printed.

PG7.2   Write a procedure which inputs two sections of mRNA, locates any matching active sections, and prints the position of the triplet at which the coincidence begins in the first string. For example:

A\$ ← AUAGUAGCUUAUUGA

will yield GCU 3

B\$ ← UAABUCGCUUAUUGA

PG7.3   Rewrite PG6.2 so that *B*\$ may be shifted along *A*\$ to find overlaps. For example, with the *A*\$ of PG6.2, and *B*\$ ← GUCGCUUAUUGC, the procedure should return GCU 3 again.

PG7.4   Write a program which will create a linked list of 15 input numbers, and *search* the list for a given (input) value.

PG7.5   Combine PG7.4 with P7.7 and do the search by **bisection.** (See PG6.9 and PJ6.3).

PG7.6   Write a program which inputs 16 numbers (8 positive and 8 negative) in random order and stores them in an array, linked in *two* lists, one for positive numbers in entry sequence order, and the other for negative numbers in entry sequence order. Print the two lists side by side.

PG7.7   Write a program which inputs 16 numbers into a single array as two linked lists, one for the first 8 numbers, and the other for the last 8. Then **merge** the lists to be in the order: 1st, 9th, 2nd, 10th, ..., 8th, 16th and print them in list order.

PG7.8   Write a program which inputs ten character strings of length 5–25 characters into an array and prints them in lines which contain *no more* than 40 characters. The number of spaces in the output is to be minimized, and no words are to be split. (You may assume that the input contains no split words.) Hence each line is to contain as many words as possible without causing a split. When looking for *word boundaries*, one may deal with commas, periods, etc. by either considering them to be part of a word, or as separate words.

PG7.9   Write a program which inputs three character strings (sentence fragments) of length 10–40 characters, separates them into words, and stores the words in a linked list of words.

PG7.10   Rewrite PG7.8 so that it inserts spaces between the words on a line in order to *right-adjust* the output (a non-blank character in column 40). The output should be acceptable typesetting.

PG7.11   Write a program which will create a linked list of 15 input numbers, then sort them *as a list.* This differs from previous sorting problems in that the progress through the list is done by following the links, and the exchange operations involve the links. Note that the numbers do not *physically* move—only the links change!

PG7.12   A *Caeser cipher* of shift N is a cipher in which each letter is replaced by the letter that is N places farther along in the alphabet. For example, shift 3 will produce

WKLV LVSL CDCC

from

THIS IS PIZAZZ

(The alphabet is considered to be arranged in a circle.) Write a program which will encipher messages from an input *plaintext* with an input value of N. Break the resulting *ciphertext* output into groups of four letters, ignoring word boundaries.

PG7.13   Write a program which will input up to 20 lines of text, and print the distribution of *letter frequencies* within the text. This is the first step in deciphering messages encoded in some unknown way. (See P7.8.)

PG7.14 Write a program which will input a plaintext, remove the blanks, break it up into groups of four letters, and print the ciphertext after an interchange of the vowels in the following manner:

   1st and last
   2nd and next-to-last
   .   .
   .   .
   .   .

PROJECTS

The comments at the beginning of the projects section of Chapter 3 apply to the following:

PJ7.1 Write a program which creates a linked list of up to 20 numbers in an array, and supports file maintenance and updating as though the values were records. Input all of the values by appending, and allow the user to choose between the operations of listing, updating, appending, and deletion.

PJ7.2 Write a program which inputs 15 pairs—name and score—and creates a linked list of *records*. Sort them by name, then sort the scores *indirectly* (using a different pair of links), and print them in the order of either the values or scores upon user demand.

PJ7.3 It is possible to represent polynomials as a linked list of their coefficients. For example:

   $5 \rightarrow 3 \rightarrow -7 \rightarrow 2 \rightarrow 0$ represents $5 + 3X - 7X**2 + 2X**3$
   $0 \rightarrow 4 \rightarrow 2 \rightarrow 0 \rightarrow -1$ represents $4X + 2X**2   - X**4$

Write a program which will input two polynomials, store them as linked lists of coefficients, and add them algebraically. The two examples above would produce:

   $5 + 7X - 5X**2 + 2X**3 - X**4$

A more challenging problem is to create a program which will add or subtract or multiply the polynomials at the user's request.

PJ7.4 Write a program which keeps the body of a form letter in DATA statements, inputs a name, and mentions the name in the heading and two or three places in the letter which it prints. The letter should be typographically correct, without excessive white space associated with the name.

PJ7.5   In files which are actively manipulated, it is possible to run out of storage space even though deletions have kept the number of active records within the capacity of the storage provided for the file. The problem has been dealt with in this text through the use of procedure SPACE and procedure AVAIL. If the file is large, the search for available storage can become a major task, and AVAIL uses storage itself. Finding the available storage is called **garbage collection**. One way to handle the problem is to keep the active records and the inactive storage in two separate lists. Then a deletion or an addition is a transfer of a record from one list to the other, but only involves relinking, not moving. The initial FLINK for the garbage may be kept in the otherwise unused BLINK(0). Rewrite enough of the procedures for the example list in this chapter so that a file may be created, appended, and deleted from, using this scheme of automatic garbage collection, without AVAIL.

PJ7.6   Develop a program which will maintain a hotel directory, using linked lists. There should be separate lists for occupied rooms (with the name of the occupant), empty but uncleaned rooms, and clean rooms. The user should be able to register and check out guests, and get a listing of the guests (in alphabetical order), and the numbers of occupied, used, and clean rooms.

Chapter 8

STACKS AND QUEUES

8.1 STACKS

Many card games involve a *discard pile,* on which a player must deposit a card in each round of the game, and may also draw from it. Cards are put on top of the pile, and withdrawn from the top of it, sometimes several at a time. As the game progresses, the discard pile may grow and shrink, but the first card that is deposited can only be withdrawn if the cards placed on top of it are removed first. Such a pile is modeled by a data structure called a **stack** or LIFO (Last-In, First-Out) list in Computer Science. Stacks are valuable for much more than simulating card games, as we shall see.

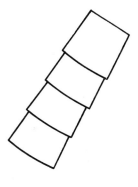

In many computers, two numbers are added together by copying one into a register in the CPU, adding the other to it there, and storing the result from the register into a memory cell. The addition instruction itself must specify the location of the second number and (usually) the register which is to be used for the operation. Some computers have an architecture designed around stacks with a contrasting method of performing an operation like addition. In this alternate approach, items are put into a stack, and whenever addition is called for, the top two numbers in the stack are added together, the result replaced in the next-to-top spot in the stack, and the top spot deleted. In analogy with the discard pile, the top two items are removed (drawn) and a new item placed (discarded) on the stack.

It is quite common in both of these computer architectures (and others), to use stacks for the return addresses of subprograms. Assume that the return address is kept in some single place in the computer, and consider what would happen if the first subprogram called another one. The first return address could be wiped out by the second one, and control might not get back to the original call location! Stacks are used as one of the ways to get out of this dilemma. If the return addresses are stacked, then the number of addresses in the stack is increased by one with each call, and decreased by one for each return. Because of the order in which items are added and deleted in a stack, control will be returned to the proper location. This is the secret of the GOSUB ... RETURN structure in BASIC, and the more general **call** procedure in other languages.

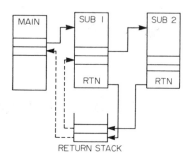

8.2 RECURSION

In a system in which return addresses are taken from the top of a stack when a RETURN is executed, subroutines may call themselves. Such subroutines are said to be **recursive**. In languages in which variables may be local (redefined within the subroutine), stacks are required to keep track of their values at the time of each call. In BASIC, such stacks, called parameter stacks, are not necessary (but the lack of them limits the value of the GOSUB ... RETURN structure. An example of an interesting use of recursion is a routine which removes *all* of the occurrences of blanks from a string $A\$$, by calling itself. Each call removes another blank, and the return is to the *last* calling position. All of the blanks must be removed before an exit from the procedure is made. Here is a pseudocode description of it:

procedure CLEANUP
  procedure MATCH($A\$$, " ", S)
  if $S = 0$ **then return**
  $A\$ \leftarrow$ LEFT$(A\$, S - 1)$ + RIGHT$(A\$, S + 1)$
  procedure CLEANUP
end CLEANUP

Because recursion is not explicitly provided for in BASIC, it is usually not possible to implement a recursive algorithm directly in BASIC. However, such algorithms can be rewritten without recursion. For example, CLEANUP can also be written:

```
procedure CLEANUP
  repeat
    procedure MATCH(A$, "  ", S)
    if S = 0 then exit
    A$ ← LEFT$(A$, S − 1) + RIGHT$(A$, S + 1)
  forever
end CLEANUP
```

It may be possible to implement a procedure like CLEANUP in a recursive *fashion* in BASIC, because the current values of A$ and S do not need to be retrieved after a later call of the procedure. In one personal computing system, in which RIGHT$(A$, K) returns the rightmost K characters of A$, a partial listing of a program which implements CLEANUP in recursive fashion looks like this:

```
 10 INPUT A$
 20 GOSUB 510
 30 PRINT A$
 40 IF A$ = "*" THEN STOP
500 REM ... PROCEDURE CLEANUP
510 GOSUB 1000
520 IF S = 0 THEN RETURN
530 A$ = LEFT$(A$, S − 1) + RIGHT$(A$, LEN(A$) − S)
540 GOSUB 510
550 RETURN
1000 REM ... PROCEDURE MATCH(A$, "  ", S)
  .
  .
  .
```

On the system in which this program was run, it removed 18 blanks from A$, but not 19, which indicates that the system allows a maximum of eighteen addresses in the RETURN stack. (This code will not work properly in all versions of BASIC.)

8.3 POP AND PUSH

Specialized procedures are required for dealing with stacks, just as they are with strings and lists. In order to see what might be required, we will model a discard pile. An array, CARD$(52), will hold the pile, which will contain no more than 52 items like "3-SPADE", "A-HEART", "J-CLUBS", "10-DIAMONDS". In order to draw from the pile, the current top of the pile must be known. Since CARD$ holds character information, we shall use TOP for a pointer to the top of the stack. In order to create an empty stack, it is only necessary to set TOP ← 0. In order to push a new card, $A$$, onto the stack, all that is required is:

TOP ← TOP + 1
CARD$(TOP) ← $A$$

However, it is valuable in some situations to check for extreme cases, such as no room in the stack, which in this example would correspond to more than 52 cards. We could set a special flag in that case, but the stack counter TOP itself will serve the purpose, by being compared to a limit. What should be avoided by the push procedure itself is exceeding the subscript range of the stack array. (On some systems, the program will be aborted if a subscript range is exceeded unless the program avoids that error explicitly.) Here is a suitable routine:

procedure PUSH($A$$, TOP)
  TOP ← TOP + 1
  if TOP > 52 **then exit**
  CARD$(TOP) ← $A$$
end PUSH

All that is needed in order to delete the top of the stack is:

TOP ← TOP − 1

unless TOP = 0, which is a case that must be dealt with in a manner determined by the application. This differs from copying the top element as it is deleted:

procedure POP(POP$)
  if TOP = 0
    then
      POP$ ← ""
    else
      POP$ ← CARD$(TOP)
      TOP ← TOP − 1
    endif
    end POP

With these procedures, let's begin our discard pile with:

PUSH("3-HEARTS", TOP)
PUSH("*A*-SPADE", TOP)
PUSH("10-DIAMOND", TOP)
POP(POP$) : **print** POP$
POP(POP$) : **print** POP$
PUSH("7-CLUBS", TOP)

Here is what happens to the discard pile:

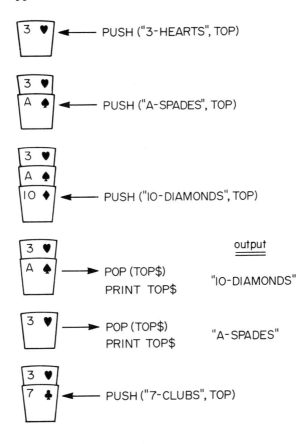

8.4   A MAZE

A stack can be used in games and simulations for organized backtracking: returning to a previous point of choice and choosing again. It is one of the techniques applied in Artificial Intelligence. Without attempting a formal definition, by Artificial Intelligence we mean the study of non-living devices which solve problems that they are not *explicitly* programmed for: they must adapt to the natural logic of an individual task in some way, and be capable of handling a variety of similar situations.

Consider the problem of finding a way through a maze. One simple model of a maze is a table, say MAZE(M, N), with 1's in locations through which it is legal to pass, and 0's in locations which are closed off. We shall use MOUSE to thread this maze, for historical reasons. MOUSE may move along rows and columns from 1 to 1, but not diagonally. A convenient shorthand for MAZE(I, J) is (I, J). With that notation, a possible path from (2, 3) to (7, 4) would be the one indicated in the figure below:

	1	2	3	4	5	6	
1	O	O	O	O	O	O	
2	O	O	1	O	O	O	
3	O	O	1	1	1	O	
4	O	1	O	1	O	O	
5	O	1	1	1	1	O	
6	O	1	O	O	1	O	
7	O	O	O	1	1	O	

If it is possible to program MOUSE to find its own way through such a maze, then s/he can be used to discover if there *is* such a path, and perhaps to remember one of them. If some randomness is introduced into the way in which MOUSE searches out its paths, then it will explore the set of *possible* paths, and not always find the same one, although s/he might also repeat paths.

A stack shall be its memory, and the path it takes (if it exists) shall be its final stack. That is sufficient reason to name the stack PATH. Then PATH must keep track of locations in the table. For example, the top of the stack might contain (3, 4), and if MOUSE then steps to (3, 5), that pair of indices is pushed onto the stack. It is convenient to use a table for PATH, with a column for each index. PATH ← (3, 5), sometimes indicated by: PATH(TOP, *) ← (3, 5) will be implemented as:

PATH(TOP, 1) ← 3
PATH(TOP, 2) ← 5

8.4.1 Which Way?

If MOUSE is in location (I, J) then it must have a systematic method for trying to go one step further. There are only four possible moves from a location that is not in the first or last row or column. Starting from the border rows and columns there are less than four. If the actual maze is restricted to be confined within rows 2 to $M - 1$ and columns 2 to $N - 1$ of MAZE, and if the border rows and columns are loaded with 0's, then there will always be four possible moves. With the assumption that we do have a bordered maze, the possible steps are:

$(I - 1, J)$
$(I, J - 1)$
$(I, J + 1)$
$(I + 1, J)$

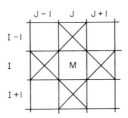

One of these may be the backtrack—the square from whence MOUSE came. MOUSE should attempt the other three possibilities first in order to make progress. If no step other than the backtrack is possible, then the current location should be *erased*—it was a *dead end*. MOUSE is followed for a few steps below:

the stack contents

(2, 3)
(3, 3)
(3, 4)
(3, 5) ← TOP

(2, 3)
(3, 3)
(3, 4) ← TOP

MOUSE reaches a deadend at (3, 5), is forced to backtrack to (3, 4) again, but erases the 1 in (3, 5). It will never take that particular dead-end road again. It does have two choices, but (3, 4) is now the top of the stack, since backtracking not only erases, but also deletes. Hence, (3, 3) appears to MOUSE to be its backtrack, which in a sense, it is. The position (3, 3) would not be on the stack if MOUSE had not already stepped through it. MOUSE will go to (4, 4) next.

This process of hunting for a path with a stack deserves a bit of amazement before MOUSE is programmed to carry it out. When the path is found by eye (and a very young child can do it), *some* process, this one or another, is carried out very quickly and largely unconsciously in the mind. However, a very complicated maze cannot be solved at all by simply looking at it. MOUSE, however, can do very large mazes as "easily" as a very small one—but can do nothing else.

8.4.2 The MOUSE Algorithm

Suppose that the procedure which describes the search algorithm for finding a path is called MOUSE also. As a procedure, MOUSE must first initialize the stack to a starting point, then loop through the four possible steps which could be taken from there. If one of them is a backtrack, it keeps on searching, but if it finds a legal step (a step containing 1, not 0), then it is ready to take that step and repeat the procedure. If it finds only a backtrack, then it takes the backtrack step and repeats. Looping continues until either there is neither a backtrack or a forward step (nowhere to go), or it reaches its goal. The procedure MOUSE uses $(I0, J0)$ for the initial position, and (IG, JG) for the goal position. Here is an initial description:

```
procedure MOUSE
    PATH(TOP, *) ← (I0, J0) //initialize the stack//
    while PATH(TOP, *) ≠ (IG, JG) do
        //look for a possible step from the current position,//
        //then check it to see if it is a backtrack. If it is//
        //a backtrack, then continue to look until the other//
        //possibilities are exhausted, otherwise stop looking.//
        //After the search, react to the results: no path avail-//
        //able, only a backtrack is located, or a forward move//
        //is possible.//
    endwhile
    print PATH(I, *) for I = 1, 2, ..., TOP
end MOUSE
```

The description of the body of the **while** ... **do** loop breaks naturally into two parts. One of these is the search for the next move, and the other is the reaction to that move. The first part must pass information to the second part so that it can deal with three possible cases. One way to do this is to set a flag, say F, which can be used to distinguish between the cases in the second part of the body. The search portion must look in four directions, and so becomes:

$F \leftarrow 0$
$K \leftarrow 1$
while $K \leq 4$ **do**
    //locate a possible step to (IS, JS) from the top of the//
    //stack. If MAZE$(IS, JS) = 0$, then F remains 0, otherwise//
    //F is set to 1 for a backtrack and 2 otherwise.//
    if $F = 2$ **then exit** //(IS, JS) was a forward move//
    $K \leftarrow K + 1$
endwhile

The search procedure in the body of this loop has two functions, which can be separated into two procedures: FINDSTEP which locates a step in one of the four directions from the position indicated by the top of the stack, and CHECKSTEP which checks MAZE and sets the flag F to 1 for a backtrack and 2 for a forward move. Hence it becomes:

$F \leftarrow 0$
$K \leftarrow 1$
while $K \leq 4$ **do**
    procedure FINDSTEP(IS, JS, K) //locate a possible step to (IS, JS)//
    procedure CHECKSTEP(IS, JS, F) //$F \leftarrow 1$ if (IS, JS) is a backtrack.//
                                  //$F \leftarrow 2$ otherwise.//
    if $F = 2$ **then exit**
    $K \leftarrow K + 1$
endwhile

After coming out of the search loop above, control should pass to one of the following three cases:

    If $F = 0$ then print "NO PATH" and exit the search.

    If $F = 1$ then deal with a backtrack by erasing the appropriate square of MAZE and unstack its coordinates from PATH. We may call this procedure BACKTRACK.

If $F = 2$ then add (IS, JS) to the stack PATH. We may call this procedure FORWARD.

This logic is handled neatly by the **case** structure, and so we have:

procedure MOUSE
  PATH(TOP, *) ← $(I0, J0)$
  while PATH(TOP, *) ≠ (IG, JG) **do**
    F ← 0 //flag which indicates the type of step to be//
            //taken in this pass//
    K ← 1
    while $K \leq 4$ **do**
      procedure FINDSTEP(IS, JS, K) //locate possible step//
                            //to (IS, JS)//
      procedure CHECKSTEP(IS, JS, F) //F ← 1 if (IS, JS) is//
                                //a backtrack. F ← 2//
                                //otherwise.//
      if $F = 2$ **then exit**
      K ← $K + 1$
    endwhile
    case of F
      : $F = 0$: **print** "NO PATH"
               exit
      : $F = 1$: **procedure** BACKTRACK
      : $F = 2$: **procedure** FORWARD(IS, JS)
    endcase
  endwhile
  print PATH$(I, *)$ **for** $I = 1, 2, \ldots,$ TOP
end MOUSE

Three of the detail procedures are straightforward.

procedure FORWARD(*IS, JS*)
  TOP ← TOP + 1
  PATH(TOP, *) ← (*IS, JS*)
end FORWARD

procedure BACKTRACK
  (*IB, JB*) ← PATH(TOP, *)
  MAZE(*IB, JB*) ← 0
  TOP ← TOP − 1
end BACKTRACK

procedure CHECKSTEP(*IS, JS, F*)
  if MAZE(*IS, JS*) = 0 **then exit**
  if PATH(TOP − 1, *) = (*IS, JS*)
    then *F* ← 1
    else *F* ← 2
    endif
end CHECKSTEP

The final detail procedure is FINDSTEP. Even to search the four possibilities clockwise is a bit awkward, because of the way in which the indices change from one direction to the next. The search can be done from (*I, J*) by adding (*DI, DJ*) where (*DI, DJ*) indicates one of: (−1, 0), (0, 1), (1, 0), and (0, −1) in turn. These step adjustments can be put into a table of the form:

−1	0
0	1
1	0
0	−1

which we shall call STEP. With STEP defined, FINDSTEP becomes simpler than it would be without it:

procedure FINDSTEP(*IS, JS, K*)
  (*I, J*) ← PATH(TOP, *)
  IS ← *I* + STEP(*K*, 1)
  JS ← *J* + STEP(*K*, 2)
end FINDSTEP

Stacks and backtracking are both useful in solving many applications problems, some of which appear in the exercises.

8.5   QUEUES

Stacks are a useful tool for holding information and releasing it in some order which is related to the order in which it is stored. There are others, and one of them is a model for a theatre ticket line, or the check-out lane of a grocery store. It is a **queue**, which follows a first-in, first-out (FIFO) rule, in contrast to the last-in, first-out (LIFO) rule for stacks.

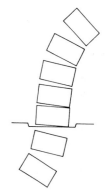

A queue is an idea about how data is to be managed, not a physical means of storage. It can be created in an array, or in a list, both of which are data structures in their own right. Lists themselves were imposed upon the primary data structure of the array by programming, since, unlike arrays, they are not part of the BASIC language itself. We shall use arrays to implement queues also. The more elegant list-structure queues appear in the exercises. The comments about the storage support of queues are specific to BASIC, however, since there are languages which allow the programmer to specify lists directly (notably the language LISP). In such a language, the translator itself sets up the machinery for storage and retrieval in the list. In languages designed for simulation, queues are created (and managed) by the language translation process, but we shall do these things ourselves, using the program structures available in BASIC.

8.6   A RESTAURANT LOBBY

Consider the case of the small but popular restaurant, which has but 50 tables, and a lobby which can hold 20 hungry patrons. As each patron (or party thereof) comes in the door, they are given an identifying number. The holders of the numbers are assigned to tables by the FIFO rule. This situation may be modeled within an array, Q, of maximum index 20. For example, suppose that three patrons enter after the tables are full, then one is seated, and another enters. If waiting slips are numbered beginning at 40 tonight, then snapshots of the queue might look like this:

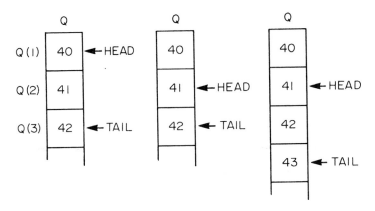

The queue is really the items between those pointed to by HEAD and TAIL. One may think of the queue as an inchworm, working its way along Q. Deletion from a queue actually means moving HEAD, and adding to the queue moves TAIL.

Adding an item to the queue decreases the space still available in Q, but deleting an item from the queue does not, in itself, increase the space available in Q. There is a sharp difference between Q and the queue—the former is the physical storage for the latter. In the second snapshot above, the queue is 41, 42 although 40 is still in Q(1). At that point, HEAD = 2 and TAIL = 3. If more additions and deletions are made, the queue will move down the array until addition is requested into Q(21), which cannot be done. At that point, there are really two possible situations:

1. The queue has 20 members and no more can be added (no room in the lobby).

2. The queue has less than 20 members. There are several options for dealing with this situation, before or after it arises. We will take the simple route, and simply shift the whole queue back down the array until HEAD points to Q(1) again. (Getting a new pad of waiting slips is *not* modeled by this, since the queue is not rebuilt, it is merely shifted in its *physical* location.)

We shall treat the overall task of creating and managing a queue from user commands, R$, which are *request options* for addition, deletion, and listing: With appropriate instructions to the user, this general model could serve as a simulation of the restaurant waiting line in the example above. The general plan of attack is:

procedure LOBBY
    print (instructions and available options)
    repeat
       HEAD ← 0 : TAIL ← 0
       input $R\$$ //$R\$$ is the request option//
       case of $R\$$
         : addition :
         : deletion :
         : listing :
       endcase
       if (task complete) **then exit**
    forever
end LOBBY

The addition case must first check to see if the queue is full (TAIL = 20 and HEAD = 1). If it is, then the program should let the user abort the run or enter a new request. If the queue is not full, but Q is full (TAIL = 20 but HEAD ≠ 1), then the queue should be shifted within Q (by procedure SHIFT, say). Given room for the entry of a new ID (a value stored in a queue position), a procedure called ADD can make the actual addition.

The deletion case should delete the head of the queue and display the deleted ID.

The listing case should list the currently active members of the queue.

When the cases are detailed (in terms of the procedures which they call), LOBBY becomes:

procedure LOBBY
  print (instructions and available options)
  repeat
    HEAD ← 0 //initialization required for some of the//
    TAIL ← 0 //queue-managing routines//
    input $R\$$ //$R\$$ is the request option.//
    case of $R\$$
      : addition : **if** (queue is full)
              then print "NO ROOM IN THE ARK"
                   exit
              endif
             if (Q is full)
              then procedure SHIFT //moves the entire//
                            //queue within Q//
              endif
             procedure ADD //input ID and add it as//
                    . //the new tail//
      : deletion : **procedure** EXTRACT //deletes the head of//
                        //the queue and dis-//
                        //plays the deleted ID//
      : listing :   **procedure** LISTING //lists the currently//
                        //active members of//
                        //the queue//
    endcase
    if (task complete) **then exit**
  forever
end LOBBY

We are left with the definition of the subtasks used in managing the queue. They may serve as models for general queue handling.

8.7 QUEUE HANDLING

The subtasks of management are simplified because the managing routine LOBBY creates the queue and checks for space limitations in both Q and the queue itself.

The ADD procedure does not need to change HEAD, unless ID is the initial entry into the queue:

procedure ADD //$R\$ \leftarrow$ "A"//
   input *ID*
   if HEAD $= 0$ **then** HEAD $\leftarrow 1$
   TAIL $\leftarrow$ TAIL $+ 1$
   Q(TAIL) $\leftarrow$ *ID*
end ADD

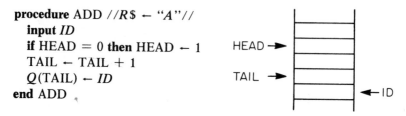

The SHIFT procedure begins with TAIL $\leftarrow 20$, and HEAD $\leftarrow 1$. It must copy Q(HEAD) to $Q(1)$, Q(HEAD $+ 1$) to $Q(2)$, ... Hence the shift is of the form: $Q(I) \leftarrow Q(I + J)$, where I is initially 1 and $I + J$ is initially HEAD, and I is incremented by 1 each time through a loop. The process should stop when $Q(20)$ is copied. The position into which $Q(20)$ moves is the new TAIL position:

procedure SHIFT
   $I \leftarrow 0$
   $J \leftarrow$ HEAD $- 1$
   while $I + J < 20$ **do**
      $I \leftarrow I + 1$
      $Q(I) \leftarrow Q(I + J)$
   endwhile
   HEAD $\leftarrow 1$
   TAIL $\leftarrow I$
end SHIFT

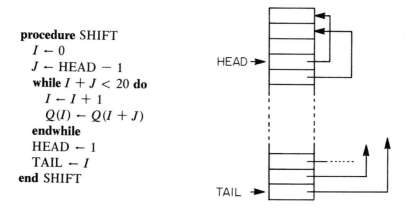

If the request option, $R\$$, is "X" for extraction, then not only will the head of the queue be moved, but the deleted item will be displayed. The procedure EXTRACT must take care of the problem of an already empty queue and one which this operation empties:

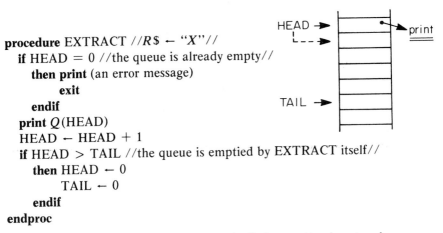

procedure EXTRACT //R\$ ← "X"//
   if HEAD = 0 //the queue is already empty//
     then print (an error message)
         exit
     endif
   print Q(HEAD)
   HEAD ← HEAD + 1
   if HEAD > TAIL //the queue is emptied by EXTRACT itself//
     then HEAD ← 0
         TAIL ← 0
     endif
endproc

If the request option, R\$, is "L", then the listing routine is entered:

procedure LISTING //R\$ ← "L"//
   I ← HEAD
   while I ≤ TAIL **do**
     print Q(I)
     I ← I + 1
   endwhile
end LISTING

With appropriate variations of LOBBY and the subtasks it uses, any queue of this type can be similarly managed, and so we will not be explicit about queue handling in the applications which follow. The general routines for adding and deleting from a queue will be referred to by **enqueue** and **dequeue** in pseudocode.

8.8 SIMULATION

A technique for the computer modeling of realistic situations which is spreading into many fields is computer **simulation**. This means simply that a computer is used to emulate some process by modeling its behavior. Generally the pretense is carried out again and again, with some aspects of the model changed for each pass through the process. Quite often, some of the **parameters**, variables which help to define the model, are randomly chosen for each pass. Then statistics may be gathered about what happened how often in so many runs. In a **game simulation**, the program may pretend, for example, to be a covered wagon trek across the American plains. Events are chosen at random, with reasonable probabilities of occurrence. The player gathers statistics about how often hostile raiders or dry water holes are encountered simply by playing many times and gaining a feel for their effects within the model. In other simulations, the program loops through the model many times, and prints only a final report of the frequencies with which various values of the parameters occur.

We shall develop a minimal simulation in which a queue is involved, and the program reports its average size during a run. Once this basic model has been developed, however, it is possible to upgrade it to a more sophisticated model.

8.9   A GROCERY STORE SIMULATION

Consider a very small grocery store. This store has one door by which customers enter, one rack of carts, one long aisle, and one checkout lane, in which a queue of impatient customers form. The owner would like to know how long the waiting line generally is, in order to help decide whether to add another checkout lane, or not. The store operates as follows:

Customers enter the store, take a cart from the rack, dawdle along the aisle for some length of time, get into the queue (if it is not empty) in front of the checker, and when the customer in front of them is finished, go through the checkout process for a while, and then return the cart to the rack. If they do not pass each other, the customers in the aisle and the checkout lane form a queue. If customers always leave before another arrives, then the store owner has problems that our simulation can not help, and there would be no checkout queue anyway.

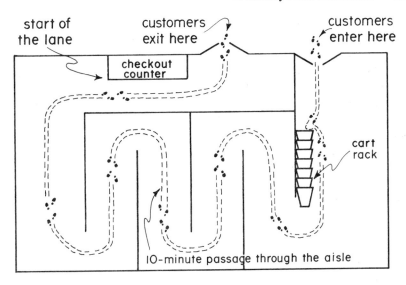

start of the lane

customers exit here

customers enter here

checkout counter

cart rack

10-minute passage through the aisle

The waiting line (together with the aisle) can be modeled as a simple queue, like the lobby of a restaurant. The queue model can be turned into a simulation by simply choosing random arrivals (additions) and departures (deletions), both chosen within reasonable ranges of values which represent the times between arrivals and the times between departures. The time between arrivals is called the **interarrival time**, but that is not the same as the time between events in the simulation. Departures are also events of interest, and in most simulations there are many kinds of events involved, often associated with random occurrences which are *independent* of the arrivals. The simulation is managed by looking for the *next* event, whether an arrival, a departure, or something else. The time between an event which has just occurred and the next event is the **event time**. All of the possible sources of events must be searched to find the next event, and it is event time which drives the simulation from one state of the system to another. By a **state** of the system, we mean a set of the contents of those stacks, queues, and counters which are affected by the events. If two such sets are affected the same way by every possible event, then they would be considered to be the same state. If such a set can be affected in more than one way by an event, then it would be taken to describe more than one state.

The statistics that can be generated by simply managing a queue which represents the waiting line are the average number of customers in the line, and the maximum size of the line. Each run of 100 customer arrivals (or departures) will generate an answer to these questions, and multiple runs will yield information concerning the *reproducibility* of such statistics. There are other aspects of the situation which can be added to the model. For example, one limitation of the capacity of the store to serve customers is the number of shopping carts, which may behave as a stack (the last cart added will be the one removed by the next customer to arrive). Again, there are statistics of interest, such as how many times there were no carts available for a new customer during the run, and on the average how many carts are available (hence unused) during the run.

A parameter of very real interest for a grocery store simulation is the average length of time that a customer spends in the store. The simple queue with unidentified arrivals and departures cannot yield this informa- tion. If a *mark* (customer) is added as the seventh item in a queue, it may eventually reach the head of the queue and be removed, but that gives no indication of how *long* it took for seven departures to occur. It is possible to determine this information (the *residence time* in the queue) in more than one way. For example, a time associated with the mark may start at 0 when it enters the queue, and whenever another event occurs, the amount of time which has elapsed since the previous event could be added to the mark's time. On exit from the queue, the mark's time is the total time spent in the queue. With such an approach, if there is more than one queue, one must derive average total times of passage through the system from the sum of average times through individual queues. An alternate approach, naming (or numbering) the marks individually and tracking each of them through the entire system, also has complications when there is more than one queue in the system.

The grocery store simulation will be handled in a way which differs from those mentioned above. The grocery store *model* we will implement has a single queue, the waiting line, and a single stack, the carts. The model is designed to determine the average number of customers in the line and the average number of inactive carts. One complication will be added to the *simulation,* however: a 10 minute delay, chosen arbitrarily as a reasonable number, will be introduced to represent the passage through the aisle. The aisle then becomes the queue of interest, and customers enter it with 10 minutes to spend in it. As events occur, a customer in the aisle has less and less time to spend there. The amount of time left for a mark before departure from the aisle queue is kept up to date by subtracting the time since the previous event each time an event occurs in the simulation. Since only the average number of customers in the waiting line is of interest, the line becomes simply a counter which is incremented by arrivals from the aisle and decremented by check outs. Becoming a counter is often the fate of the queues of a real-world model when it is simulated by a program.

The reason that the aisle must be programmed using a queue instead of a counter is that the customers are individualized by having varying amounts of time left before their exit from the aisle. Furthermore, the *number* of events between entry and exit will differ from one customer to the next because the interarrival times and checkouts are randomly chosen.

Before an algorithm for the simulation is developed, it is worthwhile to determine the parameters and the events of interest. The logic of the algorithm will then be determined by relationships between them:

If customers arrive 1 to 5 minutes apart (an arbitrary choice), then the interarrival time, say CAT, will satisfy $1 \leq CAT \leq 5$. CAT will be randomly generated within this range. An arriving customer will take a cart from the rack, and so the number of available carts is RACK. One of the statistics of interest is the average value of RACK at customer-arrival times. To determine that value, we may sum the values of RACK in a variable CART, and then divide by the total number of customers involved in a simulation run.

CUSTOMER ARRIVALS

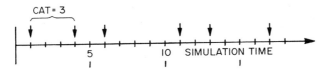

If customers are checked out in 2 to 10 minutes (an arbitrary choice), then the time from one checkout to the next, CKT, will satisfy

$$2 \leq CKT \leq 10.$$

CKT will be randomly generated within this range. Let LANE be the waiting-line counter, and let the number of customers actually checked out be LANENO. LANENO may not be the number of customers involved in a run, because the run may stop while customers are left waiting for checkout. One of the statistics of interest is the average value of LANE, and so (like RACK above) it may be summed in a variable, say WAIT. At the end of the simulation, WAIT/LANENO is the average of LANE.

The heart of the model is SQUEUE, the shopping queue of customers in the aisle, which is stored in the array SQ. A mark enters SQUEUE simply as a value, 10 (minutes), and leaves when it has the value 0. At each event, the value of the mark is diminished, but is always larger than the values of the marks behind it in SQUEUE, since they entered later.

The value of a mark is always the time left until it will leave SQUEUE, and it is updated at every event. The time at which it reaches zero *causes* an event to happen. Hence, the value of the mark at the head of the queue, say ST, is of special interest because it helps to determine the next event to occur: CAT is regenerated each time a customer arrives, and CKT is regenerated each time a customer leaves the checkout lane. *The minimum value of CAT, CKT, and ST should determine the next event, hence it is the event time.* Each time that an event occurs, then,

1. The event time calculated at the previous event is subtracted from CAT, CKT, and the marks in SQUEUE.

2. The appropriate counters and sums are updated.

3. The new event time is calculated from CAT, CKT, and ST.

The simulation consists of examining the three possible events (customer arrival, checkout, and a move from the aisle to the checkout lane), deciding which comes next, making the adjustments in the counters, queues, and times which that event represents, and repeating this cycle until some number, say 100, of customers have arrived. In order to see how the simulation might progress, consider the following choices of interarrival times for the first six customers:

customer	initial CAT
1	1
2	3
3	2
4	5
5	2
6	4

Suppose also, that the first two choices of the next checkout value CKT are 5 and 7. With these values, events will occur as shown in the table which follows. The time to the next event is circled, and the head of SQUEUE is underlined. We have been careful to avoid adjusting the check out time when no checking is being done: when no one is actually in the checkout lane.

Customer	Time	Next Arrival (CAT)	Next Checkout (CKT)	(LANENO)	Next Lane Entry (SQUEUE)
–	0	①	5	0	empty
1	1	③	5	0	10,
2	4	②	5	0	7, 10
3	6	⑤	5	0	5, 8, 10
4	11	2	5	0	⓪, 3, 5, 10
	11	②	5	1	0, 3, 5, 10
5	13	4	3	1	0, ①, 3, 8
	14	3	②	2	0, 0, 2, 7
	16	1	7	1	0, 0, ⓪, 5
	16	①	7	2	0, 0, 0, 5

EXERCISE

E8.1 Continue this table as far as possible, given that the next five initial values of CAT are 3, 1, 4, 2, 3 and that the next three initial values of CKT are 2, 6, 5.

The simulation may be blocked out by:

procedure STORE
  //initialize SQUEUE, the counters and the sums, and choose//
  //initial values for CKT, CAT, and ST//
  $I \leftarrow 0$
  while $I \leq 100$ **do**
    procedure NEXT //determine the next event ET to be one//
                     //of CAT, CKT, or ST//
    case of ET
      : CAT : **procedure** ARRIVE //I is incremented by ARRIVE//
      : ST :   **procedure** PAY
      : CKT : **procedure** LEAVE
    endcase
  endwhile
  CART $\leftarrow$ CART/100
  WAIT $\leftarrow$ WAIT/LANENO
  print (an output report)
end STORE

In order to move from one event to the next, any one of CAT, CKT, or ST must be subtracted from every item in SQUEUE and from the other two. It is worthwhile, then, to provide a single routine for this operation:

procedure SHAVE(X)
  if HEAD $= 0$ **then exit**
  $I \leftarrow$ HEAD
  while $I \leq$ TAIL **do**
    SQ(I) $\leftarrow$ SQ(I) $- X$
    $I \leftarrow I + 1$
  endwhile
  ST $\leftarrow$ SQ(HEAD)
end SHAVE

When the treatment of counters and sums are added, along with SHAVE, to STORE we have:

```
procedure STORE
  LANENO ← 0 : LANE ← 0 : RACK ← 50 : WAIT ← 0
  ST ← 0 : SQ(0) ← 0 : HEAD ← 0 : TAIL ← 0
  CKT ← INT(2 + RND*9)
  CAT ← INT(1 + RND*5)
  I ← 0
  while I ≤ 100 do
    proc NEXT //determine next event ET. If LANE = 0 then//
              //ignore CKT. In case of a tie do CAT, ST,//
              //CKT in that order.//
    case of ET
      : CAT : ARRIVE //adjust CKT, do SHAVE(CAT), enqueue//
                     //SQUEUE, adjust CART, decrement RACK,//
                     //generate CAT, and increment I//
        : ST : PAY   //do SHAVE(ST), dequeue SQUEUE, adjust//
                     //CAT and CKT, increment LANE//
      : CKT : LEAVE  //adjust CAT, do SHAVE(CKT), adjust WAIT,//
                     //decrement LANE, increment LANENO,//
                     //generate CKT, and increment RACK//
    endcase
  endwhile
  CART ← CART/100
  WAIT ← WAIT/LANENO
  print CART, WAIT, LANE, LANENO, RACK
end STORE
```

The detail procedures ARRIVE and LEAVE are almost direct translations of the comments in the pseudocode above:

procedure ARRIVE
    if LANE $\geq$ 1 **then** CKT $\leftarrow$ CKT $-$ CAT
    procedure SHAVE(CAT)
    enqueue SQUEUE
    $I \leftarrow I + 1$
    CART $\leftarrow$ CART + RACK
    RACK $\leftarrow$ RACK $-$ 1
    CAT $\leftarrow$ INT(1 + RND*5)
end ARRIVE

procedure LEAVE
    CAT $\leftarrow$ CAT $-$ CKT
    procedure SHAVE(CKT)
    WAIT $\leftarrow$ WAIT + LANE
    LANE $\leftarrow$ LANE $-$ 1
    RACK $\leftarrow$ RACK + 1
    LANENO $\leftarrow$ LANENO + 1
    CKT $\leftarrow$ INT(2 + RND*9)
end LEAVE

Procedure PAY requires some special care because SHAVE changes the values in SQUEUE, and in fact will change SQ(HEAD) to 0 by subtracting it from itself. Hence in this case, the new ST is incorrectly computed by SHAVE. We must be careful to use the old value of ST to update CAT and CKT, then apply SHAVE, then move the head of the queue, then finally derive the correct new ST from the new head of the queue (if there is one).

procedure PAY
    CAT $\leftarrow$ CAT $-$ ST
    if LANE $\geq$ 1 **then** CKT $\leftarrow$ CKT $-$ ST
    LANE $\leftarrow$ LANE + 1
    procedure SHAVE(SQ(HEAD)) //SQ(HEAD) is the old ST, which//
                                        //will be set to 0 by SHAVE.//
    dequeue SQUEUE //this will determine a new HEAD//
    if HEAD $\neq$ 0
      then ST $\leftarrow$ SQ(HEAD)
      else ST $\leftarrow$ 0
      endif
end PAY

The simulation STORE could be upgraded by making the shopping times random over an interval from 5 to 15 minutes, and by keeping track of the *time* spent in the lane. The first of these improvements might require keeping shopping times sorted in a list. The second would use a queue for the checkout lane instead of a counter. It is more standard procedure to run the simulation until a set number of entries *finishes* it, rather than begins it. Finally, the ranges of times for CKT, CAT, and shopping should be under user control instead of set within the program. Adding more checkout lanes becomes a major project, hence a simulation language GASP, GPSS, or SIMSCRIPT would normally be used to make the programming easier.

8.10   STATISTICS

The information gleaned from the simulation STORE was valuable, but more can be gotten without much difficulty. For example, we have ignored what happens when all of the carts are gone. Most likely, the customers go away or become annoyed. We could count disgruntled customers as a hidden cost. If we were to keep track of the time customers spend in the lane, then we could generate a *distribution* of waiting times: so many wait

no time, so many wait more than 0 minutes but less than 4, etc. Similar information could be generated for the number of carts available. In both cases, what is needed is a whole family of counters, perhaps in a one-dimensional array. For example, $C(1)$ might be used to count the 0-time waits, $C(2)$ the waits of 0 to 4 minutes, and so on.

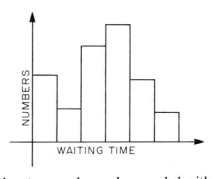

We began with no customers in the store, and may have ended with some still in SQUEUE and in the check-out lane. It is common to run such a simulation for a while in order to let the store (or whatever is being simulated) arrive at "normal" conditions, then begin counting without reinitializing. The point of delaying the start of statistics gathering is that the specialized conditions set up by the initialization may affect the statistical results of the simulation. The question of what is "normal" and how long to wait before gathering statistics has no easy answer. Simulations are normally run many times, and a statistical analysis is made of the output. That analysis must be done with care to prevent it from being misleading.

8.11 SIMULATION LANGUAGES

Simulation is an important area of research, and a number of programming languages have been developed to make simulation of real world models easier. These simulation languages tend to be "command languages," in which simple commands create queues and counters and generate random values. Furthermore, a great deal of statistical information can be kept and reported by them through simple commands. Most simulation language translators are very large, however, and such languages are not available on many systems, or cheap. The only recourse for the user of a small system that is available at the present time is to write simulations from scratch, as we have done in this chapter. Such a project is not feasible without a great deal of attention to the careful structuring of the program.

SELF-REVIEW

1. The replacement cost of a given item in the inventory of a business may vary with receiving date. If reordering is done before an item is out of stock, the items in stock will not all have cost the same amount. What are the advantages and disadvantages of treating the inventory (items and costs) as a stack? as a queue?

2. Are the magazines at a doctor's office a stack, a queue, or a combination of the two?

3. How do you determine the average size of a stack during a procedure in which it is activated more than once? the average size of a queue? the maximum and minimum size of a stack or a queue?

4. In procedure MOUSE (page 216), why is **if** $F = 2$ **then exit** placed outside of procedure CHECKSTEP?

5. In procedure LOBBY (page 221), is it possible to switch the check for a full queue and a full Q? If so, would any of the routines of LOBBY need to be altered?

6. Is it possible to switch the order of routines CAT, ST, and CKT chosen in NEXT when there is a tie in event time?

7. What is the purpose of the condition LANE $\geq$ 1 on the adjustment of CKT in procedures ARRIVE (page 232) and PAY (page 232)?

PROBLEMS

Write the following in pseudocode.

P8.1 Rewrite procedure FINDSTEP so that the next step is determined randomly rather than in clockwise order.

P8.2 Write **enqueue**, **dequeue**, and listing procedures for a list-supported queue.

P8.3 Write **enqueue**, **dequeue**, and listing procedures for a queue supported by an array which appears to be circular: $Q(1)$ follows $Q(\text{maximum})$.

P8.4 Write **enqueue**, **dequeue**, and listing procedures for a queue supported by a list which is in turn supported on an array which appears to be circular. Note that this is not really a circular list in the sense of *linking* the last item to the first.

P8.5 Write the procedures required for an initialization run of STORE, prior to the start of statistics gathering.

P8.6 Write the procedures required to keep track of waiting times of patrons in the restaurant simulation.

P8.7 Write the procedures required to find the distribution of time spent in the lane and the distribution of cart availability in STORE.

PROGRAMS

PG8.1 Write the program required to simulate the pop-up tray holder in a cafeteria. Customers arrive at random intervals, a load of clean trays is added occasionally, and the holder has a maximum size. Run it.

PG8.2 The bins of a warehouse can be modeled as stacks. Write a program which models a five-bin warehouse. The user of the program should be allowed to input an item for bin storage and withdraw an item using a simple description of the item. The program itself should sort the items into the correct bin, or locate them. Addition to full bins is to be denied, as is deletion from empty bins. Empty (or low) inventories generated by a deletion are to produce reorder messages. The program is to keep data on the average size of the stacks, the frequency of reorder messages for each bin, and the number of overfull stacks.

PG8.3   Write a program to manage a stack, *S,* containing marked items, which may need to be retrieved when they are not on top of the stack. Retrieval is done by popping from *S* and pushing the popped item onto an auxilliary stack, *S'*, until the desired mark is located, then removing it, then reversing the pops and pushes in order to empty *S'*. For example, m2 is retrieved in this manner from *S* below:

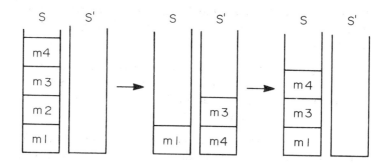

Such a program simulates some of the operations of a long-distance moving van which can hold the belongings of several customers at one time. It also serves as a model for almost any storage area around the house, or the local lumber yard.

PG8.4   Write a program for the retrieval problem of PG8.3 with the additional assumption that *S'* is also an active stack and hence the roles of *S* and *S'* switch back and forth upon demand.

PG8.5   It is possible to combine the stack and the queue into a single data structure, which is called a **deque**. This is a queue which behaves as a stack at the tail end. Such a structure can be emptied from the tail end as well as the head. Write procedures to manage a deque, and run them.

PROJECTS

The comments at the beginning of the project section in Chapter 3 also apply to the following:

PJ8.1   Code and run one of the simulations described in this chapter. Run it ten times and observe the variations in the output. (Do not forget to use RANDOMIZE.)

PJ8.2   The restaurant queue procedures in this chapter may be incorporated into a simulation by providing arrivals at random intervals, table vacancies at random intervals, and keeping track of some statistics. Table vacancies may also be generated as random values within a reasonable range of time spent eating. Some suggested statistics are:

   a. The average number of people in the lobby, the maximum number, the percentage of time the lobby is full, and the percentage of time it is empty.
   b. The average length of time spent in the lobby (individual entries must be tracked.)
   c. The average total length of time spent in the restaurant.
   d. The average number and the maximum number of people stacked up at the door, unable to get in.
   e. The number of people who become impatient after a too-long wait and leave, either outside of the door, or while in the lobby.

PJ8.3   Write a restaurant simulation in which the seating capacity of the tables is taken into account. Separate queues may be kept for each size, but if, for example, the parties-of-2 queue gets large enough, such parties may be seated at parties-of-4 tables even though the parties-of-4 queue is not empty. Run it.

PJ8.4   In STORE, if customers spend randomly chosen amounts of time in the aisle, then a sorted, linked list can be used to keep track of ST instead of SQUEUE. Write the procedures for creating and managing this list. Run them.

PJ8.5   Assume in STORE that there are two check-out lanes, and customers always choose the shortest line to join. Write the procedures required to manage this simulation. Run them.

PJ8.6   Model a railroad switching yard with whatever stacks queues, or deques are required.

PJ8.7   Telephone switching provides a whole family of simulation problems. As one simple example, simulate a trunk-line with five circuits. Generate calls at random, with random lengths for the calls, and keep them in a sorted, linked list. They may be adjusted by event time, as were the items in SQUEUE. When all five circuits of the trunk line are tied up, the call is denied. When a call is over, it frees a circuit. Generate statistics on the usage of the circuits.

A more challenging variation of this problem involves destination phones (which may be busy), as well as trunk-lines.

PJ8.8   Develop a *simulation* of PJ7.6, over a month, with reasonable numbers of (random) check-ins and check-outs. Report the percent occupancy of single rooms, double rooms, and suites.

PJ8.9   Write a program which simulates a one-barber shop with five chairs during an eight-hour day. Randomly generate customer arrivals (15 ± 5 minutes) and haircut times (12 ± 4 minutes). Report the number of customers that are immediately served, the amount of time the barber is busy, and the average number of customers who must wait for service. It is more challenging to determine the average amount of time that customers who wait must spend in the shop.

Chapter 9

TREE-LIKE STRUCTURES

9.1 GENERAL TREES

The data structures which have been discussed in previous chapters are convenient and natural models for many situations which can be studied with computer programs. Arrays, tables, lists, stacks, queues, and files are natural data structures in a variety of situations, and may be useful in many more. None of them are appropriate, however, for a large class of widely-used models—trees. For example, a tree is a 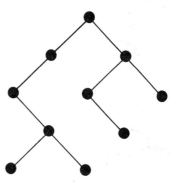 suitable model for the kind of relationship which occurs in the following examples:

> genealogy (family trees)
> the derivations of languages, species, or peoples from a root stock
> the taxonomy structure used to develop field guides to plants or birds
> tournament pairings
> the table of contents of a book
> possible move sequences in a game
> the structure of a record in a file

The geometrical model for these structures looks something like the following:

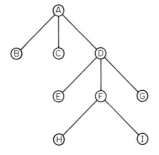

A—Student record
B—Name
C—Number
D—Scores
E—Test 1
F—Test 2
G—Test 3
H—Part 1
I—Part 2

The linking between the **nodes** A, B, ..., I is not clear in the simple list at the right of the tree, but it can be indicated by appropriate numbering, indenting, and ordering as was done in Chapter 6 where this record structure was initially outlined. The *relationships* between the nodes (fields) of the record are easily seen in the geometric model. If these relationships are important, then they need to be expressed in *any* model of the record. However, the geometric content of a tree model needs to be dispensed with when a tree is formally defined, and when it is represented within a computer program. Removal of the geometry requires the determination of the pattern of relationships between nodes that is common to all trees.

Trees have nodes and links, but so do linked lists. Trees, however, differ from linked lists in that a tree node may have more than one successor, or **child**. In the record example, A has *three* children: B, C, and D. A common feature is that both a tree and a linked list have a first element, which for a tree is called a **root node**. The root node is distinguished by the property that it is not the child of any other node. The node A in our example is a root node. Finally, a tree differs from a more general collection of linked nodes like the following:

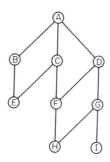

This structure is called a **graph**, and a tree is a restricted form of graph. The essential restriction is that in a tree, a child of a parent node has no links to another child (**sibling**) of the parent, or to a child of a child of a sibling, etc. For example,

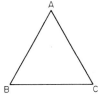

is not a tree because of the link between B and C.

Neither is 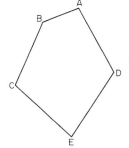 because there is a sequence of

links and nodes which connects A to E through D, and another which connects A to E that does not involve D. The node E is said to be **reachable** from
A by either sequence A, D, E or by A, B, C, E. In a tree, all of the nodes
reachable from one child are different from the nodes reachable from a sibling of that child. This in turn implies that each child is itself a root node of a
tree, a **subtree** of the original tree. For the student record example, the subtrees beginning with the children of A are:

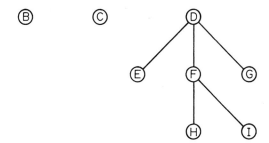

With all of this in mind, a definition of a tree can be given:

A tree has the following properties:

1. There is a root node R, linked to a (possibly empty) set of children $C_1, C_2, \ldots, C_n$ of R.

2. Each child C_i (if there are any) is itself the root node of a tree T_i.

3. The trees $T_1, \ldots, T_n$ are all *disjoint*—they have no nodes in common.

This is a **recursive definition** in the sense that if we are given a collection of nodes and links and wish to find out if the collection forms a tree, we would apply the definition to the root node, then to each child of that node, then to each child of each child, etc. This definition is rather difficult to use in practice, since with its direct application, eventually one of two things would happen:

1. Every branch leads to distinct nodes with no children (**leaf nodes**), which *do* satisfy the definition. If every child of a node is a leaf node, then that node roots a tree. The *parent* of such (disjoint) roots is the root of a tree. Eventually we could work our way back to the root node of the entire collection. Consider the following tree:

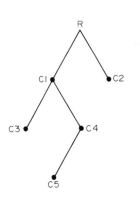

1. R is linked to $C1$ and $C2$.

2. $C2$ is a leaf node, hence the root of a tree with an empty set of children.

3. $C1$ is linked to $C3$ and $C4$.

4. $C3$ is a leaf node.

5. $C4$ is linked to $C5$.

6. $C5$ is a leaf node.

7. By 5 and 6, $C4$ is the root of a subtree.

8. By 3, 4, and 7, $C1$ is the root of a subtree.

9. By 1, 2, and 8, R is a tree.

2. Two subtrees, with root nodes X and Y for example, have a node in common, in which case the subtrees rooted by the *parents* of X and Y are not disjoint, hence their parents do not root disjoint subtrees, and

so on. Eventually we arrive at children of the root node of the entire collection which do not root disjoint trees, and hence the collection does not satisfy the definition. For example:

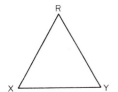

X is the child of Y (as well as of R), hence X and Y have a common node, namely X. (Similarly, Y is a common node of these subtrees.) Hence R does not root a tree.

If the definition of a tree is carried out on a graph of arbitrary complexity, then the problem of forming and carrying out an organized search which follows paths down to the leaves, all of the leaves, once and only once, can be impractical. For example, if a graph has N nodes, there may be as many as $N - 1$ paths to follow from the root node. For each of these there may be $N - 1$ paths to follow further. This are already $(N - 1)^2$ possible paths. As the search continues, the number of possible paths which must be checked for common nodes gets to be too large to deal with in a reasonable time and in a storage area of reasonable size. One of the useful things about trees themselves is that they are more reasonable to search through than is a graph. Each node is linked to children, and they in turn are linked to other children, but each path eventually leads to a leaf node. With N nodes, at one extreme we have one root and $N - 1$ children ($N - 1$ paths), and at the other extreme, one path with one child per root:

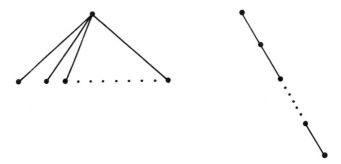

There are no more than $N - 1$ paths, and the more there are, the shorter they are.

The algorithms for searching or otherwise processing a tree-like structure are greatly simplified if the nodes are reorganized into a somewhat different, but related form, called a binary tree. (We will use the acronym *bitree* for binary tree in the sections which follow.)

9.2 BINARY TREES

A **binary tree (bitree)** is a tree-like structure with the property that there are only two possible children for any node, a **left child** and a **right child**. The children of the nodes of a (general) tree are not necessarily considered to be ordered. (An ordering convention can be adopted, if desired.) For example, the following *trees* are usually considered to be the same:

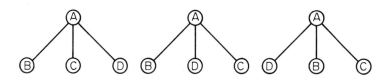

In contrast, the following, as *binary trees*, are distinct:

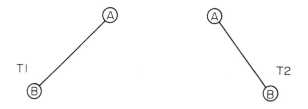

The distinction is that node *A* in *T*1 has a *left* child but no right child, whereas in the bitree *T*2, node *A* has a *right* child but no left child.

A tree is a natural pattern to use for many applications, but a binary tree is a more convenient and efficient pattern to use as a data structure, because each node has precisely two links—one to the left child, and one to the right child. (A special link value is used to indicate that a child is missing.) Fortunately, there are ways to transform a tree into a bitree. Here is one such transformation:

1. Draw the tree, or otherwise determine an order for the siblings of each node.

2. The linkage for the corresponding bitree is as follows:

    a. The left child of a node *N* of the bitree is its first child (if any) in the tree, and

    b. the right child of a node *N* of the bitree is its adjacent tree *sibling* (if any) on the right.

Consider the student record of the previous section. It is transformed from a tree into a bitree in stages as follows:

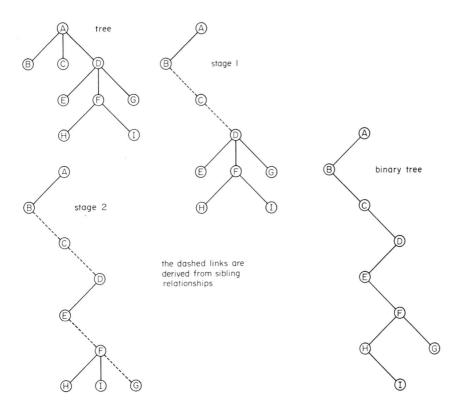

the dashed links are
derived from sibling
relationships

A binary tree like the one above has the advantage for program storage that each node requires only three storage cells—the node cell, a link to the left child, and a link to the right child. The multiple siblings of a general tree require links to an arbitrary number of possible children. We will denote the links to the children of a node N of a binary tree as LCHILD(N) and RCHILD(N). We can then store the nodes and the links of the binary tree above in three arrays as indicated below:

I	NODE(I)	LCHILD(I)	RCHILD(I)
1	A	2	0
2	B	0	3
3	C	0	4
4	D	5	0
5	E	0	6
6	F	8	7
7	G	0	0
8	H	0	9
9	I	0	0

9.3 BINARY TREE TRAVERSAL

Suppose that the original tree structure is to be recovered from the corresponding binary tree. For example, it may be desired to print all of the children of a given node. This involves two tasks:

1. Search through (traverse) the binary tree until the given node is located.

2. Print the left child of the found node, and then the right child of that left child, and then the right child of that right child, etc., until it is no longer possible to traverse to the right. (Traversal stops when a link value of zero is encountered.)

Item 2 is similar to following a linked list, using RCHILD(P) rather than FLINK(P) to follow the links. Item 1 requires procedures which are different from those involved in searching other data structures. It differs because of the branches which must be taken, and the paths which must be retraced after a leaf node is reached. When one branch is taken from a node, N, during a traversal, it will generally be necessary to return to N later in the traversal in order to take the other branch. The necessary backtracking information is provided by using a stack, either with explicit programming, or with the use of programming languages which support recursive procedures (those which may call themselves). The support for the recursive procedures is itself done through the management of transparent stacks.

In the design of a traversal there are three things which can be done when a node is reached: traverse left (L), traverse right (R), or process the node (P). By "process the node" is meant "to carry out the purpose of the search"; print the contents of the node, or compare the node value to another value, etc. There are six ways to permute these three operations:

LPR, LRP, PLR, RLP, PRL, or RPL

The usual convention is to always traverse left before traversing right, which leaves only the first three options, and they differ from each other only in the position of the processing step. These three standard types of traverse are called **inorder** (LPR), **preorder** (PLR), and **postorder** (LRP). The left-right visitation process itself is common to all three standard forms of bitree traversal, and may be described as:

1. Traverse left as far as possible (until the LCHILD link is zero).

2. Backtrack to the last node at which a left branch but no right branch was taken. If there is no such node, then stop.

3. Move right one node if possible, and repeat at step 1, else repeat at step 2.

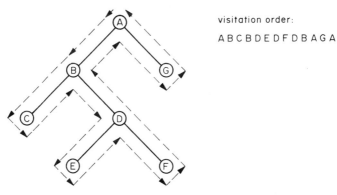

visitation order:

A B C B D E D F D B A G A

The central programming problem involved in the writing of a procedure to carry out a traversal is the development of an algorithm which backtracks properly. This is done with a stack, STACK, which is managed with essentially the same routines discussed in Chapter 8:

```
procedure POP(P)                    procedure PUSH(P)
    if TOP = 0 then exit                if TOP ≥ (maximum index)
    P ← STACK(TOP)                          then print (warning message)
    TOP ← TOP − 1                               exit
return                                  endif
                                        TOP ← TOP + 1
                                        STACK(TOP) ← P
                                    return
```

The items which are kept in STACK are the addresses—indices of cells in the array(s) in which the nodes are stored. Each standard type of traversal has its natural applications, and deserves some discussion.

9.3.1   Inorder Traversal

If we assume that a bitree is to be stored in an array NODE, then the LPR traversal may be described by:

0. Initialize a node pointer P to LCHILD(0). (a pointer to the root node).

1. Traverse left by repeating $P \leftarrow$ LCHILD(P) while $P \neq 0$. The values of the pointer P are pushed onto the stack as they are encountered.

2. If TOP $= 0$ then stop. Pop the top value of the stack as P (it points to the last node which led to LCHILD(P) $= 0$ and also has not yet been processed). Process NODE(P).

3. Set P to RCHILD(P), and repeat at step 1.

The resulting procedure is:

```
procedure LPRT
  P ← LCHILD(0) //a pointer to the root node//
  repeat
    while P ≠ 0 do //traverse left as far as possible//
      push P
      P ← LCHILD(P)
    endwhile
    if TOP = 0
      then exit //stack is empty—all nodes processed//
      else pop P
        process NODE(P)
        P ← RCHILD(P) //traverse right one node//
    endif
  forever
endproc
```

Consider the binary tree at right:

If **process** NODE(P) is interpreted as **print** NODE(P), then the LPR traverse order should produce:

    C B E D F A G

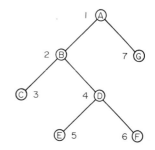

The action of procedure LPRT on this bitree may be traced by displaying the value of P and the stack each time **endwhile** and each time **forever** are reached. Here is such a trace, which assumes the indices indicated for the nodes:

	P	2	3	0	0	4	5	0	0	6	0	0	7	0	0	0
STACK	**endwhile**	1	1 2	1 2 3			1 4	1 4 5			1 6			7			
	forever				1 2	1			1 4	1		1	—		—	exit
OUTPUT					C	B			E	D		F	A		G	

9.3.2 Preorder Traversal

The PLR traversal differs from the LPR traversal in that nodes are processed as they are encountered, rather than when they are unstacked. The PLR traversal may be described by:

0. Initialize the node pointer P to LCHILD(0). (a pointer to the root node).

1. Traverse left by repeating $P \leftarrow$ LCHILD(P) while $P \neq 0$. As each node is encountered, process it and then push its pointer value onto the stack.

2. If TOP $= 0$ then quit. Pop the top value of the stack as P.

3. Set P to RCHILD(P), and repeat at step 1.

The resulting procedure is:

procedure PLRT
  $P \leftarrow$ LCHILD(0) //a pointer to the root node//
  repeat
    while $P \neq 0$ **do** //traverse left as far as possible//
      process NODE(P)
      push P
      $P \leftarrow$ LCHILD(P)
    endwhile
    if TOP $= 0$ //stack is empty—all nodes processed//
    then exit
    else pop P
        $P \leftarrow$ RCHILD(P) //traverse right one node//
    endif
  forever
endproc

If **process** NODE(P) is interpreted as **print** NODE(P), then the PLR traversal order for our example bitree should produce:

    A B C D E F G

Procedure PLRT may be traced just as was LPRT:

		P	2	3	0	0	4	5	0	0	6	0	0	7	0	0
STACK	endwhile		1	1 2	1 2 3			1 4	1 4 5		1 6			7		
	forever					1 2	1			1 4	1	1	—			exit
	OUTPUT		A	B	C			D	E		F			G		

9.3.3 Postorder Traversal

The LRP traversal differs considerably from both the LPR and the PLR traversal. For the latter two, node pointers are stacked with the first visit and then unstacked with the second, and they are processed at one visit or the other. The LRP traversal must visit a node to make the left traversal, then leave the pointer stacked while it makes the right traversal so that the node can be processed after the right traversal is complete. The top of the stack is examined twice at each node, and the two examinations must be distinguished. One way to do this is to stack the pointer value to a node when traversing left, then stack the *negative* of it when traversing right, so that when a negative pointer value is unstacked, processing is indicated. The LRP traversal may be described as:

0.   Initialize the node pointer P to LCHILD(0). (a pointer to the root node).

1.   Traverse left by repeating $P \leftarrow$ LCHILD(P) while $P > 0$. The pointer values are pushed onto the stack as they are encountered.

2.   If TOP $= 0$ then stop. Pop the top value of the stack as P.

3.   If $P \geq 0$ then push $-P$ and set P to RCHILD(P). If $P < 0$ then process NODE($|P|$), and repeat at step 1.

The resulting procedure is:

procedure LRPT
   $P \leftarrow$ LCHILD(0) //a pointer to the root node//
   repeat
     while $P > 0$ **do** //traverse left as far as possible//
       push P
       $P \leftarrow$ LCHILD(P)
     endwhile
     if TOP $= 0$ **then exit** //stack is empty—all nodes processed//
     pop P
     if $P < 0$ **then** $AP \leftarrow -P$ //both branches have been traced//
            process NODE(AP)
          else push $-P$
             $P \leftarrow$ RCHILD(P) //traverse right one node//
         endif
   forever
endproc

If **process** NODE(P) is interpreted as **print** NODE(P), then the LRP traversal order for our example bitree should produce:

   C E F D B G A

Procedure LRPT may be traced just as were LPRT and PLRT:

P	2	3	0	0	-3	4	5	0	0	-5	6	0	0	-6	-4	-2	7	0	0	-7	-1	-1
STACK — endwhile	1	1 2	1 2 3				1 -2 4	1 -2 4 5			1 -2 -4 6						-1 7					
STACK — forever				1 2 -3	1 2	1 -2		1 -2 4 -5	1 -2 4	1 -2 -4		1 -2 -4 -6	1 -2 -4	1 -2	1	-1				-1 -7	-1	exit
OUTPUT					C					E				F	D	B					G	A

9.4 A BINARY TREE SORT

A bitree can be created so that if **print** replaces **process** in LPRT, the result is
an ordered list. Such a binary tree is called an **ordered bitree**. An ordered
bitree has the property that the node values to the "left" (processed earlier by
LPRT) of any node N are smaller than the value of N, and the values to the
"right" are at least as large as the value of N. The node values may be
ordered alphabetically rather than numerically with the same algorithm
through the use of NODE$ instead of NODE, using the collating sequence
for characters. Consider the following example:

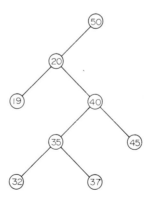

Procedure LPRT applied to this ordered bitree will produce:

   19   20   32   35   37   40   45   50

Suppose that new entries are to be inserted into this bitree so that LPRT will print the amended bitree in order. The insertion for some example entries should be:

Entry	Insertion Position
18	LCHILD of 19
21	LCHILD of 32
33	RCHILD of 32
36	LCHILD of 37
38	RCHILD of 37
41	LCHILD of 45
46	RCHILD of 45

The algorithm required for such additions must search the bitree for the correct position of the addition, and then link it to the existing bitree. Suppose that the value to be inserted into the ordered bitree, say A, is physically stored in NODE(N). Then A must be repeatedly compared to NODE(P), where P is generated by a visiting process which searches for the proper position of A in the bitree. If A < NODE(P) then the process should traverse to the left, otherwise to the right. If the appropriate traversal cannot be made because LCHILD(P) = 0 or RCHILD(P) = 0, then NODE(N) is linked to NODE(P) as its LCHILD or RCHILD, respectively. If the appropriate link is not zero, then the search must continue down the bitree. A procedure for sorting up to MAX positive numbers in this manner is as follows:

procedure BORDER
   $N \leftarrow 1$
   NODE(0) $\leftarrow$ 0 : LCHILD(0) $\leftarrow$ 0 : RCHILD(0) $\leftarrow$ 0
   repeat
     if $N >$ MAX **then print** //array-full message//
                        exit
              endif
     input NODE(N)
     if NODE(N) $<$ 0 **then exit**
     $P \leftarrow 0$
     procedure ALIGHT(N, P) //locate position for NODE(N), and//
                               //link it to the bitree//
     $N \leftarrow N + 1$
   forever
endproc

procedure ALIGHT(N, P)
   repeat
     if NODE(N) $<$ NODE(P)
       then if LCHILD(P) $\leq$ 0
          then proc PLEFT(N, P) //attach NODE(N) as//
                        //LCHILD of NODE(P)//
            exit
         else $P \leftarrow$ LCHILD(P)
         endif
       else if RCHILD(P) $\leq$ 0
          then proc PRIGHT(N, P) //attach NODE(N) as//
                        //RCHILD of NODE(P)//
            exit
         else $P \leftarrow$ RCHILD(P)
         endif
       endif
   forever
return

procedure PLEFT(N, P)   **procedure** PRIGHT(N, P)
   LCHILD(P) $\leftarrow N$ RCHILD(P) $\leftarrow N$
   LCHILD(N) $\leftarrow$ 0   LCHILD(N) $\leftarrow$ 0
   RCHILD(N) $\leftarrow$ 0   RCHILD(N) $\leftarrow$ 0
return   **return**

If a sequence of entries for procedure BORDER is:

50   20   19   40   35   45   32   37

then the process may be traced by displaying the crucial parameters each time that **forever** is reached in ALIGHT.

A	N	P	insertion	A	N	P	insertion
50	1	0	RCHILD(0) ← 1	32	1		
					2		
20	1				4		
	2	1	LCHILD(1) ← 2		5		
					7	5	LCHILD(5) ← 7
19	1						
	2			37	1		
	3				2		
	3	3	LCHILD(2) ← 3		4		
					5		
40	1				8	5	RCHILD(5) ← 8
	2						
	4	2	RCHILD(2) ← 4				
35	1						
	2						
	4						
	5	4	LCHILD(4) ← 5				
45	1						
	2						
	4						
	6	4	RCHILD(4) ← 6				

Procedure BORDER provides a form of insertion sort (see PJ4.3, PG6.7, and PJ6.3), supported on a structure which may be treated in many ways like a file. In that context, BORDER creates a file, but the subprocedure ALIGHT forms a basis for appending, updating, and searching a bitree file. Procedure LPRT serves for listing. The nodes of a bitree may themselves be structures of some complexity, in particular they may be records of a file which is linked as a bitree and stored physically in several arrays. The logic of the processes of creating, adding to, updating, and listing of a file which is linked as a sorted bitree is not altered by the structure of the nodes themselves—it is determined by the linkages of the nodes. Given that the simplicity of our example bitree does not truly limit the generality of our procedures, then we have dealt with all but one of the major areas of file maintenance for ordered bitree files: deletion.

9.5   BINARY TREE DELETION

Deletion of the nodes from a bitree requires *relinking*, and relinking involves the **predecessor** of a node in the visiting order. Consider the ordered bitree of the previous section:

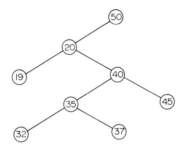

Deletion of the leaf nodes 19, 32, 37, and 45 presents no difficulties. Leaf nodes can be located and processed with a procedure that is similar to ALIGHT, although the PLEFT and PRIGHT equivalents involve the predecessor of NODE(P). Deletion of 40 or of 35 could be done by replacing a node by the root of its right subtree. Node 20, however, cannot be treated in this manner because it has a LCHILD, and so does the root of its right subtree, 40. Replacement of a node by the root of its left subtree leads to similar difficulties. Suppose that we call the node to be deleted D, its RCHILD RD, its LCHILD LD, and the index of its predecessor PRED. Then a study of examples soon reveals that the relinking depends upon whether D is itself the RCHILD of NODE(PRED) or the LCHILD of NODE(PRED). In the example above, if 40 is D, then LD is 35, RD is 45, and NODE(PRED) is 20. Here D is the RCHILD of NODE(PRED), so LD should be visited before RD in order to retain the visiting order. That will occur if RD is attached in the right subtree of LD. In fact, RD must be to the right of the "rightmost" in the chain of right children of LD, since the entire subtree rooted at LD is traversed before LD in the original bitree. On the other hand, if 35 is D, then LD is 32, RD is 37, and NODE(PRED) is 40. Here D is the LCHILD of NODE(PRED), and the entire subtree which it roots must be traversed before the RCHILD of

NODE(PRED). Hence *LD* should replace *D* as the LCHILD of NODE(PRED),
and *RD* must be to the right of the "rightmost" in the chain of right children
of *LD*. In either case, *RD* may be attached to the *LD* subtree with a process
similar to ALIGHT. Here are the two cases:

1. *D* is the RCHILD of NODE(PRED).
   a. Attach *RD* to the subtree rooted at *LD*.
   b. Link *LD* as the (new) RCHILD of NODE(PRED).

2. *D* is the LCHILD of NODE(PRED).
   a. Attach *RD* to the subtree rooted at *LD*.
   b. Link *LD* as the (new) LCHILD of NODE(PRED).

These may be illustrated on our example tree by:

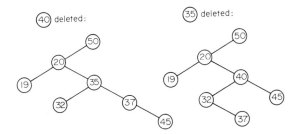

The remaining program difficulty lies in locating a given value in the
bitree, determining its index and the index of its predecessor, and setting
a flag which indicates which of the two cases above are to apply. The resulting procedure is:

```
procedure DENODE(A)
    P ← LCHILD(0) : PRED ← 0
    proc LOCATE(A, P, PRED, FLAG$) //Given the value A, LOCATE//
                                    //determines its index P, the//
                          //index PRED of its predecessor, and sets FLAG$//
    if FLAG$ = " " then print "no such node"
                        exit
                    endif
    RDP ← RCHILD(P)
    procedure ALIGHT(RDP, P)
    if FLAG$ = "LEFT" then LCHILD(PRED) ← LCHILD(P)
                        else  RCHILD(PRED) ← LCHILD(P)
                    endif
endproc
```

The effect of this scheme is diagrammed below:

CASE 1: A is the LCHILD of its predecessor:

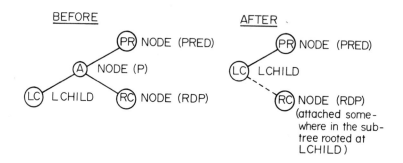

CASE 2: A is the RCHILD of its predecessor:

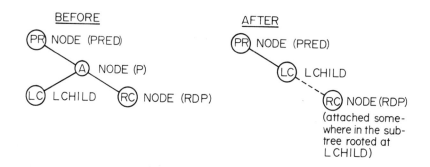

ALIGHT will actually make a "rightmost" attachment in both cases, and there is no need to design a specialized procedure when this more general routine has already been developed.

LOCATE is similar enough to previous traversal procedures that it is included without further discussion:

```
procedure LOCATE(A, P, PRED, FLAG$)
  repeat
    while P ≠ 0 do
      process NODE(P)
      push P
      PRED ← P
      P ← LCHILD(P)
      FLAG$ ← 'LEFT'
    endwhile
    if TOP = 0
      then FLAG$ ← " "
           exit
      else pop P
           PRED ← P
           P ← RCHILD(P)
           FLAG$ ← 'RIGHT'
    endif
  forever
return
```

Finally, **process** NODE(P) reduces in this case to:

    if A = NODE(P) **then return**

9.6 A TREE FILE

The maintenance of a tree structure, stored as a bitree, differs from the maintenance of an ordered bitree in that the links between nodes are pre-determined by the tree structure itself. Because of the fixed linking, the position at which a new node is to be attached to the tree cannot be determined by a traversal, but must instead be supplied along with the node value. The communication that is required between the user and a tree-file management program is simplified if nodes are numbered and their children are displayed upon request. The user can then add children to an existing tree in order to extend it. One approach, in which the tree is displayed after every entry of children, is adopted in the creation procedure which follows.

```
procedure OAK
   RCHILD(0) ← 1
   N ← 1
   input NODE$(1) //What is the root node?//
   RCHILD(N) ← 0 : LCHILD(N) ← 0
   print //entry instructions//
   repeat
      print "PARENT NODE"
      procedure DISPLAY(1)
      input A$ //Add to the tree?//
      if A$ ≠ "YES" then exit
      procedure EXTEND TREE
   forever
endproc

procedure EXTEND TREE
   input NP //Number of the parent?//
   repeat
      input A$ //potential child//
      if A$ = "*" then exit
      NODE$(N) ← A$
      procedure BRANCH(NP, N) //increments N after attaching//
                                //NODE$(N) to NODE$(NP)//
   forever
return

procedure DISPLAY(P)
   repeat
      print P, NODE$(P), "CHILDREN"
      P ← LCHILD(P)
      while P ≠ 0 do
         print P, NODE$(P) //display beneath header//
         push P
         P ← RCHILD(P)
      endwhile
      if TOP = 0
         then exit
         else pop P
         endif
   forever
return
```

procedure BRANCH(*NP, N*)
  $P \leftarrow NP$
  if LCHILD(P) = 0
    then LCHILD(P) $\leftarrow N$
    else while $P \neq 0$ **do** //search for the last RCHILD of//
        $Q \leftarrow P$ //the LCHILD of the parent node//
        $P \leftarrow$ RCHILD(P)
    endwhile
    $P \leftarrow Q$
    RCHILD(P) $\leftarrow N$
  endif
  LCHILD(N) $\leftarrow$ 0
  RCHILD(N) $\leftarrow$ 0
  $N \leftarrow N + 1$
return

With this routine, the display
for the tree at right would be:

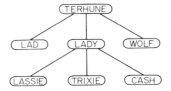

PARENT NODE :
1   TERHUNE   CHILDREN
                        2   LAD
                        3   LADY
                        4   WOLF
4   WOLF   CHILDREN
3   LADY   CHILDREN
                        5   LASSIE
                        6   TRIXIE
                        7   CASH
2   LAD   CHILDREN

9.7   HEAP STRUCTURES

A data structure called a **heap** is commonly used for sorting records, and
it is often implemented as a bitree. It is then a bitree with the property
that the values of the subtree rooted at a node N are no greater than the
value of N. A heap differs from an ordered binary tree, as can be seen by
the examples below:

HEAP

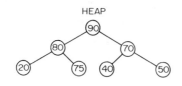

Note that:

1. 90 > 80, 90 > 70
2. 70 > 40, 70 > 50
3. 80 > 20, 80 > 75

ORDERED B - TREE

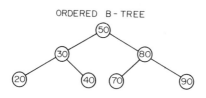

Note that:

1. 50 > 30 but 50 < 80
2. 80 > 70 but 80 < 90
3. 30 > 20 but 30 < 40
4. Everything to the left of 50 is less than every entry to the right of it.

Both structures vary a great deal with the entry order of the node values into a program which creates the structure, but a heap is normally kept *balanced*. A **balanced bitree** is balanced in the sense that no more levels than necessary are used in its structure. (A level is the number of links that are required to reach a node from NODE(0).) Balance is maintained by restructuring the bitree as much as necessary after insertions and deletions. The effect of balancing is to minimize the length of the search path from the root node to a leaf, and hence it is a more efficient structure on which to base some algorithms. A heap is awkward to search, however, and so an alternate scheme for listing a heap in order is called for. The standard scheme involves the *storage* of the bitree which supports the heap. A bitree may be simply stored in a linear array, say H, so that the *position* of the left and right child is determined directly from the position (index) of the parent. In short:

$$\text{LCHILD}(P) \leftarrow 2P \qquad \text{RCHILD}(P) \leftarrow 2P + 1$$

For the ordered binary tree above:

P	1	2	3	4	5	6	7
$H(P)$	50	30	80	20	40	70	90

With this scheme it is possible to directly determine the parent of $H(P)$ for a given P. The parent is $H(Q)$, where $Q \leftarrow \lfloor P/2 \rfloor$, using the notation $\lfloor K \rfloor$ for the largest integer less than or equal to K. In effect, $Q \leftarrow \text{INT}(P/2)$ for the BASIC function INT. (The same effect may be gotten in BASIC by using $P\%$ and $Q\%$ instead of P and Q, in which case $Q\% \leftarrow P\%/2$).

A heap may be created one entry at a time as follows:

1. Input a value A and attach it at the bottom of the heap.
2. Shift A up the heap levels by exchanging it with its parent as long as the parent has a smaller value.

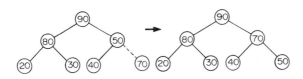

The physical exchange of records is the price paid for the lack of explicit links in the linear storage of a bitree. A simple heap containing positive numbers may be created by:

procedure HEAPIN
   $N \leftarrow 1$
   while $N \leq$ MAX **do**
      input $H(N)$
      if $H(N) < 0$ **then exit**
      $P \leftarrow N$
      procedure CLIMB(P)
      $N \leftarrow N + 1$
   endwhile
endproc

procedure CLIMB(P)
   while $P > 1$ **do**
      $Q \leftarrow \lfloor P/2 \rfloor$
      if $H(P) > H(Q)$
         then $T \leftarrow H(P)$
            $H(P) \leftarrow H(Q)$
            $H(Q) \leftarrow T$
      endif
      $P \leftarrow Q$
   endwhile
   return

The heap may be used for the sorting of records by first creating a heap from them, then by repeatedly deleting the top record of the heap and welding the two subtrees back together into a single heap. To see how this may be done, consider the heap:

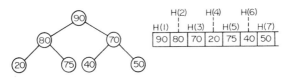

with the storage scheme in which LCHILD of $H(P)$ is $H(2P)$ and RCHILD of $H(P)$ is $H(2P + 1)$. Then the value to be retrieved is always in $H(1)$. A new heap can be constructed from the remaining entries by applying procedure CLIMB to them: One of the remaining entries can be moved to

$H(1)$ as soon as $H(1)$ has been processed, and the others attached to it one by one to form a new heap. For the example above, we may process 90, then form a (nonheap) by assigning $H(7)$ to $H(1)$. Now, however, if N is set to 1, CLIMB(2) will take the simple heap formed entirely from $H(1)$, and attach $H(2) = 80$ to it to form a heap of two entries. Then CLIMB(3) can be used to attach $H(3) = 70$, and so on. After $H(6)$ has been attached, the heap has been reconstructed without the old $H(1)$. The result will be:

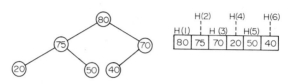

The value 50 is still in $H(7)$, but now the heap has only six elements, and $H(7)$ is no longer a heap cell. This process is repeated until all of the heap values have been removed:

procedure HEAPOUT
  while $N \geq 1$ **do**
    process $H(1)$
    $H(1) \leftarrow H(N)$
    $P \leftarrow 2$
    while $P \leq N - 1$ **do**
      procedure CLIMB(P)
      $P \leftarrow P + 1$
    endwhile
    $N \leftarrow N - 1$
  endwhile
endproc

For the purpose of sorting, **process** $H(P)$ may involve moving NODE(P) to a file which is stored in linear order. For the purpose of listing, it may be replaced by **print** $H(P)$.

9.8   THREADS

The linear storage technique introduced with heaps is one means of avoiding the creation of a stack during bitree traversals. Such stacks can require a large amount of storage for a complicated bitree—as many cells as there are nodes in the bitree in the worst case. Another way to avoid the traversal stack is to build **threads** into the bitree. A thread is a pointer to some node in the bitree other than LCHILD or RCHILD. One standard scheme is to place threads in those LCHILD(*P*) and RCHILD(*P*) which would be zero in an unthreaded tree (these are called **null links**). Then RCHILD(*P*) is set to the value which would be taken from the top of the stack upon leaving NODE(*P*) during an inorder traverse of the unthreaded bitree—the inorder *successor* of *P*.

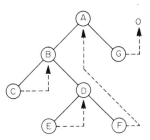

It is convenient to use the LCHILD null links to point to the inorder *predecessor* of a node, which gives us:

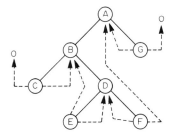

Distinguishing between threads and links during a traversal is easy if the threads are set to the *negative* of an index. If the threads are in place, an LPR traversal may be made by:

procedure LPRTH
  $P \leftarrow$ LCHILD(0) //a pointer to the root node//
  repeat
    while $P > 0$ **do** //traverse left as far as possible//
      $Q \leftarrow P$
      $P \leftarrow$ LCHILD(P)
    endwhile
    if RCHILD(Q) $= 0$ **then exit**
                    else process NODE(Q)
                              $Q \leftarrow$ RCHILD(Q)
                              $P \leftarrow Q$
                              if $Q < 0$ **then** $Q \leftarrow -Q$ **endif**
                    endif
  forever
endproc

One advantage of threads is that the inorder successor index Q of any NODE(P) can be found without traversing the binary tree from the root:

procedure SUCCESS(P, Q)
  $Q \leftarrow$ RCHILD(P)
  if $Q \leq 0$ **then return**
            else while $Q > 0$ **do** //traverse left//
                  $R \leftarrow Q$
                  $Q \leftarrow$ LCHILD(Q)
                endwhile
                $Q \leftarrow R$
                return
            endif
endproc

The process of creating a threaded tree is simply a modification of procedure BORDER of 9.4. The modification is required only in ALIGHT, and an examination of ALIGHT reveals that the only required change is in procedures PLEFT and PRIGHT:

procedure PLEFT THREAD(N, P)
  RCHILD(N) $\leftarrow P$
  LCHILD(N) $\leftarrow$ LCHILD(P)
  LCHILD(P) $\leftarrow N$
return

procedure PRIGHT THREAD(N, P)
  RCHILD(N) $\leftarrow$ RCHILD(P)
  LCHILD(N) $\leftarrow P$
  RCHILD(P) $\leftarrow N$
return

The changes required for deletion are left to the reader, as part of the projects.

9.9 A CLASS SCHEDULE SEARCH

Trees are often used to *direct* a search procedure, since they are explicitly designed around branches, and branches are models for decisions. The creation of a tree itself may model a search process, and the final tree may model the set of possible solutions. As an example of a search tree, consider the process of finding a class schedule. A student begins with a list of desired classes, looks up the hours in which they are offered, and tries to schedule the desired classes when they are available so that they do not conflict with each other. Consider the following set of classes, and their scheduled meeting times:

SUBJECT	HOURS OFFERED
Math 225	11, 12
History 110	8, 10, 11
Physics 150	10
Civics 200	9, 10, 12
English 100	8, 10, 12

The possible schedules may be searched for by building a tree, beginning with the hours for Math 225 as children of the root node. Each Math 225 node represents the beginning of a possible schedule. The History 110 nodes are added as children *unless* they conflict with one of their ancestor nodes:

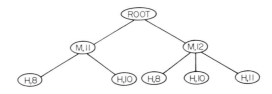

When Physics 150 is added, some of these five potential schedules *disappear* because they lead nowhere. If a node cannot lead to the desired result for a class hour, then it is marked in some manner. If none of the hours for the new class can be attached to a node, then it is **pruned**— removed from the tree:

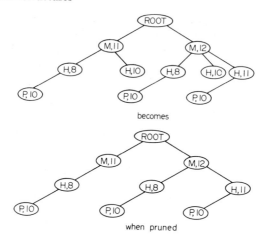

becomes

when pruned

There are now only three potential schedules, and Civics 200 is added:

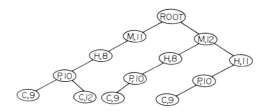

Finally, English 100 is added, leaving us with two possible schedules:

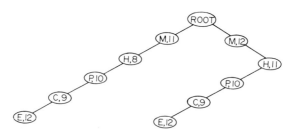

The building of the tree schedule can be handled by a procedure that is similar to procedure OAK of 9.6 in that all of the hours of a class are dealt with before any hours of the next class. Modifications are required because of the necessity for pruning, however. The nodes also differ in an essential way: the Pth node consists of *two* items, NODE(P), and NODE(P). The class identification is in NODE(P), and NODE(P) contains one of the hours at which NODE(P) is offered. The pair is actually a *record*, NODE$[P]$. The major considerations for the managing of this tree are as follows:

1. NODE(1) is set to "ROOT", which (in the singular form) does not coincide with academic class titles.

2. The tree is searched with a PLR traverse for *all* leaf nodes to which an input class hour H may be attached. If H coincides with the value of a node, no traversal beyond it is taken.

3. If the traversal carries beyond a node (or attaches H to it), then that node is marked by setting NODE(P) to its negative value. Attachment of leaf nodes is also made with negative values. The marking of successful nodes (which lead on toward the desired goal of a full schedule), rather than the unsuccessful ones, allows the hours associated with a class to be dealt with one at a time.

4. After all of the possible hours for a class have been attached, then the tree is searched for unmarked nodes, and they are deleted. The marking may be erased either during or after this traversal. The parent of an unmarked node is also deleted unless it has another child, and its parent is treated the same way, and so on.

Some of the management may be done as follows:

```
procedure SCHEDULE
  N ← 1
  NODE[1] ← ("ROOT", 0)
  RCHILD(N) ← 0 : LCHILD(N) ← 0
  repeat
    input A$ //Add more classes?//
    if A$ ≠ "YES" then exit
    procedure HOURS
  forever
endproc

procedure HOURS
  input C$ //Class title//
  print //entry instructions//
  repeat
    input H //potential hour for class C$//
    if H < 0 then exit
    NODE[N] ← (C$, H)
    procedure SLOT //add NODE[N] to all possible leaf nodes//
  forever
  procedure PRUNE //remove all subtrees rooted at unmarked//
                  //records, then erase marks//
return
```

Procedure SLOT turns out to be merely procedure PLRT with **process** NODE(P) replaced by the following:

```
process NODE(P):
   if H = |NODE(P)| then exit //no solution—back up.//
                            //(this is an exit from the//
                            //while ... do loop in PLRT)//
   if NODE$(P) = NODE$(N) //a match denotes an alternate//
                            //hour for the same class//
      then while P ≠ 0 do      //search for rightmost sibling//
         Q ← P
         P ← RCHILD(P)
      endwhile
      RCHILD(Q) ← N
      procedure BUD(N)
   else if LCHILD(P) = 0 //attach only at a leaf//
         then LCHILD(P) ← N
               procedure BUD(N) //increments N//
         endif
   endif

procedure BUD(N)
   NODE(N) ← −|NODE(N)|
   LCHILD(N) ← 0
   RCHILD(N) ← 0
   N ← N + 1
return
```

9.10   A ROUTING PROBLEM

The routing of people or goods from one place to another, usually by way of several possible intermediate places, is a common problem in business and industry. There is usually a cost or distance associated with moves from one place to another, and the *optimal* route is the desired choice. For the sake of a simple example, consider the following map of cities (with simplified names) and distances between them:

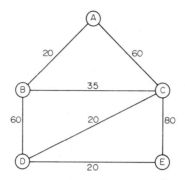

The object is to travel from *A* to *E* with a route of minimal distance. As in the case of trees, multiple links are required to represent this graph as a data structure. In this case, a bitree will not serve to describe the links, because a graph contains *cycles,* that is, it is possible to find a path which returns to its starting point. Fortunately, we are interested in paths which do not have this property, because returning to a node is clearly not optimal. What is required is a tree which describes *all* such *acyclic* paths from *A* to *F*. This, however, can be treated as a scheduling problem, in which the cities that are reachable from a given node (its *neighbors*) play a role similar to that of the possible class hours of the previous section. The neighbors of a city are its potential children, but no child of a node may be an ancestor of that node. When treated in this manner, the desired tree will be:

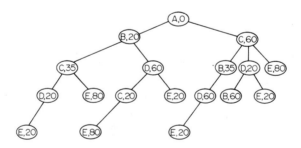

The major considerations are:

1. A branch which has the target city *E* as a node value is not extended beyond it.

2. A tree search is made for all leaf nodes to which a city *C$* may be attached. It can be attached only to those leaf nodes which have city

values that are neighbors of $C\$$, and which are not E. The search does not traverse along a path beyond the first occurrence of $C\$$ in that path, and so cycles are avoided.

3.   When all of the cities have been tried in turn without extension of the tree by any of them, then the tree is complete. If any node is extended by any city, then they must all be tried again.

All of the cities and the distances between them need to be in memory before the tree can be constructed. The crucial information is the linking of neighbor to neighbor. One clean way to store this information is in a table, usually called an **incidence matrix**. For N cities, it is an N by N table which contains a one in the (I, J) position if the Ith city is a neighbor of the Jth city, and a zero otherwise. For the present file, the ones may be replaced by distances. Hence for the example above:

	1 (A)	2 (B)	3 (C)	4 (D)	5 (E)		1 (A)	2 (B)	3 (C)	4 (D)	5 (E)
1(A)	0	1	1	0	0	1(A)	0	20	60	0	0
2(B)	1	0	1	1	0	2(B)	20	0	35	60	0
3(C)	1	1	0	1	1	3(C)	60	35	0	20	80
4(D)	0	1	1	0	1	4(D)	0	60	20	0	20
5(E)	0	0	1	1	0	5(E)	0	0	80	20	0

The details of the programs which may be used to manage this file are left to the projects at the end of the chapter.

9.11   MAZE REVISITED

The problem of finding a path through a maze that was discussed in Chapter 8 may be restructured in terms of trees. For that purpose, it is convenient to store a table containing only ones and zeroes as a bitree, with the root being any given non-zero entry. For example, if branching along rows and columns but not diagonals is allowed, and if no child of a node can be one of its ancestors, then the array below may be considered as a tree with root at $(1, 1)$:

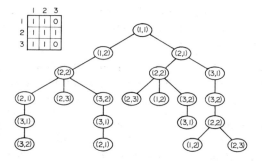

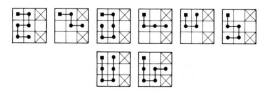

The leaf nodes correspond to the following paths:

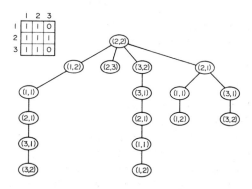

Considered as a tree with root (2, 2), the same array yields:

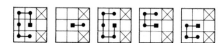

The leaf nodes correspond to the following paths:

These trees are constructed as follows:

Any node, indicated by a table position (I, J), is linked to the adjacent positions as children of (I, J) in the tree. (For the sake of simplicity, diagonal links have been ignored, and so there are only four possible children of any node, instead of eight. This restriction of movement was also a part of the previous pathfinder, MAZE.) An algorithm may be constructed by using a backward link to the parent of each node, and *four* forward links, one for each possible child. It searches the (general) tree for leaf nodes. If (I, J) is adjacent to the leaf node in the table, and if it has the value 1, then it is a potential child. Cycles of the form: $(1, 1)$, $(1, 2)$, $(2, 2)$, $(2, 1)$, $(1, 1)$, ... are avoided by attaching only those potential children which do not appear as ancestors of the leaf node. The backward links serve to check for that possibility. In the example above, the three possible paths from $(1, 1)$ to $(3, 2)$ are located in the tree by tracing paths from the root node with value $(1, 1)$ to the leaf nodes with value $(3, 2)$. In effect, the creation of the tree (or perhaps, the bitree which represents the tree within the program) takes care of the backtracking which was done with a stack in Chapter 8. By the principle of the conservation of effort, the procedure for creating the tree requires the same amount of dithering that was used by MOUSE to find a path.

The algorithm for constructing maze trees must develop a systematic way of moving through the array, MAZE(I, J), beginning at an arbitrary entry. This is a tree-directed search, similar to the previous two examples. Major considerations are:

1. The leaf nodes which were attached in the *previous* stage are the ones to be extended with their children. New leafs must be marked, so that they can be processed at the next stage. If NODE[P] is a pair of indices (I, J), then the marking may be done by setting $J \leftarrow -|J|$ during attachment. When all possible children have been attached to a leaf, then it is unmarked. Since it is unmarked, even if it has no children, there will be no attempt made to extend the tree at this leaf in succeeding stages.

2. A bordered maze with zero-entry outside rows and columns may be used, just as it was in Chapter 8. It is convenient to use the array STEP, below, to look for children:

$K = 1$	-1	0
2	0	1
3	1	0
4	0	-1

Most of the details for developing such a tree search are left for the projects at the end of the chapter. It should be noted that the four forward links of a node to its children in the general tree generate the *only* right links in the corresponding binary tree.

SELF-REVIEW

1. Draw a pairing tree for a tournament of 8 people, playing a game without draws. Now add one person, and draw the tree for 9 players. What is the root node of a tournament pairing?

2. Draw the following as binary trees if possible:

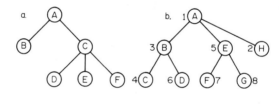

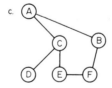

3. Test the trees in 2. for conformity to the recursive definition of a tree by moving down the tree, marking nodes which do not yet violate the definition, then unmarking them in reverse if a violation occurs.

4. Suppose that the b graph in item 2 is converted to a binary tree, and the nodes are stored in the cells of NODE according to the numbers beside

them. Construct a table of the node cells, and their LCHILD and RCHILD links of the form:

I	NODE(*I*)	LCHILD(*I*)	RCHILD(*I*)

5. What is the visitation order for:

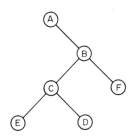

6. If **process** NODE(*P*) is simply **print** NODE(*P*), what will be the output of the following when applied to the binary tree in item 5?

   a. PLRT   b. LPRT   c. LRPT

7. The actions of LPRT (page 248) can be thought of as a series of *pop, push* or *print*. If a **pop** requires 18 microseconds, a **push** requires 17 microseconds, and a **print** requires 50 microseconds, how long will LPRT require to produce the output asked for in 6.b.?

8. What are the distinctions between:

   a. a tree   b. a bitree   c. an ordered binary tree
   d. a heap   e. a graph

9. Convert the graphs below into trees, and also into bitrees, by removing the *minimum* number of edges (connecting links). All of the edges incident to a node may not be removed.

10. Draw the ordered bitrees which would be created by procedure BORDER for each of the following possible entry sequences:

a. 1, 2, 3, 4, 5   c. 1, 5, 2, 4, 3
b. 5, 4, 3, 2, 1   d. 4, 1, 3, 5, 2

11. What ordered bitree will result from the operations below, applied to the ordered bitree at right?

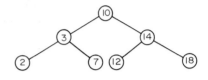

a. Addition of 11
b. Deletion of 3
c. Addition of 13 followed by the deletion of 12
d. Deletion of 14 followed by the addition of 14

12. What does a heap look like (draw a picture) at each stage with the following entry sequence? (The top of the heap should be first alphabetically.)

JOE, ABE, GABRIEL, ALI, LI, BILL, AARON

13. Suppose that a heap contains 17 entries, and the 18th entry is entered and moves to the top of the heap. Where will the 4th one end up? The 5th one?

14. Supply the threads for the following binary tree:

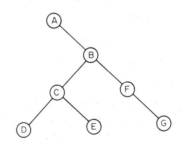

PROBLEMS

P9.1   Trace the operation of the stack in PLRT for the bitree below:

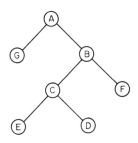

P9.2   Trace the operation of the stack in LPRT for the bitree in P9.1.

P9.3   Trace the operation of the stack in LRPT for the bitree in P9.1.

P9.4   Trace the action of procedure ALIGHT for the entry sequence d. in self-review item 10.

P9.5   Trace the changes in linkage which occur during the action of part d of self-review item 11. Assume that the original nodes are stored in a linear array in the order: 10, 3, 14, 2, 7, 12, 18.

P9.6   If the heap of self-review item 12 is stored in a linear array with linking by position only, what is the final order of the entries?

PROGRAMS

PG9.1   Write a program which inputs 20 names into a linear array, sorts them by linking them as an ordered bitree, and then prints them in alphabetical order. (See PJ9.1 also.)

PG9.2   Write a program which inputs the ancestry of a person or a pet, and displays it. The program is to create a bitree which reflects the structure of the tree.

PG9.3   Write a program which will act as a guide to an identification file of trees or birds, progressing only one stage at a time, upon request. (See PJ9.2 also, where the guide itself may be altered by the user.)

PG9.4   Write a program which sorts 20 numbers by creating a chosen heap from them, and then prints them in order. (See PJ9.3 also, where the heap itself may be altered by the user.)

PG9.5   Write a program which will search a chosen heap for every occurrence of an input value, and replace it with another input value, adjusting the heap if necessary.

PG9.6   Rewrite the program for PG9.1 using a threaded binary tree.

PG9.7   Rewrite the program for PG9.2, with the tree supported as a threaded binary tree.

PG9.8   Rewrite the program for PG9.3, with the tree supported as a threaded binary tree.

PROJECTS

The comments which precede the projects in Chapter 3 also apply to the following:

PJ9.1   Write the programs (GOSUB ... RETURN structures) that are required to manage a file of records that consist of both an identifier and a numeric value, supported as an ordered bitree. Routines are required for creation, addition, deleting, updating, and listing. For a complete system, sort the records both by name and number (with separate ordered bitrees), one of them indirectly.

PJ9.2   Write a collection of programs (GOSUB ... RETURN structures) which will serve as a guide to the identification of trees, birds, micro-organisms, etc. (See PG9.3.) Routines must be available for addition, deletion, updating, and listing.

PJ9.3   Write a collection of programs (GOSUB ... RETURN structures) which manages a heap. Routines are required for creation, addition, deletion, and listing. An addition should be made in the location of minimum index which was previously freed by a deletion, if there are any.

PJ9.4   Write and run a class-scheduling program, supporting it on a threaded binary tree.

PJ9.5   Write and run an optimum-route program which will handle as many as 10 nodes.

PJ9.6   Write and run a program which will find all paths from one location to another in a 5 by 5 (or 10 by 10, etc.) table by constructing a search tree. Diagonal moves may be allowed or not allowed, as you wish.

PJ9.7   A number of the projects of the previous chapters may be restructured in tree-like form. In particular, search problems are related to PJ4.6, PJ4.8, PJ4.9, PJ4.10, PJ4.11, and PJ4.12, and tree-like records are handy in PJ6.4, PJ6.5, PJ6.6, and PJ6.7.

Appendix A

ANSWERS TO SELF-REVIEW EXERCISES

CHAPTER 1

1. The term BASIC refers to the BASIC *language*, the program which *translates* a program written in the BASIC language, the program which makes it possible for a user of the BASIC language to enter a program and *edit* it, and the *operating system* which supports operations initiated by commands such as RUN and SAVE.

2. ⟨input⟩, ⟨output⟩, ⟨branch⟩, ⟨branch on condition⟩, ⟨copy⟩, ⟨arithmetic⟩.

3. Keywords mentioned in Chapter 1 are: INPUT, PRINT, IF, THEN, GO TO, LET, STOP, END.

4. The diagram is in 1.3 on page 4. The arrow labeled 2 is to be labeled *P*. The CPU block is to be enclosed in double lines. The memory block is associated with the storage of variable values.

5. INPUT and PRINT are in 1.6 as shown on page 10, the IF is in 1.8 on page 12, and assignment is of the form:

   [*N*]   LET ⟨variable⟩ = ⟨expression⟩

6. The BASIC commands mentioned in Chapter 1 are RUN and LIST. Most readers will have encountered SAVE (and perhaps DIR, OLD, NEW, KILL, BYE, and others) in the process of operating within the specific system which they are using.

7. See section 1.8 page 13.

8. See section 1.9 page 14.

9. An IF-statement.

10. An infinite loop is one which never stops repeating. It is expressed in pseudocode by the **repeat ... forever** structure.

282

11. Pseudocode is used to *develop* a clean logical structure for a program as well as to describe program logic. Flowcharts provide an alternate description of the logic of program segments.

12. True or false.

CHAPTER 2

1. Yes. An **if** cond **then exit** can abort the process after a finite number of steps.

2. The following are equivalent:

procedure ADD__TEN
   $S \leftarrow 0$
   $N \leftarrow 1$
   repeat
      input A
      $S \leftarrow S + A$
      print S
      $N \leftarrow N + 1$
   until $N > 10$
end ADD__TEN

procedure ADD__TEN
   $S \leftarrow 0$
   $N \leftarrow 1$
   while $N \leq 10$ **do**
      input A
      $S \leftarrow S + A$
      print S
      $N \leftarrow N + 1$
   endwhile
end ADD__TEN

procedure ADD__TEN
   $S \leftarrow 0$
   $N \leftarrow 1$
   repeat
      if $N \leq 10$
      then input A
         $S \leftarrow S + A$
         print S
         $N \leftarrow N + 1$
      else exit
   forever
end ADD__TEN

procedure TABLE
   $I \leftarrow 1$
   while $I \leq 20$ **do**
      print I, I^2, I^3
      $I \leftarrow I + 1$
   endwhile
end TABLE

procedure TABLE
   $I \leftarrow 1$
   repeat
      print I, I^2, I^3
      $I \leftarrow I + 1$
   until $I > 20$
end TABLE

procedure TABLE
   $I \leftarrow 1$
   repeat
      if $I \leq 20$
      then print I, I^2, I^3
         $I \leftarrow I + 1$
      else exit
   forever
end TABLE

procedure CONTROL
   input A
   while $A \geq 0$ **do**
      print $A \uparrow 7$
      input A
   endwhile
end CONTROL

procedure CONTROL
   input A
   if $A \geq 0$
   then repeat
         print $A \uparrow 7$
         input A
      until $A < 0$
   endif
end CONTROL

procedure CONTROL
   input A
   repeat
      if $A < 0$ **then exit**
      print $A \uparrow 7$
      input A
   forever
end CONTROL

3. The structure **if** cond **then** S, where S is a block of more than one statement, and:

    if cond
       then $S1$
       else $S2$
       endif

4. *zero*: 100 IF $A > 1$ THEN LET $A = A - 1$
              110 IF $A > 1$ THEN 140
              120 LET $A = A \uparrow 2$
              130 PRINT $A \uparrow 2$
              140 ...
              .
              .
              .

    Without the use of the second IF, *one* is required:

        100 IF A > 1 THEN 140
        110 LET $A = A \uparrow 2$
        120 PRINT $A \uparrow 2$
        130 GO TO 150
        140 LET $A = A - 1$
        150 ...
        .
        .
        .

    In either case, the value .1296 of A^4 is printed.

5. A counter is a special case of a control variable. The term *control variable* is more general than *counter*.

6. Because FOR ... NEXT loops require that the initial value, the limit value, and the step value of the control variable be determined when the loop is entered, and that the step value be constant. The **while ... do** structure does not impose this restriction on the step value. It is poor programming, but possible, to change the limit value within a pseudo-code loop.

7. An increment *increases* a value, a decrement *decreases* it.

8. *None* of the cases is executed, and the effect is to execute whatever follows the **endcase** in the logic as S_{n+1}.

9. The GOSUB preserves the location [50] at which it was executed so

that the execution of a RETURN will then bring control back to the statement which physically follows [50]. The GO TO is a blind transfer for which no information is preserved.

CHAPTER 3

1. A program or algorithm is portable if it can be moved from one computing system to another without change. In the example, the cost will be eighty million dollars. In practice, the portability of algorithms (which are frequently expressed in pseudocode) reduces this sort of cost. Several means of portability between *identical* computing systems reduces it even more, but the variety of available systems is growing.

2. A literal is a string constant which has the value indicated, whereas a string variable provides storage for string values. Only a variable may be altered by the user.

3. The position of the displayed question mark.

4. Extended names, pseudocode, flowcharts, listings, remarks, instructions, prompting, explanatory output.

5. Real numbers, stored in variables with names which contain neither a % nor $; integers, which may be stored in some systems with names which end in %; character strings, stored in variables with names which end with $.

6. -9 on most systems.

7. It does not adjust for the number of digits displayed for a numerical value. Hence decimal points may not line up, dollar signs may not snuggle up to significant digits, and so on. It *is* possible to get around most of the limitations with elaborate programming, but as a tool, TAB is lacking.

CHAPTER 4

1. The statement: 10 DIM $A(11)$, $B(2, 5)$ reserves $A(0)$, $A(1)$, ..., $A(11)$ which is 12 cells, and $B(0, 0)$, $B(0, 1)$, ..., $B(2, 5)$ which is 18 cells for a total of 30. However, 10 DIM $C(K)$ is not a legal statement and reserves none.

2.   0 to 11 for *A* and 0 to 2 for the first subscript of *B*, 0 to 5 for the second subscript of *B*.

3.   Only one value of DIFF is used at a time, and then discarded—there is no need to preserve a collection of values.

4.   The numeral 2 is not a legal variable name.

5.   To initialize variables.

6.   See section 4.6 page 105.

7.   The first.

8.   A matrix is one of a set of tables to which algebraic operations are applied.

9.   ?

10. a. Determine the column of the warehouse and the row of the item. The connection between the warehouse name and the column number must be taken from a printed list (a cross-listing or catalog) or it may be looked up by the program in an internal table. The latter approach requires that the identifier of the warehouse be spelled correctly by the user. The item row presents a similar problem.

     b. Search through the item row for a non-zero entry in some warehouse column. Sophisticated routines may locate the required amount of an item split between warehouses, or locate the suitable warehouse which is to be preferred because of shipping costs. Additional information, such as shipping costs, will need to be placed in another table, indexed by warehouse and row just like the inventory table.

     c. Determine the appropriate row and column and add the received amount to the table at that location. The date of arrival or the cost of an item may be need to be retained as well as the amount for future price determination or tax purposes. This can be handled by other tables, as in b.

     d—m   These transactions lead to considerations similar to those discussed in a-c above.

CHAPTER 5

1. a. −1
   b. −5
   c. 7
   d. −6
   e. 1.5
   f. $8^2 = 64$
   g. 300
   h. 16
   i. (an approximation of) 32/3
   j. (an approximation of) 1/54

2. a. false
   b. true
   c. true
   d. false
   e. false
   f. true

3. a. $B \uparrow 3 = 1/8$
   b. $(B \uparrow 3) \uparrow 2 = 1/64$
   c. $(B \uparrow 2) \uparrow 3 = 1/64$
   d. $Y*B - 4*B = -1/2$
   e. $Y*X - 4*X = -2$
   f. $(FNA(X) + Y)/2 = (X \uparrow 3 + Y)/2 = 11/2$
   g. $(B*X - Y) \uparrow 3 = -8$
   h. The type of $A\%$ and X do not match.
   i. FNB requires two arguments.
   j. $FNA(2)*FNC(Y) - 4*FNC(Y) = 12$
   k. $X + B - INT(2.5) = 1/2$
   l. $INT(ABS((3 - 9)/2))) = 3$

CHAPTER 6

1. a. [20], [10], [30], [10], [25], [40], [25].
   b. [10], [20], [30], [40].
   c. [10], [20], [30], [10], ...

2. NEW creates the program file
   [20] adds to the file
   [10] adds to the file
   [30] adds to the file
   [10] updates a record in the file
   [25] adds to the file
   [40] adds to the file
   [25] deletes from the file

3. An array is a collection of data items, as is a *file* of records. However, all of the items in an array must be of the same data type, whereas a single record may contain data of several types. A record

has a structure in which one data item may be subordinate to another (or part of another), whereas the items in an array are all at the same level and are independent of each other.

4. The condition $J \geq 2$ is used because when the second value is guaranteed to be in place, so is the first. The condition $I \leq J - 1$ is used because with each pass another value is moved into place, and it does not need to be examined again.

5. The loop may be exhausted without the execution of $P \leftarrow I$, in which case P *should* have the value $N + 1$. If $P \leftarrow N + 1$ were placed *after* the loop, then it would always be executed and no sorting would occur.

6. Because of the use of **while** ... **do** loops, SINKING__SORT and SHIFTUP will not do anything, but PLACE will allow the entry of a new first record. Procedures like LIST and OUT should also be written to be harmless or give warning messages when $N = 0$. If I is initialized to 1 in COMPACT, and all records are deleted, then COMPACT would pass on the information that there was actually one record in CLASS. Such an error might not show up in the use of a program until long after it was considered to be debugged.

7. With MAP(I) $\leftarrow$ 1, no sorting would take place. With
$$\text{MAP}(I) \leftarrow N - I + 1$$
sorting would occur bottom-up rather than top-down.

8.

I	SCORE(I)	MAP(I) initial	pass 1	pass 2	pass 3
1	67	1	2	2	2
2	92	2	3	4	4
3	76	3	4	3	3
4	81	4	1	1	1

9. $A(0)$ is the number of data items in the file in both STASH and APPEND.

10. Values for items in the file must be retrieved from the disk, or written onto the disk, every time $A(I)$ appears in a statement. For example, **while** $I < A(0)$ **do** requires input from the disk into the program in order to have a value of $A(0)$ to compare to I. The only output onto the disk occurs when $A(I)$ appears as the target variable in an assignment, or an **input** statement. Other mentions in the program cause input from the disk to the program.

11.   Then the first new value would wipe out the last old value in A.

CHAPTER 7

1.   Omit the **exit** from: **if** $S \neq 0$ **then** ....

2.   Type is often set by partitioning a line of type into words, moving or hyphenating a word which extends beyond the desired margin, and then interposing enough spaces and half-spaces between (and sometimes within) words to fill out the line. The words and punctuation marks must be located in order to do this because they form the natural tokens (units) of typesetting.

3.   One example: to locate (by keyword or index) the laws, cases, and court decisions which bear upon a particular subject within the huge multitude that exists.

4.   One example: to locate books published after a given date within a file of books organized by subject.

5.   A letter can be broken into strings, separated at those points where the recipients' name should appear. These strings can then be catenated, using the variable which contains the name, to form a single string. The formatting of the letter (with heading, return address, etc.) is then reduced to the same problem which it would have been for *any* letter.

6.   **procedure** INSERT($A\$$, $B\$$, N)
     $M \leftarrow$ LEN($A\$$) $- N + 1$
     $A\$ \leftarrow$ LEFT\$($A\$$, $N - 1$) $+ B\$ +$ RIGHT\$($A\$$, M)
     end INSERT

   procedure EXTRACT($A\$$, $B\$$, M, N)
     TEMP\$ $\leftarrow$ LEFT\$($A\$$, N)
     $B\$ \leftarrow$ RIGHT\$(TEMP\$, $N - M + 1$)
     end EXTRACT

   The only necessary change in MATCH is the change in EXTRACT:

   TEMP\$ $\leftarrow$ RIGHT\$(LEFT\$($A\$$, N), $N - M + 1$)

7.

a.	b.	c.
100	90	20
STOP	GO TO	IF
	145	$A < B$
		THEN
		40

8. If the values of A are physically sorted, then links are required only for B and C, hence 5 columns will do (without backward links). If A is unsorted, 6 columns are needed. If backward links are required, 7 columns are needed for a sorted A column, 9 if the A column is unsorted.

9. In DELETE: Coming out of the loop, S will be the FLINK of line L, but P will point to L itself; it will not be the BLINK of line L. As a result, the FLINK of the predecessor of line L will be unchanged and line L with still be linked into the list, but declared available by $AVAIL(D) \leftarrow 0$.

   In INSERT: Coming out of the loop, S will be the FLINK of line L, but P will point to the predecessor of line L, not to L itself. The pointers involved will *delete* line L and *replace* it by the inserted line.

10. The pointers given follow the sequence:

    $0 \rightarrow 3 \rightarrow 1 \rightarrow 5 \rightarrow 2 \rightarrow 4 \rightarrow 0$

    The effect of each change in sequence is:

    a. $0 \rightarrow 3 \rightarrow 5 \rightarrow 2 \rightarrow 4 \rightarrow 0$
    b. $0 \rightarrow 3 \rightarrow 5 \rightarrow 4 \rightarrow 2 \rightarrow 0$
    c. $0 \rightarrow 3 \rightarrow 5 \rightarrow 4 \rightarrow 2 \rightarrow 1 \rightarrow 0$ (The new item is stored in the first available location.)
    d. $0 \rightarrow 3 \rightarrow 6 \rightarrow 5 \rightarrow 4 \rightarrow 2 \rightarrow 1 \rightarrow 0$

    We then have:

cell	BLINK	item	FLINK
0			3
1	2		0
2	4		1
3	0		6
4	5		2
5	6		4
6	3		5

CHAPTER 8

1. If inventory items are treated as a stack, then those on the bottom may deteriorate before they are retrieved. (Customers in a grocery store treat milk as a stack, but the milkman moves leftover containers to the front and fills in behind.) In a queue, the time spent in the system by an item depends only upon demand, the re-order levels, and re-placement time. If items do not deteriorate, then a stack may be cheaper or easier to handle. The choice of a stack or queue affects profit in times of changing prices. For example, a cheap item stacked for a long time before sale may represent a larger profit than an item passed through a queue in a time of rising prices, but also involves a longer-term investment. The choice of a stack or a queue may be affected by considerations of tax benefits and stockholder's reports. In any case, when the choice is included in a program used to manage an inventory, the *program* becomes *a statement of management policy.*

2. The monthly issues of a given magazine generally form a queue, but the physical arrangement within the queue is haphazard and tends to be a stack.

3. The average size of a stack is the sum of the values of TOP, taken at each stack transaction, divided by the number of transactions. The maximum size of the stack is the maximum of TOP, examined at each transaction. For a queue, TAIL $-$ HEAD $+$ 1 plays the role of TOP in a stack, although care must be exercised when the queue is empty.

4. Inside of CHECKSTEP, the **if** statement would need to cause exit from the **while ... do** loop which *contains* CHECKSTEP.

5. They can be switched if SHIFT can handle a full queue. As written, it will do so.

6. The realism of the model is affected in minor ways by the order of these events. For example, if a customer is leaving the lane at the same time that one is arriving, does the new customer get the cart just released? (CKT before CAT will do this.) The decision affects the statistics concerning the number of carts in the stack. In particular, suppose there are *no* carts in the stack. CAT before CKT will turn the customer away. Every permutation of CAT, ST, and CKT will have advantages and disadvantages, and require some care in interpreting the resulting statistics.

7. If LANE $=$ 0 then no customers are waiting to be checked out, and CKT is *zero.* It should not be allowed to become negative.

CHAPTER 9

1. The root node represents the winner. The solid lines represent a tournament for eight players, and the addition of the dotted lines will serve for nine players, but no *tree* is really satisfactory for nine players.

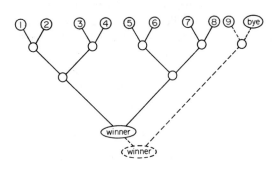

2. a.   b.   c. not possible

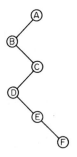   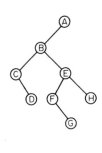

3. —

4.

I	NODE(I)	LCHILD(I)	RCHILD(I)
1	A	3	0
2	H	0	0
3	B	4	5
4	C	0	6
5	E	7	2
6	D	0	0
7	F	0	8
8	G	0	0

5. A B C E C D C B F B A

6. a. PLRT: A B C E D F
    b. LPRT: A E C D B F
    c. LRPT: E D C F B A

7. The sequence will be:

push A	17	push D	17
pop A	18	pop D	18
print A	50	print D	50
push B	17	pop B	18
push C	17	print B	50
push E	17	push F	17
pop E	18	pop F	18
print E	50	print F	50
pop C	18	This is a total of 510 microseconds.	
print C	50		

8.   A graph may have cycles and the rest may not—they are specialized (acyclic) graphs. Any acyclic graph is a tree. If each node of a tree is considered to have 0 or 1 left children and 0 or 1 right children, then it is a bitree. If each node of a bitree has a value at least as great as those of its left subtree and no greater than those of its right subtree, then it is an ordered bitree. If each node of a bitree has a value at least as great as that of its children, then it is a heap.

9.

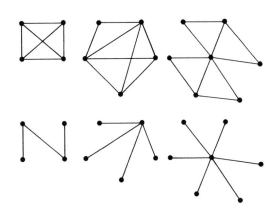

Any way you go about it, a *tree* with N nodes must have precisely $N - 1$ edges.

10.   a.

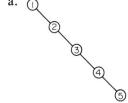

c.

b.

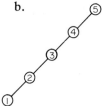

d.

11. Taken in order:

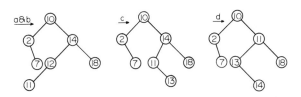

12. In normal alphabetical order with the top of the heap being the first item in the lexicographic sense we have:

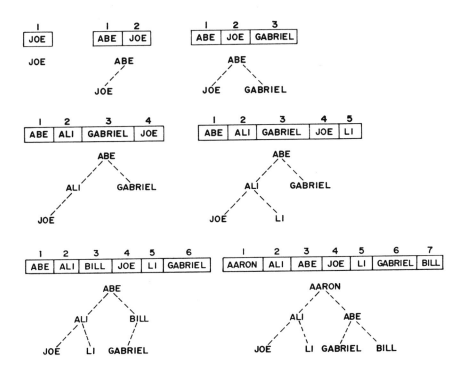

13.   The original heap:

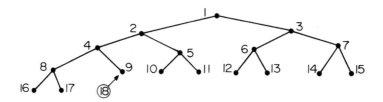

The new heap, where the old positions of moved items are indicated at their new nodes:

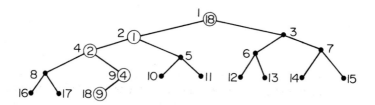

14.

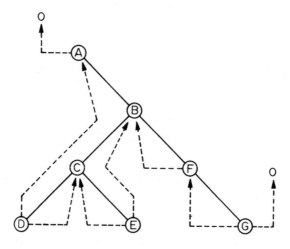

Appendix B

A BASIC STANDARD

Most languages in common use exist in many versions. Computer manufacturers often supply a version of at least one high-level language with a computer, and other versions may be created by software houses or universities. The translator used in a computer must be written specifically to translate *into* the machine language of that computer. If the language is to be "BASIC", for example, then the translation must be *from* a high-level language which closely resembles other languages called BASIC. The resemblance must be close in both syntax and in semantics. The problem faced by the designer of a translator is that other versions differ in many ways, and there are choices to be made in the design. Design options can be resolved by the existence of a **standard** for the language to serve as a guide. Programs written in a version of a language which closely adheres to a standard tend to be more portable than those written in a non-standard version. Standards exist for most of the high-level languages that are in common use.

At the time of this writing (1979), a standard exists for limited BASIC, but most commercially viable versions of BASIC extend the language outside of its formal bounds. A more comprehensive standard is in preparation by ANSI (American National Standards Institute). A new standard cannot affect the many (perhaps 50 to 100) versions now in use on several hundred thousand computers, but it may affect the design of future translators. Since programs written in available BASIC will not be affected by the new standard, the value of transmitting algorithms by way of a pseudocode description is likely to remain high, no matter how completely that standard is accepted.

What follows are some comments about the relationship of an interim report, X3J2/79-52, of the committee that is working on the ANSI standard, to BASIC as it has been presented in this text.

In the proposed standard, there are essentially two data types: numbers and strings, and numbers are stored in real form. Hence 2 is equivalent to 2.0 or to 2E1, and 2/3 is taken as 0.66 ... 67, not as 0. Some provision may be made for declaring an *integer* variable, but apparently not by appending a % to the identifier, as in $X\%$. In some current versions, the division of (apparently) integer constants does not agree with the result of assigning them to *integer* variables and then dividing them; it does agree in other versions. It is not clear how this problem will be resolved in the standard. A related problem is the choice of either truncation or rounding upon conversion from real to integer in TAB, for subscripting, for loop control, and (perhaps) upon assignment to integer variables. The standard will apparently be to *round*. The versions which the author uses most often all truncate in these situations. In general, the treatment of integers in BASIC, any BASIC, is a mess. This data type cannot be avoided internally, and must be faced by the user in several contexts. The attempt to simplify BASIC by making all numbers *real* simply fails. One solution which would be comfortable for the user is:

$X\%$ is an integer variable (just as $A\$$ is a string variable)

2 is an integer

2.0 is real

2/3 is zero

2.0/3.0 is .666 ... 67

2./3 is .666 ... 67

All of these can be explained fairly readily to the beginner, and one of the main attractions of BASIC is that it is a *beginners'* language. *The conventions above will apparently not be the ANSI standard.*

The standard for identifiers will remain ⟨letter⟩⟨digit⟩, rather than change to the EXTEND mode.

Variables are not necessarily initialized to 0 or to the null string. Doing so should be banned.

The incredibly forgiving practice of creating an undeclared subscripted variable upon the first appearance of a subscript for it in the code is to be continued. This is *very* poor training for beginners, and the addition of a DIM statement to some old programs would not be too much to ask as the price of a change in the standard.

Subscripted variables will still be limited to either 1 or 2 subscripts. This can be quite awkward in some applications.

There are no explicit LEFT$ and RIGHT$ functions, but their effect can be obtained with $A\$(M:N)$, which specifies the Mth-through-Nth characters of $A\$$. Not to be confused with $A\$(M, N)$, of course.

There are to be more library functions than those listed in Chapter 5, Chapter 7 (string functions), and Chapter 4 (MAT functions).

Several versions of PRINT USING will be acceptable.

Prompting of input is to include the keyword PROMPT as in:

10 INPUT PROMPT "WHAT IS YOUR NAME?": $A$$

An entire line may be input (commas and all) into $L$$ by:

20 LINPUT $L$$

This certainly solves an otherwise intractable problem.

The effect of attempting to display output beyond the right-hand display margin is treated in detail, and may not agree with current versions.

There is still no standard index value upon exhaustion of a FOR ... NEXT loop. Either the last used value or the **while** ... **do** equivalent would have been helpful.

Multi-line functions will probably be included.

Standards for real-time programs, parallel programs, bit manipulations, editing, and debugging are being developed.

An IF cond THEN [N] ELSE [M] statement *is* included, but it is still not the general **if** ... **then** ... **else** structure of pseudocode. The general form *may* be included as in:

100 IF cond THEN
.
.
.
150 ELSE
.
.
.
200 ENDIF

A true subprogram feature has been added to supplement the GOSUB ... RETURN structure. The lack of the SUB structure has been a major limitation in BASIC, and its inclusion is welcome. A subprogram would be a block of statements transferred to by, for example:

100 CALL CALC(X, Y, $A$$)

and defined by:

1000 SUB CALC(X, Y, $A$$)
.
.
.
1200 SUBEXIT

Here SUBEXIT includes the role played by RETURN. The arguments would be dummy arguments (as in statement functions), but *only* the information passed through the argument list would be shared with the rest of the program. Other variable names could be re-used within the SUB structure without confusion. Hence the SUB structure can be written as a much more general program module than the GOSUB ... RETURN structure. For example, one could be written to sort *any* (and every) numerical, singly-subscripted variable within the program. This is a valuable adjunct to BASIC. It also tends to increase (and require) programming sophistication by the user.

A limited form of **case** is included as:

ON expression GO TO $N1$, $N2$, ..., Nm

A more general form of **case** is also being developed.

A form of **repeat** ... **forever** has been included:

```
100 LOOP
    .
    .
    .
150 IF cond THEN EXIT
    .
    .
    .
200 END LOOP
```

File handling is treated in some detail. Many of the essentials will be recognizable to readers of Chapter 6, but file-handling in the sense proposed requires a fair amount of sophistication on the part of the user. It also makes BASIC an acceptable tool for small business and educational purposes.

Graphics is treated in some detail. This may be the wave of the future, but surfing requires a bit of practice. The size of the translator, the cost of the equipment, and the sophistication of the user will need to be fairly large in order to use graphics effectively.

Programs may be chained together, with one using the main memory, then calling in another from disk storage, which in turn brings in another, etc. A chain of programs can then be executed, even though they can not all fit into memory at the same time.

Some of the proposed features are especially welcome:
IF ... THEN ... ELSE ... ENDIF, CALL ... SUB, and
LOOP ... END LOOP. With the addition of name ... END name, and the
use of IF cond THEN EXIT within named blocks and within FOR ... NEXT,

we would effectively have BASIC structures which closely match pseudocode. Many other structures, including GOTO, could then be dispensed with, but perhaps the resulting language would not be BASIC.

To serve on a standards committee is to fail. It is not possible to satisfy everyone, and some problems to be faced have no definite resolution. **A great deal of time and effort is required for standard development, and the ANSI committee members are to be commended for serving.**

BIBLIOGRAPHY

A reader of this book is in a position to explore both programming and Computer Science, and other books are available to provide help. In fact, there are many such books, but some cannot be recommended because they are either out of date, too specific, or require more background from the reader than this book provides. For example, one of the usual directions taken from an introduction to programming in college curricula is *assembly-language programming*—programming in a symbolic language very close to machine instructions. This is normally aimed at a particular machine, and it is thus too specific to be of use to the general reader. Without an acquaintance with at least one assembler, the language-translation process itself is out of context. Nevertheless, some doors are opened by an introduction to programming, and some suggested directions and possible guides are indicated in the paragraphs which follow.

languages It is probably true that one cannot fully appreciate or understand one computer language without learning a second one. Some of the more available languages are discussed in these books:

Conway, R. and Gries, D. *An Introduction to Programming: A Structural Approach Using PL/I and PL/C.* Cambridge, MA: Winthrop, 1973.

Findlay, W. and Watt, D. A. *Pascal: An Introduction to Methodical Programming.* Potomac, MD: Computer Science Press, 1978.

Gilman, L. and Rose, A. J. *APL, An Interactive Approach.* New York: John Wiley, 1974.

Griswold, R. E., Poage, J. F. and Polonsky, I. P. *The SNOBOL4 Programming Language.* Englewood Cliffs, NJ: Prentice-Hall, 1971.

McCracken, D. D. *A Guide to FORTRAN IV Programming.* New York: John Wiley, 1972.

Weissman, G. *LISP 1.5 Primer.* Encino, CA: Dickenson, 1967.

data structures There are many useful ways to organize data that have not been discussed in this book. Well-chosen data structures can decrease the difficulty of solving a programming problem by orders of magnitude. A rather accessible treatment of this topic is:

Elson, M. *Data Structures.* Palo Alto, CA: Science Research Associates, 1975.

A more complete, but more sophisticated treatment is:

Horowitz, E. and Sahni, S. *Fundamentals of Data Structures.* Potomac, MD: Computer Science Press, 1977.

A fairly accessible view of the world of large data collections is:

Martin, J. *Computer Data-Base Organization.* Englewood Cliffs, NJ: Prentice-Hall, 1977.

simulation Although large, special-purpose simulation languages may not be available to the reader, the second reference below provides an interesting over-view, and the others a useful introduction.

Hills, P. R. *An Introduction to Simulation Using SIMULA.* Norwegian Computing Center, 1973.

Pritsker, A. A. B. and Pegden, C. D. *Introduction to Simulation and SLAM.* New York: John Wiley, 1979.

Schriber, T. J. *Simulations Using GPSS.* New York: John Wiley, 1974.

hardware The design of computers is part of *digital circuit design,* which does not really require a background in engineering or science to understand in large part (although it certainly does to practice effectively). One accessible source for this topic is:

Winkel, D. and Prosser, F. *The Art of Digital Design: An Introduction to Top-Down Design.* Englewood Cliffs, NJ: Prentice-Hall, 1980.

algorithms This topic is perhaps the heartland of Computer Science, but it is normally approached through programming itself until a certain amount of programming sophistication can be assumed. That same sophistication can be gained, however, by working through the following:

Even, S. *Graph Algorithms.* Potomac, MD: Computer Science Press, 1979.

Horowitz, E. and Sahni, S. *Fundamentals of Computer Algorithms.* Potomac, MD: Computer Science Press, 1978.

software engineering The need for careful programming becomes acute when large projects are attempted; programs are quite difficult to organize well when a *group* of programmers is involved. The books listed here sort out a number of the problems which must be considered in such a situation. They are readable, but the importance of their content, and even the content itself, is multiplied by the reader's experience.

De Marco, T. *Structured Analysis.* Englewood Cliffs, NJ: Prentice-Hall, 1979.

Yourdon, E. *Techniques of Program Structure and Design.* Englewood Cliffs, NJ: Prentice-Hall, 1975.

Yourdon, E. and Constatine, L. L. *Structured Design: Fundamentals of Computer Program and Systems Design.* Englewood Cliffs, NJ: Prentice-Hall, 1979.

INDEX